Satan the Walks the Earth as a Human Being, a Person!

Book 4

Donald Evans

ISBN 979-8-88540-481-5 (paperback)
ISBN 979-8-88540-482-2 (digital)

Copyright © 2022 by Donald Evans

All rights reserved. No part of this publication may be reproduced, distributed, or transmitted in any form or by any means, including photocopying, recording, or other electronic or mechanical methods without the prior written permission of the publisher. For permission requests, solicit the publisher via the address below.

Christian Faith Publishing
832 Park Avenue
Meadville, PA 16335
www.christianfaithpublishing.com

Printed in the United States of America

To Karen Elizabeth Williams, my eldest daughter whom Grace and I love. I want you to know you've been and still is a part of our lives. You are an inspiration in our lives, your sister Grace Marie and I.

The day you were born, I've never ceased in praying for you, your health, safety, and now your family. I've seen the results of my prayers. God does answer prayers.

I thank you for your help in preparing several years ago God's messages, which are to be read throughout the land. I believe in my heart God has seen what you did and how you helped His servant. God will reward you for your obedience through Me for what you have done.

We love you, Grace,
Dad

Contents

Preface ix
To Educational Institutions xi
Introduction and Presentation of Sin, Demon Spirits,
    and Mankind xiii
The Lord Has Set Us Free 1
To Whom It May Concern: Do Not Place Me, Jehovah, in a Box ... 8
Jehovah God and Mankind Spiritual Integrity: Sermon
    and Message 11
The Fight to Do What's Right Sermon 19
God Army Isn't Denominational 27
The Blood and the Cross of Jesus Christ Sermon 34
I. A Living Testimony! I, an Eyewitness of Satan the Devil! 42
II. A Living Testimony! I Am an Eyewitness of Satan the Devil! ... 45
III. Answer to "The Question": How Does Satan Deceive
    the Entire World? Message 50
Satan Is on the Earth as a Person—Man: What You
    Should Know! 56
"Satan, an Enemy of Everlasting Life!" Sermon and Message 62
Mankind Should Know and Acknowledge the Spirit World 74
Questions and Answers of the Spiritual Realm 81
Mankind in Spiritual Warfare 91
Spirits of the Unseen 96
Invisible Enemies in Our Government Demonization by Proxy! ... 105
How to Recognize Satan the Devil's Spirit Message and Sermon ... 117
The Other Spirit 124
Demons: Evil Spirits in the Homes 130
The Reality Is, We Live in a Spirit World 135

I Speak to Them That Are Not Seen..142
Congregation: "What Satan Does Not Want You (Us) To
    Know" Sermon..144
Mankind Must Prove Himself in the Spirit World Realm............156
Spiritual Deception 162
Spiritism and Demonologies Hidden Dangers..............................168
"Forming an Opinion: Satan's Access to the Human
    Mind" Sermon and Message...174
"Thus," Says the Lord, "Teach and Preach!": How
    Demon Spirits Enter "You" Humans..............................178
Satan's Master Plan..190
What Mankind Should Know Satan the Devil and
    Mankind's Perception Sermon and Message 197
The Holy Spirit Satan Waging War against the Holy
    Spirit Sermon and Message...204
Satanic Dictator, Dictatorial, and Dictatorship............................211
Satan's Spiritual Manifesto of Order and Rank 218
Shake Hands with the devil 224
What the World Is up Against Sermon and Message 232
The Congregation of God Has a Target on Its Back!
    Sermon and Message 255
Doctrine of Demons in the Church: The Body of Christ 260
A Doctrine of Demons..288
Acknowledging the Mind, Not the Perception of Satan..............295
Flesh: The Other Spirit Versus the Five Senses...........................301
Jesus Christ, Our Redemption and Redeemer Sermon
    and Message 307
Homosexuality...315
Homosexuality and Demons 322
Does the World Acknowledge Satan Is the World's
    Biggest Enemy? Sermon 333
Spiritual Warfare Fought through Faith......................................339
The Holy Spirit: Satan Waging War against the Holy
    Spirit Sermon and Message...347
Schizophrenia...354

Uncontrollable Spirits..361
The Lamb of God 367
Abortion: A Great Sin 373
Healing for This Generation, Mankind Can Be Made
     Whole Sermon and Message...377

Preface

Understanding oneself, all people is to acknowledge the devil; Satan is walking the Earth, appearing as a real person (human being). The revelations describe in this book how Satan's spirit transition from a spirit being into a human being, a person like you and me, and transitioning or materialize back into an invisible spirit person.

The book reveals the devil's power is used by way of the human race, but not all mankind is vulnerable machinations or his crafty schemes.

Many of Satan's secrets are revealed throughout the book, which no other person would know unless he or she experienced the realization of the spirit realm and its effect it has toward the little ones and people in general, the physical realm, as well as in the spirit realm.

This book, *Satan the Devil, Walks the Earth as a Human Being*, a person leads mankind in one direction, which is to find Christ Jesus and accept him into one's life as Lord and Savior.

The book also is the manifestation of the way, the truth, and the life, which is written that every man, woman, and child who reads this truth will get the same revelations and understanding of the spirit realm, which is real and alive in spirit and active in the spirit realm physically and spiritually and also active in and through humankind.

The book explains the other spirit's hidden thoughts of humankind, which Satan's spirit used to counter against man, you, by creating his own perception or thought for man to perceive as his or her own to act on or carry out.

You will discover your own perceptions or thoughts aren't always yours but the perceptions or thoughts of the enemies, the devil or demon spirits, or both.

Man (you) will learn or become aware to be deceive by his or her perception and will discover anything that is carnal, the devil's spirit has power to possess and control.

Child of God, Scripture tells us, "Be alert, be on watch! Your enemy the Devil, roams around like a roaring lion, looking for someone to devour."

The huge dragon was thrown out—that ancient serpent named the devil or Satan that deceived the whole world. "He" was thrown down to Earth and all his angels with him.

Scripture also says, "How terrible for the Earth and the sea! For the Devil has come down to you and 'he' is filled with rage because he knows that he has only a little time left."

Therefore, we must all wear the whole armor of God and pray on every occasion as the Spirit of God leads!

To Educational Institutions

History has been recorded and is of the past, present, and future that is being studied in all educational institutions. History is part of school's curriculum of the past, but the spiritual realm is alive yesterday, the past; today, the present; and future until Jesus Christ return.

History, spiritual history, is just as important as any of past histories because we live in a spiritual realm with real, live spirit enemies whom mankind is in spiritual war or conflict with, where age is no exception.

Spiritual combat is of past, present, today, and future with invisible enemies, whom mankind can only defeat and control in and through the name above all names, Jesus Christ.

There is no other name or person nor weapon that can defeat invisible enemies of the human race throughout the Earth other than the Name and the person Jesus Christ.

This history of yesterday, today is forever, until Jesus returns, and should be implemented and validated into the schools and all educational institutions across the Earth and taught as a creditable course.

The people, the world is at war in a spiritual realm like no other war and like no other enemy known to mankind.

We are at war in the spiritual realm like no other war in the past, present, nor in the future, which should be made known and acknowledged by all mankind throughout the future of our history books of tomorrow as well as in the Church, the Body of Christ.

Now is the time to implement, this spiritual revelation into a plan for tomorrow, for today, for all educational institutions' curriculum as a creditable course in public schools, colleges, and universities.

It should be no secret: we live in a spiritual realm with live spirit beings, the enemies of mankind that every child of God. Jehovah should know and acknowledge the beginning of adolescent years in educational institutions across the Earth beginning in America.

Note: This is a recommendation of a spiritual concept, a spiritual revelation strongly influenced by the Holy Spirit, that it may come to pass implementing according to God's will and purpose, therefore, place it on record, the plan, as it is said, "Get it started," as the spirit leads; don't delay.

Your brother in Christ,
Bro. Evans

Introduction and Presentation of Sin, Demon Spirits, and Mankind

There was a chaotic condition brought about on the Earth as a result of the sins of angels. The sin of the angels is mentioned first and occurred first. Which mean there was a devil already in existence by the time Adam was created. Therefore, sin was in existence before the creation of man.

God commanded the Earth to give life to all kinds of animals, wild animals, and reptiles. The serpent or snake is a reptile whom a certain angelic creature made himself the wicked spirit Satan the Devil by lying to Eve in the Garden of Eden by speaking through the mouth of a serpent. It was the snake that spoke first.

"Did God tell you mustn't eat fruit from any tree in the Garden?"

"Of course, we may not eat it," Eve told the serpent. "It's only the fruit from the tree at the center of the garden that we are not to eat. God says we mustn't eat or even touch it or we will die."

"That's a lie," the serpent hissed. "You'll not die. God know very well that the instant you eat it, you will become like him, for your eyes will be open. You will be able to distinguish good from evil." After lying to Eve in the Garden of Eden, he got angels to turn against God.

Some angels stopped the work that God had assigned them to perform in heaven and came down to Earth and made for themselves flesh by bodies like those of human. In essence, some angels forsook their own proper dwelling place in heaven to come to Earth. They left the spiritual realm to materialize in the physical realm into fleshly human bodies to have sexual relations with women of this world.

But such love affairs were wrong for angels. This was a sinful act of disobedience, which became mankind's way of living ungodly lives. Disobedience is now human beings' inheritance, which Satan is responsible for.

The Garden of Eden is the place that the inheritance of sin and disobedience of mankind took place in which man's spiritual predecessors were the wicked angels that forsook their own proper dwelling place in heaven to come to Earth. But not the angels that conspired with the cherub angel against God, who were cast out of heaven.

Those angels descend to Earth to became demons or evil spirits of the Earth and of the Earth's atmosphere. As Lucifer became Satan the devil, God's adversary and the enemy of mankind who is here to deceive the world.

But the angels that forsook their heaven dwelling, God did not hold back from punishing them. They were thrown into pits of dense darkness to be reserved for judgment.

I believe sin nor disobedience of mankind would not have been establish in man had not the cherub angel lied and attempted to overthrow God and the throne of God. It was Satan's failure in his attempt that he, his spirit, caused mankind to become like himself and use mankind as representative of his spirit being.

He lied to Eve in the Garden of Eden by speaking through the mouth of a serpent and that which he did, and then his spirit is still speaking and lying through the mouth of humankind of all ages.

Telling a lie comes from a spirit other than a person's own natural spirit but the spirit of Satan or a demon. Regardless how small or great a lie is or how it is told, it still come from a demonic spirit of deception. Scriptures say Satan is a liar and the father of lies; he is the originator of lies and demons as well. They perform and act as intercessors, which means all lies are revelations of the presence and manifestation of the devil or a demon by way of a person's tongue. That means the manifestation of demonic spirits are in the tongue of mankind. It's proverbial: "life and death are in the tongue." Mankind cannot control the tongue.

Believe me, lying demons are in possession of human bodies as their own throughout the nation and world. There are people that cannot tell the truth. It's not that they don't want to, they cannot because a spirit or spirits greater than their natural spirit is in possession of mind and body.

A lying demon or evil spirit speaks in its own language of deception by way of a person's tongue. It is a person's tongue that manifest the presence of a demonic spirit or spirits in a person. Something man has no control over because he does not acknowledge it that isn't his natural spirit but a spirit of deception greater than his or her own speaking through him or her, which confirms we live in a world of deception.

Evil spirits or demons are here to deceive the world in which they are succeeding by performing through mankind. The entire population is vulnerable to deception spiritually and physically both by way of the human race.

They cause mankind to become deceptive to himself just imagine if Satan or demons can cause a person to be deceptive to him or herself, you can imagine the state of mind the world is in.

Let no one fool you, even though Satan and demons are defeated foes or spiritual beings. They still possess great power of influence over the world population because of human ignorance and lack of knowledge of spiritual warfare and the existence of demons dwelling among in the body of mankind and in the Earth's atmosphere.

They are powerful evil spirits in the lives of multitudes, and even you if you lack knowledge of their presence and existence in which they know because of their invisibility, they see and hear everything we do and say. They are with us and in the presence of you at this very moment spiritually and physically or both. Demon spirits are assigned to us individually, forever lasting, including myself twenty-four hours a day.

People, I stated earlier: they are persons without bodies in search of human bodies to dwell in to perform the work of the devil. Once they enter you, only the Name of Jesus Christ and prayers for some can make them depart from your body. Satan nor demons will not obey no other name but the Name of Jesus. "This is spiritual warfare!"

Demons that has entered and possess human bodies as their own are causing people to act violently, commit and perform acts never before committed. I said it before and I say it again: more people are demonized, demon-possessed, or under the influence of the devil's power and control than ever before including some Christians.

All mankind is under the attack of the devil or demons in their lives. Every man, woman, or child is vulnerable until the duration of one's life. There isn't a person dead or alive in which Satan or demons has not come against spiritually or physically through the flesh of mankind.

I cannot express strong enough the reality of demon spirits in observance waiting in the Earth's atmosphere for the opportunity to enter and possess human bodies as their own, in which many already has.

You know, if Satan's spirit enters a person's body sitting in the presence of Jesus Christ, the King of kings and Lord of lords imagine what his spirit is doing to those which are lost in the world. And believe me; he isn't alone when his spirit enters a person's mind and body.

Note: Read John 13:27. "As soon as Judas took the bread, Satan entered into him. Jesus said to him, 'Hurry and do what you must.'"

Their purpose is to steal, kill, and destroy and cause mankind to be deceptive to himself as well as the world by creating and fooling the world population by lies of deception and his human transitional appearance of a person, a real, live human being, still yet a spirit person that walks the Earth among us.

Church, the Holy Spirit is my witness, I've defeated sin, Satan, demons, and the spirit realm. I believe I've defeated every wicked demonic force the world had come against me with. However, I'm still in spiritual warfare in this wicked world against persons without bodies, demons, evil spirits in the Earth's atmosphere.

But we, the believers, have the authority and the power in the Name of Jesus Christ to defeat Satan and cast out demons throughout the world. Believers' power is in the Name of Jesus. I, as a believer, use the power Jesus Christ gives us to defeat the enemies of the spirit world, Satan, and every demon and wicked spirit that inhabit the Earth, atmosphere, and the world's population.

"There is no other name Satan or demons will obey but the Name Jesus Christ." The devil and demons glorify God in their obedience when hearing the Name of Jesus, which I've witnessed and experienced.

Church and humankind, without the Resurrection of Jesus, would live in vain, which the devil and demons or the spirit realm acknowledge. The spirit world realize mankind lives because Jesus Christ lives. The Church lives because the Body of Christ lives.

But the enemies of the spirit world want to destroy God's divine will and purpose of all mankind through man. They are attempting through the living to condemn or bring condemnation on the world's population through the body the Church, the Body of Christ.

The enemy realize every child of God has a divine will and purpose for their lives as did the first man and woman God created. That is to serve and be a servant of God on Earth as is in heaven all the days of our lives because of Jesus Christ our redeemer.

Jesus Christ is the seed that brought redemption of sin and death. Even though Jesus died, had it not been a resurrection, mankind would have lived and died in vain, never to live again. Thus, had it not been a resurrection Satan and demons would be in control of many if not all lives.

But by Jesus's life, death, burial, and resurrection Jesus paid the price that set people free from the devil's power over our lives. It is Jesus's death, burial, and resurrection that gives us believers life after death. Just as Jesus lives again, we shall also live again to serve God. The same Spirit that raised Jesus from the grave shall someday raise us, mankind from the grave.

Scriptures says when Jesus died on the cross, at once, the curtain in the temple was torn in two from top to bottom. The Earth shook and rocks split apart. Graves opened and many God's people was raised to life.

The dead left their graves to live again after Jesus had risen to life; they went into the Holy City where they were seen by many people. Which mean those souls came back to life but did not raise up on their own. It was God's Spirit that raised them to life again, never to die again.

The same Spirit that raised the dead and Jesus will someday raise us from sleep. It's Jesus resurrection that gives life and eternal salvation with God.

Jesus came as a human being, yet he was the image of God the Father in spirit. God is Spirit whom we worship in Spirit and truth. We are who we are in the flesh, yet we are God's image in spirit. For we surely know that we are God's temple and that his Spirit lives in us.

I'm in the flesh, but I'm God's spiritual child in spirit. I am in God's image in spirit just as Jesus Christ is God in Spirit but yet was hung in flesh in the Earth. However, it was not known to humankind until after Jesus's death that Jesus Spirit lived in us since the creation of humankind.

This was God's sacred secret the mystery that was reveal by way of the dead coming back to life. It wasn't by power or might but by God Holy Spirit, the Spirit that raised Jesus from the grave that weren't reveal until after Jesus's death on the cross when the graves open up and the dead came to life.

For ages and ages, this mystery was kept secret from everyone and now it has been explained to God people. The mystery is that Christ lives in our heart and is our hope of salvation and everlasting life with God, sharing God's glory.

Sharing the glory of God is through Jesus Christ, the promised seed that brought the redemption of mankind and salvation of sharing everlasting life with God. Jesus was the first to die, buried, and raised to everlasting life with a new immortal body, never to die again.

We, mankind, are seeds being prepared for burial in the ground and someday be raised to life again by the same Spirit that raised the seed of Jesus to life; and we, too, will have new immortal bodies. Without physical seeds, man cannot plant because he has nothing to sow. Likewise with God, without human seeds, God cannot sow.

Therefore, God created the first human seed, the first Adam made of soil came from the Earth, yet he was a seed, a created being. But not the spiritual seed that gives eternal life after the first death. The second Adam, Jesus in his prehuman existence, was the life-giving spiritual seed of God.

Remember, it is not the spiritual life that comes first but physical life and then the spiritual life after the first death, which means mankind must die before he is sowed and returned to soil but then become spiritual sons and daughters of God after the first death.

However, all will not die but be changed in an instant as quickly as the blinking of an eye. What I'm saying is, that which is made of flesh and blood cannot share in God's Heavenly Kingdom and that which is mortal, our body the seed cannot possess immortality until it dies and returns to dust.

We are seeds to be buried and resurrected. The last Adam, the seed from heaven, the life-giving seed was the most important seed ever walk the face of the Earth. He was the life-giving seed, his Name, Jesus Christ.

It became clear in light of the Christian Scriptures that the promised seed of the woman would have to be more than human in order to bruise the head of this spiritual enemy this angelic person, the devil. The seed would have to be a mighty spirit person.

Jesus is the promised spirit seed that is to bruise the devil's head. Jesus came as a human being; he had a physical body and a physical birth and human mother, Mary, whom God's Holy Spirit planted the seed of Jesus in the womb of.

It is through Jesus Christ we as seeds has the power to bruise the devil's head as well as demon forces. Church as seeds of God we have the power through Jesus Christ over every demonic force as well as the devil himself.

Church, as seeds of God, we must be like Jesus which is God's will to be him in every way and someday see him as he really is. But it is through Jesus Christ who is the truth, the way, and the life; and through him, the promise that we will someday as seeds of God shall be with him.

But as seeds, we are to die as Jesus died and be raised from death by the same Spirit that raised our Lord. As seeds of God, one must live as God wants us to live that is to live as Jesus lived to become spiritual sons and daughters in heaven. God wants every seed that dies to be resurrected and to have eternal life with Him and the Lord in heaven.

The Holy Spirit proved that Jesus is the powerful Son of God, the spiritual seed that is to bruise the serpent head, because he was raised from death. Jesus's death made it possible for humankind to become spiritual sons and daughters of God, when God raised him from the dead by his Spirit. Hence, when we die, we are raised by the same Spirit that raised Jesus and then we become spiritual sons and daughters of God as well as heirs of God and joint-heirs of Christ.

But unfortunately, all humankind weren't born to be spiritual sons and daughters of God. Scriptures say some children are of the wicked one, the devil. There are seeds of the devil throughout this world, which you can distinguish between the two, God seeds and seeds of Satan. A person knows who's in control of one's life by that person's performance in life.

He or she is either a servant of God or Satan. Mankind cannot serve the two. Church, Jesus's congregation, is one seed with one Body and one Head, which branches out to bear fruit. But it still remains one Head and one Body, which is in Christ.

The Lord Has Set Us Free

I am a living testimony of what the Lord can and will do for anyone who seeks his help to be set free of worldly and demonic bondage. Demonic captivity in today's world is more prevalent than ever before by demonic forces, forces that mankind has no power over not even himself.

Worldly bondage is a sign of world slavery which slavery is a sign of a person bound in worldly servitude. Spiritual bondage is that man servitude is with the Lord but worldly bondage is bound in the world and a worldly system.

However, mankind has a perception he or she is in control of their lives and no one else. But how far from the truth are they? Man is either control by the Spirit of God, that which all children of God are or he or she is controlled by the lust of the flesh that which Satan or demonic forces have the power of influence over.

Believe me brethren demonic spirits are in control of the world. Jesus said, "I come not to save the world but the world may be saved through me," which means to save the world Satan and demon forces would be save.

We well know Satan and demon forces are doomed to eternal hell in the "Lake of Fire" in which hell is created for which mean the world cannot be save, however, Jesus has defeated the world, Satan and every demonic force that exist in the world. And it is through Jesus Christ mankind is save but not the world.

Jesus can and will set anyone free in and of the world that comes to him and from where Satan and demons has control. You see it isn't the world that hold mankind captive, Jesus has defeated the world, mankind is held captive by demonic forces dwelling within human bodies, forces no human being can control under their own strength.

People is the world whom demon spirits possessed and which Satan power of influence cause the world to sway in their direction. We live in a wicked world and society where Satan attempt to prove he's greater in the world than God that is in Christians.

The devils spirit tells man and the world he's greater in him than he (speaking of Jesus) that is greater than the world. The devil like all mankind to believe he's greater in them than Jesus

Christ. There are many that accept his spirit false perception and lie. The Holy Bible says, "Satan is deceiving the world causing it to sway. He is the great deceiver and the truth isn't in him."

Satan isn't alone, he has followers, demon spirits in the millions inhabiting the Earth's atmosphere assisting the devil's spirit in deceptiveness. The question is how do they operate to succeed? By the power of influence of the devil's spirit and great demonic forces that dwell in the body and mind performing as a person own natural spirit.

That's why you, mankind must be set free internally of the mind, man's mental nature, body, and soul before you become a new creature in Christ Jesus. You see the devil and demon power are your enemies within yourself which you, mankind has no control over.

The devil's spirit and demons are more active in people today than ever before because there are more avenues and accesses created by the spirit realm that allows Satan to enter demons into the minds and bodies of the world. But man does not acknowledge nor recognize their bondage nor captivity is within control by the manifestation of evil spirits.

The world does not know and does not want to know Jesus Christ as Lord and Savior over one's life and is their only way of being victorious over the forces of evil that are here to steal, kill, and destroy mankind any way possible.

In this victory, mankind can possess through Jesus Christ victory over the elements of the world that which condemn the lost in and of the world. Brethren, do not be deceived by the world devices that the spirit realm uses as deception to deceive to snare the world.

There are more worldly events that Satan has created through some elements of the world such as alcohol, drugs of all kind and through worldly events such as vice of all kind, homosexuals, gay parades, a public procession now held on ceremonial occasion. Which give possessive demons the opportunity to shout out, "We're out and we're proud."

Now the world use several discourses to dialogue with the spirit realm by internet, psychic hotline, dial a person but speak to a demonic voice in disguise as a human voice (dial a demon-psychic hotline) spiritualism, witchcraft, voodoo, satanism, sects, occultism and a host of others not mention.

People are experiencing with their minds for the sake of the devil. While some have literally consented to Satan and demon forces the use of their minds, bodies, and souls to perform against God and Jesus Christ. Satan knows man's weakness; therefore, his spirit manifests in man to use his weakness for power and influence over man himself, holding him captive in his or her own body and mind.

"Remember, Jesus came to set the captives free and whom he set free is free indeed." The world cannot set you free, only Jesus Christ, the Son of the Living God. Even though Jesus defeated the world, it is wicked. Man cannot live in and be of the world and have victory over death, sin, the devil, and demonic forces, not even in himself.

World! The spirit realm does its wickedness and evil deeds through the human race. There are no exceptions. There is no respecter of person Satan nor demons do not use to represent their spirit being. You are no exception including some Christians.

There are Christians characters performing in disguise as sheep but are really wolves in sheep clothing. So beware of characters they are no more than Christians shows off attempt to fool God but in retrospect they only fooling themselves.

Remember Satan is a deceiver out to deceive the world through the human race. There is no respecter of person his spirit being will not attempt to use. Human vulnerability is great among the world which he and demon forces seek out every second of the day. "Discrimination nor age is no exception in the spirit realm."

Its evidence is visible in people of all ages of what they do and speak. The world is under seized by demonic forces; it is being controlled by these forces through mankind. Through denominational and nondenominational persons, including some Christians and nonbelievers. We all become vulnerable in the spirit world during a period of one's lifetime. Because man isn't focus on the spirit realm or because he and Christians think the spirit world ignores us.

Christians, people, you are in for a rude awakening. Many Christian characters of all denominations and nondenominations are parading the church grounds demonize or under the influence of Satan but does not recognize their condition but yet they think they are free of the devil and demons in which the spirit realm won't touch them.

These individuals or Christians characters are ignorant of Satan's demonic power and spirit realm all because of their denominational views of other denominations that teach and preach the full gospel of Jesus Christ. The characters are lost in a spirit world we all live in. Demon spirits parading in the body of mankind while others waiting in the atmosphere for the opportunity of anyone whom their spirit can enter.

I was in and of the world. Well, over forty years in which not one Christian nor Christian character administer or inform me of the spirit world nor the existence of a real devil and demons that are real and alive, nor the power of influence they possess over human lives. No one, not even family members.

However, one family member jokingly said, "I had a demon in me!" How right he was; at that time, I was possessed with a legion of demonic spirits. I was demoniacal, or demon-possessed had been for nearly forty years. Which I had heard voices in my head for as many years and was hearing voices at the time he jokingly made the accusation. Congregation beware of yourself and those around you, neither Satan nor demons has no respecter of person to manifest their spirit through. We are all vulnerable of their attack and devices on human lives and the church. "Age is no exception."

I was six years of age when Satan enter demons into my body through the use of alcohol. I took my first of drink of alcohol at the age of six which I became intoxicated, drunk. After years of drinking I became an alcoholic possessed with alcohol demons that was alive internally in my body using my mind well over thirty years while demon-possessed over forty years which I had no control over.

But Jesus set me free of both alcohol demons and demon possession. Demons that spoke internally to me. I heard demonic dialogues in my head for over thirty years. Jesus set me free of both along with the voices in a matter of minutes. Friends, there isn't a stronghold God cannot overcome in a person's life. I'm a living witness and testimony of the truth.

Mankind must acknowledge all strongholds are under the influence of the devil and demonic powers. Something no human being is capable of overcoming under his or her own strength. Only Jesus Christ living in you as Lord and Savior can defeat strongholds and demon possession in one's life.

Ask Jesus Christ to come into your life to be Lord and Savior open up you heart invite him in at this very moment. Ask Jesus to deliver you from any habits (strongholds) or anything that which you are a slave or cannot control in your life.

Jesus Christ will set you free of any demonic strongholds. I was set free of alcohol demons something I thought could not ever happen. The devil had me fool with his spirit perception that I could not be free of alcoholism.

The world won't tell you but I am, the entire world is in a stronghold. While under the influence and sway of the devil's devices and demonic powers, powers that exist in the body of the world population. These spirit powers are real and alive; they aren't a figment of imagination. Demon spirits are real and alive moving about in the Earth and in the body of humankind of all ages.

Remember strongholds of the devil and demonic powers are being under the influence of the devil's spirit and demonic powers such as habits or anything a person is a slave of or anything a person does or says without their will or the will of God is being manifest and perform by a spirit or spirits that is greater than their natural spirit.

I know what it's like to be held in bondage or stronghold by demonic forces manifesting and performing through which you have no control over. I was victimized without I though no hope well over forty years in which the devil told me I was going to die at the age of thirty-six. He literally said, "You're going to die at the age of thirty-six!" which he tried because I thought I had no hope. "Church he tried."

Therefore, mankind needs Christ living in him as Lord and Savior. Jesus Christ is the only way mankind can live a holy and normal life God want us to live. Before the world was made God had already chosen us to be his through our union with Christ so that we would be holy and without fault before him.

Back sliders and sinners whom the devil and demon forces have in bondage, God says, "I've blotted out your sins, they are gone like morning mist at noon. Oh! return to me for I have paid the price to set you free."

Therefore, Jesus will set you free to live the life that our Father want us to live. But you and mankind must have Jesus Christ as Lord and Savior to accomplish their life.

Backsliders and sinners you are compromising with a phenomenon, an occurrence, a circumstance, or a fact that you aren't perceptible to your senses because you aren't in your rightful mind but under the power of influence of Satan or demonic forces or both. The perceptions you perceive is that of the world, the spirit of Satan or a demon or both.

Which mean you must be set free of demonic bondage and to be set free of demonic bondage is to be set free of the world after being set free of the world through Jesus Christ, God returns you to your rightful mind and senses that the devil and demons spirits used for their wicked purposes.

You are now set free of the world that made you live as you used to; the old self that was being destroyed by deceitful desires. Jesus Christ has set you free and will keep in perfect peace all those who trust in him and whose thoughts turn often to the Lord.

Trust in our Lord and God always for your heart and mind are made completely new. And in the Lord Jehovah is everlasting strength.

Once you receive Jesus Christ into your heart, this same power working in you and in me is the same as the mighty power that God used to raised Christ from death and seated him at his right side in the heavenly world.

Church, I believe the world belong to the church, the Body of Christ, I also believe that's why Jesus said, "I did not come to save the world but the world may be save through me," the Church, the Body of Christ.

To Whom It May Concern Do Not Place Me, Jehovah in a Box

Thus, says the Lord, to the congregation of all denominations throughout the entire world, "Do not place me, Jehovah God in a box nor my name; nor my Word or works in a box, nor behind closed doors for which My servants has to say of My Word or works through them."

There isn't anything about Me, Jehovah is so important which cannot openly be discuss or spoken of, not anything on the Earth, in the Earth nor under the Earth, that's more important to what I say or do.

My Word and My works are to be public throughout the Earth, not put or discuss in a "box," nor behind closed doors.

Note: "Everyone, I mean, everyone" is to hear that which I speak to and through My servants that which he or she speaks for Me.

Again, never place Me, Jehovah God, My Word nor My works in a box nor behind closed doors.

My congregation of all denominations are to hear My Word and see works of their God, Jehovah. I have spoken these words, even though written by man, My servant who speaks in behalf of Me, Jehovah God.

"Thus," says the Lord, "my Word and neither My works is to be compromised, nor laugh at. I have spoken, to whom it may concern."

No devil nor demon, in spirit or flesh will return My Word nor My works "void" unto Me, Jehovah God.

Doctrine of demons has Jesus Christ as being His own Father, but woe upon you who teaches and preaches such, to make it sound good to the ears of congregations, which is being traditionally preached to this day and time but are afraid or embarrass to teach that which is true, "You will be held accountable," says the Lord.

A Doctrine of Demons

Note: Children of God, "doctrine of demons," is a system or principle which scripture or scriptures which are preached or taught, which are nonbiblical. Scriptures which clergies and ministers who were called to preach, turn "true" biblical Scriptures around or alter to change the true biblical meaning to comply with their carnal mind (flesh) to preach or speak what the congregation is itching to hear. "But woe upon them that does such."

To God's congregation, I'm just a forerunner, who speaks in behalf of Jehovah God, which only a "fool" would make fun or comedy remarks (jokes) of God's servants or attempt or would try to prevent or hinder the works of God. Only a "fool" in or out of the Body of Christ, the Church.

Note: Congregation of God, without any doubt, I know who I've seen. Without any doubt who spoke to me in Jesus's presence. Without any doubt who spoke to me in Jehovah God's presence. Without any doubt who called me. Without any doubt who ordained me and without any doubt who is in me and instruct me.

Note: Now to whom it may concern, if any in doubt, go to Him, Jehovah God, that sent me, don't go to man, not even come to me, His servant, go directly to Jehovah God to ask anything you wish to know of me, anything.

Mankind know and recognize me in the flesh, but no one knows me of the Spirit.

Your brother in Christ,
Bro. Evans

Congregation, this letter or message is written in respect of the Kingdom of God.

Jehovah God and Mankind Spiritual Integrity Sermon and Message

I

Note: Congregation of God, spiritual integrity began with a challenge of mankind integrity toward Jehovah God which brought about spiritual warfare into the spiritual realm in which we live.

Spiritual warfare began with a challenge of mankind integrity toward Jehovah God. When Satan charged Jehovah God with unrighteously giving Job everything along with full protection so that he, Satan could not test Job to show what was really in his heart. Satan said that Job served God for selfish reasons.

Brethren, it is Satan the Devil that cause mankind to become enemies of God as well as man himself.

You can't imagine the multitude of people whom the devil is responsible for turning away from God and abandoning faith in the Lord Jesus Christ.

Note: Did they turn away from God under their own power? "No," they turn by the powerful influence of the devil.

Satan is still challenging mankind integrity toward God. Therefore, you must stay alert at all time, learn to recognize the enemy or enemies attack in the body which is the temple of the Holy Spirit. Listen to your words spoken as you and the other person speak.

Recognize being yourself, acknowledge when using the tongue and mouth to speak and others as well.

Read James 4:7–8. "So then, submit yourselves to God. Resist the Devil, and he will run away from you. Come near to God, and he will come near to you."

The tools and devises of Satan is the human mind, against man, is man himself and also his spirit.

Read John 13:2. "The Devil put into the heart of Judas one of the twelve Disciples the thought of betraying Jesus, and which he did."

Note: Servants, brothers and sisters, who has been born spiritually again from above into the Kingdom or family of God, a time and place is coming when your spiritual integrity of the fruitage of God's spirit in you will be tested, love, joy, peace, patience, longsuffering, kindness, goodness, faithfulness, humility, and self-control.

Congregation, your spiritual integrity of each will be tested, you will come under the attacks of Satan the Devil through members of your own family, relatives, friends, or associates.

Satan alone will attack you internally and externally in and of the body, in the Earth atmosphere.

There aren't no ifs, ands, nor buts, all will be tested, "however the Scripture says in 1 John 4:4. "He that is in you is greater than he that is in the world."

I believe all Christians have read this verse of Scripture. But how can one on an individual basis say, "greater is he in me, than he that is in the world," unless tested.

Note: Spiritual integrity and spiritual warfare, both take place or exist in the spiritual realm. Spiritual warfare covers all areas of life, there isn't anything left out.

II

How to Recognize the Devil's Spirit

Children of Jehovah God, Satan the Devil is two, a spirit and a person. He is a devour in many areas of mankind's life. He, his Spirit is the representatives of two living beings, the devil, or Satan as spirit in the spiritual realm or supernatural realm and as a human or a materialize being, person. Who is the manifestation of a spirit being in the physical realm who roams the Earth seeking whom he can devour or use to steal, kill, or destroy?

Recall, the devil's spirit approached and appeared to Eve through a snake (serpent). Today he appears to mankind in the "flesh" as a human being, a person yet approaching mankind with venomous words.

Satan is an enemy of all mankind, evil words taste so good (mouth) to him, that he keeps some in his mouth to enjoy its flavor, venomous of whom he chooses to manifest through.

Children of God, you should always remember the devil's spirit, approaches you in the "flesh" of mankind as a human being (person) to steal, kill, or destroy.

Testimony of Myself

Note: "Man can't see the devil in his natural form in spirit. Which I did at the age of six, through the vision of the Holy Spirit. Satan at that time telepathically communicated with me and commanded me to curse God but the Holy Spirit led me not to."

Congregation of God, this is the "good part," acknowledging who Satan is and who represent Satan spirit being.

Never forget, the devil is two, a spirit being, person that represent himself and a human being, a person which represent his spirit being through the manifestation of the "flesh" of either gender, male or female.

Note: It is extremely important to recognize Satan spirit approach through manifestation of the flesh of mother, father, son, daughter, sister, or brother or by other means. There aren't any exceptions which is to steal, kill, or destroy.

Note: Jehovah God is my "Witness," as an adult Satan appeared again in the dining room of my home as a materialize human being, a person whom I saw with my natural vision, which I conveyed to him, "I see you," before he dematerializes back into spirit.

Man cannot see Satan as himself, spirit; therefore, a person must listen for his or demon spirit's approach by means of a person's mouth and speech, the manifestation of their spirit approach is by way of mouth and tongue of a person's vocal expression or utterance (*speech*).

Note: The devil is representative of two realms, so are demons, one is the spiritual realm or atmosphere and the other as a human being, a person in the physical realm so are demons.

He appears as both a person and an angel of (deception) light, so does his demons. He is devoured in many areas of human life. He constantly seeking out whom he may devour through manifestation of his spirit, so are his demons.

Read 1 Peter 5:8: "Be alert, be on watch! Your enemy, the Devil roams around like a roaring lion, looking for someone to devour."

Note: Congregation, remember, the devil is here to steal, kill, and destroy human lives. They are adversaries of the spiritual and physical world.

Remember, they are here to steal, kill, or destroy, you must stay alert to recognize who (*the devil*) or (*demon spirits*) may manifest through father, mother, son, daughter, brother, sister, relatives, friend, associates, even oneself, or an animal.

Jesus gave a clear and comprehensive example of Satan the Devil's spirit when he spoke to Jesus through the articulation of the vocal expression of Peter, which Jesus knew and recognize his spirit by addressing him. While making it known to the other disciples, that Satan can and will use anyone to represent him and his evil and wicked works.

Example, Jesus spoke to the disciples about his suffering and death.

Read Mark 8:32–33.

> He made this very clear to them. So, Peter took him aside and began to rebuke him.
> But Jesus turned around, look at his disciples, and rebuked Peter, "Get away from me, Satan," he said, "your thoughts don't come from God, but from human nature."

Note: It may be noted that Jesus looked at the other disciples when doing this likely indicating that he knew Peter spoke sentiments ("as an angel of light") shared by the others.

Note: Children of Jehovah God, mankind didn't choose to represent Satan nor demons, nor their devious, heinous wicked works. He chose (man) humankind and so does demons for delegates as representatives for their demonic wicked works.

However, there are children of the devil.

Read 1 John 3:9–10.

> Those who are children of God do not continue to sin, for God's very nature is in them, and because God is their Father, they cannot continue to sin.
> Here is the clear differences between God's children and the Devil's children, those who do not do what is right or do not love others are not God children.

Note: I believe all mankind unknowingly while some knowingly represented demonic behavior or activities at some point in one's life.

However, we must not forget their approach is in the flesh as a person which cannot be seen with natural vision but you can hear their invisible spirit approach through a person mouth and words; however, you must listen for their approach in the tongue which reveals the manifestation of the spirits presence in vocal articulation (speech) or expression.

Note: Congregation, by the eternal Word of God, Christians are enlightened to realize Satan and demon forces power, designs, and purposes, have all been defeated in the Name of Jesus Christ and with the spiritual weapons God provides, "His Word."

Read Ephesians 6:13–18.

> So put on God's Armor now. Then when the evil day comes you will be able to resist the enemy's attacks and after fighting to the end, you will still hold your ground.
>
> So stand ready, with the truth as a belt tight around your waist, with righteousness as your breast plate.
>
> and as your shoes the readiness to announce the Good News of peace.
>
> At all times carry faith as a shield, for with it you will be able to put out all the burning arrows shot by the Evil one.
>
> Do all this in prayer, asking for God's help. Pray on every occasion, as the Spirit leads.

Note: So pay attention, child of God, Satan's approach is in and through man's words, the manifestation of Satan spirit is in and through the person's tongue.

Don't ever forget, you don't see his spirit approach, you must listen for his approach through one vocal articulation and expression.

Note: Satan does not discriminate, he transforms into the spirit of that of a human being, male and masquerade as a female, age nor gender is no exception to accomplish his objectives or goals which is to steal, kill, or destroy in the spiritual or physical realms.

Note: Child of Jehovah God stand your ground and remember. "Greater is He in you, than he that is in the world and he that is in them who belongs to the world."

Remain vigilant in the world, wear at all times the whole armor of God, and remember, "He is in you, is greater than he is in whom is speaking to or coming against you!"

Amen.

Note: A testimony, one of many encounters I've experienced with Satan the Devil and just as many or more encounters with his cohorts, demon spirits in the flesh of people of the physical realm and as many more in the spiritual realm.

My testimony of Satan being two, a spirit and a spirit person. Over the years, I've experienced many encounters with the devil, Satan in the spiritual realm and as a spirit person in the physical realm.

I am a bona fide witness of Satan materialization as a human being whom I dialogue with not knowing who he was until he left, whom I thought never to be seen again until he appeared in the dining room of my home.

I left the kitchen and upon entering the dining room which was dark with a little illumination coming from a den light of another room.

Upon entering, I saw the figure and outline of a person (man) standing between the dining table and china cabinet. I stopped to pause. I said, "I see you, I see you"; as I got a better fix on him, he would move out of the illumination of the light coming from the den.

I walked past him and the dining room table between us. I went into the bedroom, but upon returning, he had dematerialized back to spirit.

I stood across from where he stood and told him he was a defeated "foe," and I possess authority and power over him in the Name of Jesus Christ.

I reiterate.

Congregation, by the eternal Word of God, Christians are enlightened to realize Satan and demonic forces, existence, their power, designs, and purpose are defeated, with the spiritual weapons God provides, "His Word in the Name of Jesus Christ."

Amen.

Declaration

I proclaim this decade and the duration of mankind upon the Earth will be the exposing of demons and demonic activities throughout the nations. It will be exposing of demon spirits in the homes as well as in human lives.

Congregation of God, more people will be delivered of demonic bondage and oppression and demon possession of spirits in the flesh than ever before.

This declaration and revelation, I believe, parents will become husbands and wives again; boys and girls will become sons and daughters again.

Husbands and wives will become fathers and mothers again, sons and daughters will become, brothers and sisters again. "All will unite in the presences of Jehovah God as families again." May we all be in agreement, for this is what the Lord wants.

Amen.

The Fight to Do What's Right Sermon

Note: Congregation, as long as Satan's world exists, Christians must fight to keep free from its wicked influences. The Apostle Paul wrote, "Put on the complete suit of armor from God that you may be able to stand firm against the crafty work of the devil."

Read Ephesians 6:11–18.

> For we are not fighting against human beings but against the wicked spiritual forces in the heavenly world, the rulers, authorities, and cosmic powers of the dark age.
>
> So put on God's armor now! Then when the evil day comes, you will be able to resist the enemy's attacks, and after fighting to the end, you will still hold your ground.

Note: Our (your) fight is not only against Satan and his world, it is also against our own desires to do what is bad. The Bible says the inclination of the heart of man is bad from his youth up.

Read Genesis 8:21. "The Lord said, 'Never again will I put the Earth under a curse because of what people do. I know that from the time they are young their thoughts are evil.'"

Note: Because of the sin inherited from the first man Adam, the heart craves to do what is bad; therefore, with the word of God, the armor, Christians fight to do what is right.

The Apostle Paul had such a fight, as he explained: Read Romans 7:21–23.

> So I find that this law is at work, when I want to do what is good, what is evil is the only choice I have.
> My inner being delights in the law of God.
> But I see a different law at work in my body, a law that fights against the law which my mind approves of. It makes me a prisoner to the law of sin which is at work in my body.

Note: Christian you to may have a powerful conflict going on within you, while thinking what to do. You must come to know God and Jesus Christ.

Note: Some persons studying the Bible may actually be engaging in such bad practices, though they know that these things are condemned by God.

Note: The fact that they do wrong when they wish to do right demonstrates the Bible truth. "The heart is more treacherous than anything else and is desperate." Scripture says in Jeremiah 17:9, "Who can understand the human heart? There is nothing else so deceitful, it is too sick to be healed."

This does not mean that a person has no control over strong desires to do wrong. You can strengthen your heart so that it will lead you in a right way. But it is up to you to do this. Nobody else can win the fight for you.

You must take in life-giving Bible knowledge of the true God, it must also sink into your heart, so that you really want to act upon it to gain appreciation for God's law and world.

Note: A person need to think deeply about them, meditate on them and obey them. Obedience is better than sacrifice. Obeying God really make a different in one's life.

Note: Think of the teenage girl, who wrote, "I've had venereal disease three times. The last time it cost me my right to bear children because I had to have a hysterectomy." It is truly sad to consider all the trouble that is caused when people disobey God's laws.

Note: Here a woman who had committed fornication sadly said, "It's just not worth the pain and emotional breakdown that comes with disobedience. I'm suffering for that now."

This fight can be won through obedience, congregation, obedience to God is essential in this life and eternal life. God has first claim to the obedience of all his creatures. We rightly owe God obedience as our Maker and the Source from whom our life derives and on whom life depends.

Read Psalm 95:6–7.

> Come let us bow down and worship him,
> let us kneel before the Lord, our Maker.
> He is our God, we are the people he cares
> for, the flock for which he provides. Listen today
> to what he says.

Note: Yet you will hear people say that fornication as well as getting drunk and taking drugs is fun. But the so-called fun is only temporary. So do not be misled into a course of action that will rob you of your obedience and happiness.

Note: Counteracting disobedience due to sin and imperfection, Jehovah God has mercifully provided the means for combating "the fight to do what is right."

To win the fight against the many pressures to do wrong, we (mankind) need to have a close relationship with Jehovah God.

Note: A twenty-year-old youth who was faced with the temptation to commit fornication, said, "My hope for everlasting life was too valuable to lose for a few moments of immorality."

Note: Congregation, Christians, "the fight to do, what is right," you can't never let down your guard in this fight, as King David once did.

Read 2 Samuel 11:1–17.

> King David happened one day to be looking from his rooftop, and in the distance, he saw beautiful Bath-sheba bathing herself. Rather than turning away, improper thoughts grew in his heart, he kept looking. His desire to have sexual relation with Bath-sheba became so strong that he had her brought to his palace.
>
> Later she became pregnant and he was unable to have their adultery covered up, he arranged to have her husband killed in battle.

Note: That indeed was a terrible sin, and King David really suffered for it. Not only was he distressed by what he had done, but Jehovah punished him with trouble in his household for the rest of his life, but first Jehovah God says to David in 2 Samuel 12:9–12:

> Why, then have you disobeyed my commands? Why did you do this evil thing? You had Uriah killed in battle, you let the Ammonites kill him, and then you took his wife!
>
> Now, in every generation some of your descendants will die a violent death because you have disobeyed me and have taken Uriah's wife.
>
> I swear to you that I will cause someone from your own family to bring trouble on you. You will see it when I take your wives from you and give them to another man, and he will have intercourse with them in broad daylight.
>
> You sinned in secret, but I will make this happen in broad daylight for all Israel to see.

Note: David's heart was more treacherous than he had realized, his wrong desires overpowered him. David confessed, "I have sinned against the Lord, David said" (2 Sam. 12:13).

Read Psalm 51:5: "I have been evil from the day I was born, from the time I was conceived, I have been sinful."

Congregation, the bad thing David did with Bathsheba did not have to happen. His problem was that he kept looking, he did not avoid the situation that caused his sexual appetite to grow for another man's wife.

Note: Brethren and sisters, we should learn from King David's experience, "The fight to do what is right" is through the Lord Jehovah God. Therefore, be alert and on guard against situations that excite improper sexual feelings.

Note: For example, think what will happen if you read books and watch television programs and movies that put emphasis on sex? Your sexual desires are sure to be stimulated. So avoid activities and entertainment that work up sexual appetite.

Read Colossians 3:5. "You must put to death, then, the earthly desires at work in you, such as sexual immorality, indecency, last, evil passions, and greed also the Scripture says."

Read 1 Thessalonians 4:3–5:

> God wants you to be holy and completely
> free from sexual immorality.
> Each of you should know how to live with
> your wife in a holy and honorable way.
> Not with a lustful desire, like the heathen
> who do not know God.

Note: Congregation, hear this, "Do not put yourself in a situation with another person that can lead to fornication."

Anyone can say, "We know when to stop." True, a person may know when, but how many can do it?

Note: "It is better to avoid the situation."

Note: Here's another example, "If David had kept in mind the example of Joseph, he would never have committed that great sin against God."

Read Genesis 39:7–12.

> Remember Joseph had been put in charge of Potiphar household.
> Potiphar was away, his wife tries to seduce Joseph, but he refused.
> Then one day she grabbed him and tried to make him lie down with her. But Joseph broke free and fled.
> He kept his heart strong by thinking, not of satisfying his own sexual desires, but of what was right in God's sight.
> Joseph ask himself, "How could I commit this great boldness and sin against God?" Joseph fled from the immoral advances of Potiphar's wife.

Note: Congregation, to win the fight, to do what is right, you must let Bible knowledge sink down into your heart so that you are moved to act upon it. And with its help, the "Bible," no matter how deeply you may have been involved in wrongdoing, you can change with Bible knowledge.

Note: The Apostle Paul wrote do not be misled.
Read 1 Corinthians 6:9–11.

> Surely you know that the wicked will not possess God's Kingdom. Do not fool yourselves, people who are immoral or who worship idols or are adulterers or homosexual perverts,
> or who steal or are greedy or are drunkards or who slander others or are thieves—none of these will passes God's Kingdom.
> Some of you were like that. But you have been purified from sin, you have been dedicated to God, you have been put right with God by the Lord Jesus Christ, and by the Spirit, our God.

Note: Brothers and sisters, think of yourselves today some of us Christians had formerly been fornicators, adulterers, homosexuals, thieves, and drunkards. But with help from the Christian organization, the Body or Church we have changed.

Note: The Apostle Paul himself had once practiced bad things.

Read 1 Timothy 1:15: "This is a true saying, to be completely accepted and believed, Christ Jesus came into the world to save sinners. I am the worst of them."

Note: Titus also wrote to his fellow Christians: "For we ourselves were once foolish, disobedient and wrong. We were slaves to passions and pleasure of all kinds. We spent our lives in malice and envy, others hated us and we hated them" (Titus 3:3).

Note: Apostle Paul had a lifelong battle against the wrong desires and pleasures to which he had once been a slave.

Paul got tough with himself. He would force himself to do what is right, even when his body desired to do wrong. Paul says, "I harden my body with blows and bring it under complete control to keep myself from being disqualified after having called others to the contest" (1 Cor. 9:27).

Note: Brothers and sisters, you too can do as Paul, get tough with yourself, to fight to do, what is right. And if you do as he did, you also can win this fight through Christ.

Note: Congregation, if you are finding it hard to overcome some bad habit, like myself once had and like many other persons were once part of this world in which fornication, adultery, drunkenness, homosexuality, smoking, drug addiction, theft, fraud, lying and gambling, are so very common. All these things we once practice.

Read 1 Peter 4:3–4.

> You have spent enough time in the past doing what the heathen like to do. Your lives were spent in indecency, lust, drunkenness, orgies drinking parties and the disgusting worship of idols.

And now the heathen are surprised when you do not join them in the same wild and reckless living, and so they insult you.

Note: But be of good cheer.

Read 1 John 5:4. "Because every child of God is able to defeat the world. And we win the victory over the world by means of our faith."

Note: We, Christians, are among persons who are fighting to overcome the same practices we ourselves once desired. We must encourage them; it takes courage in winning the fight to do what is right with God's help.

Note: Our responsibility as Christians is to shepherd the flock of God. We must not hesitate to go to them to help to overcome some habit that is contrary to God's law.

Read 1 Peter 5:3. "Do not try to rule over those who have been put in you care, but be examples to the flock."

Also, read Acts 20:28. "So keep watch over yourselves and over all the flock which the Holy Spirit has placed in your care."

Note: Congregation, the pressure to do wrong is on us, not only in Satan's world but from within our sinful selves. So be fruitful to God in our daily fight to do what is right.

Amen.

God Army Isn't Denominational

I was baptized into the Body of Christ at the age of eleven. Obviously, I did not realize nor acknowledge life of becoming a Christian. Neither a demonized demon-possessed alcoholic nor spokesperson for God the Creator. However, in later years I became all three but not in that order.

I was six years of age when I drunk to experience alcohol after the first of many encounters with the devil, demons, and the spirit world, which last over forty years even though I was baptized at the age of eleven.

Satan the Devil attempts to bring condemnation upon me before I knew he or demons existed. He visited me three times at the age of six. I initially witnessed his spirit being emerged from beneath the ground while visiting my grandmother. However, I did not realize I was seeing a demonic form nor the devil's spirit. After the dark shadowy figure of a person emerged, it appeared to float in midair just above the surface floating away from me and vanished.

It was dark when my parents came and got me as we drove off, I look back in the direction of the area. I saw the shadowy figure and there he was riding on the rear bumper staring me in the face. He was in bodily form wearing dark clothing and a large dark hat, having a face and head; however, I could only see his large white eyes. And as he stared me in the face, he rode on the rear bumper until we were near home that's when his dark shadowy figure leap from the bumper. I was so frightened, I never told anyone of the encounter.

Several days later, he appeared in the back yard of our home in transparent bodily form. I still did not realize nor recognize whom or what I was seeing in the spirit realm. However, he telepathically communicated with me commanding me to curse God. I did not know any better, but the Holy Spirit led me not to. "This spiritual encounter I witnessed through the vision of the Holy Spirit." The question is, "Why the devil followed me home and why he command me to curse God?"

Several days later, I was out alone playing not very far from the area the devil had spoken to me when a white cloud descend onto my head and vanish. I ran into the house and told my mother what had happen, she looked at me with a smile as though it was a child's prank. It was over forty years later when God revealed the revelation and significance of that cloud, which I'll reveal later.

Since the encounters a host of demonic spirits has physically came to harass and followed me since the first time, I witnessed the devil's spirit being emerge from beneath the surface of the ground. Since then I've been physically slapped and punched on several times just to name a few.

Since the age of six, I've been demonized, and demon-possessed for over forty years in which I heard demonic voices in my head, thirty of those forty years I was under demonic influence.

Over forty years of the sixty years of my life, I was under demonic domination and demonic influence. I was an alcoholic for over thirty years, controlled by alcohol demons and influence by demonic voices in my head by their spirit intellectual perceptions for many years.

However, that did not stop God's calling upon me to become His servant. It was until God cured me of demon possession, demon domination and alcohol demons that Jesus Christ cleansed me of demonic personalities, voices, demonic perceptions, and fornication.

Upon my calling (recruitment) I was alcoholic, demonized possessed fornicator. I was the lowest of the least of sinners. Still yet God recruited me into His army, and it was Jesus Christ that cleansed me and made me worthy of becoming a servant of God.

I've been involved with demons and the devil in the Earth's atmosphere and in people my entire life. My last major demonic encounter, "I've had many since then," was with Satan himself. They acknowledge I'm a servant of God. However, he came to do that which demons failed to do that is to stop or turn me away from serving God. However, he failed as well. This happen after the revelation and significance of the cloud.

Remember he appeared just before the cloud forty years earlier. This time he appeared after the revelation was revealed to me forty years later in my home in a materialized human body but he would not show his face neither did he speak. He just stood motionless in the semidark dining room not doing a thing. I told him several times before I left the room, "I see you." I return shortly but he could not be seen.

Now the significance of the cloud was a revelation of God calling me to become His servant in His universal army. Even though I was a young boy of six years of age it was a divine revelation of God's recruitment and enlistment which came to past over forty years later. Now I'm a servant of the Most High and a member of God's universal army.

However, it is imperative mankind acknowledge Satan has an army, a spirit of fallen angelic beings, angels who have become demon's person without bodies, wicked evil spirits in the Earth's atmosphere and dwelling in the bodies of the demon-possessed throughout the world.

Satan is a nondenominational devil; he is neither bias nor unbiased. He does not discriminate; he uses all human beings on an equal basis. Therefore, it's imperative that we mankind remember that which God said of judging others, "Man judges from appearance but I look at his heart, says God of all and who is in all and Father of all."

People, Satan, and demons are real and alive in the spirit world around us and in people. The spirit realm is beyond mankind comprehension or perception. However, I see into the spirit realm as well as any person but it never amazes me to see that which are in people and around us in the atmosphere.

But I'm a member of God's army for this is what we are up against in this evil and wicked world. I've come a long way over the years from being the least of the lowest of sinners to the highest rank in the army of God whom Jesus himself picked up to ordain and anointed.

Since then I've come a long way since Jesus came into my life to mold me to be whom God called me to be even though I'm nondenominational and various times I'm Pentecostal.

What I'm expressing, people who are Christians are in the Body of Christ's congregation as members or disciples, so we shall all come together to that oneness in our faith and in our knowledge of the Son of God reaching to the very height of Christ's full stature.

By way of Jesus Christ, I discovered there is one army but several branches serving under one God. Categorically and collectively speaking God is not a denominational God. God put every different part denominational and nondenominational in the Body just as He wanted it. There would not be a Body nor army if it were all only one part. As it is there are many parts but still one army or Body of Christ.

God Himself has put the Body together in such a way as to give greater honor to those parts or denominations that needs it. And so there is no division in the Body but all the branches or denominations have the same concern for one another. We are all supposed to serve One God and Lord.

Whenever the Body preach a denominational God, it preaches a crossless gospel and wherever a crossless gospel there is no power to change a life. The salvation of mankind is the work of the cross of Jesus Christ.

The Apostle Paul said, "The gospel of Christ is the power of God unto salvation and the preaching of the cross is the power of God to us that believe." (The demons believe.)

Remember we, the army, cannot preach the gospel without preaching the cross and the blood of Jesus Christ whereby we are crucified, washed, purified, sanctified, and perfected in Christ and raised up in newness of life to serve God.

This is the gospel of truth; we are not risen with Christ if we are not crucified with Christ. Crucifixion is the work of salvation. It is a finish work at the cross of Calvary for all that believe the gospel. The gospel is in the cross. If we ever move away from the simplicity of the Gospel of Jesus Christ, there is no help for neither the church of America nor the army of God. For there is only one army of God but many branches serving under one God.

It was the death of Christ that broke down the wall of partition between Jew and Gentile or Jews and denominations. Jesus's death on the cross was the basis for removing denominations and law separation that which separated the Jews from the non-Jews. There by Jesus death brought denominations together that became one body to God.

Jesus came to save all. Remember what Jesus said to the Samaritan woman, "But the time is coming and is already here when by the power of God's Spirit people will worship the Father as he really is offing Him, the true worship that he wants. God is Spirit and only by the power of His Spirit can people worship Him as he really is. God is worship in Spirit and in truth."

We know about being baptized into Christ, don't we? There is one body and one spirit, just as there is one Hope to which God has called you and me. There is one Lord, one faith and one baptism. There is One God and Father of all who is Lord of all, works through all and is in all. For by one Spirit are we baptized into one Body.

Yet it is the cross that we are reconciled to God in the body of Jesus Christ through death. When we were baptized into Jesus we were baptized into His death. Everything that was accomplished for us, mankind was through Jesus's death, burial, and resurrection. Therefore, it is a finish work at the cross when we are crucified with him buried with him and resurrected with him, ascend with him, and seated with Him in heavenly places.

That's why all denominations and nondenominations must preach the death, burial, and resurrection of Jesus Christ as the wisdom and power of God to free mankind from sin and birth them into the Kingdom of God.

In the same way all of us whether Jews or Gentiles, whether slaves or free, denominational, or nondenominational have been baptized into the one body and one army of God by the same Spirit, and we have all been given the one Spirit to drink.

I'll use the functioning of a human body categorically and collectively to illustrate denominational and nondenominational operations of the Christian congregation and army. All are baptized by Holy Spirit into Christ and into his death. Thereby we are all baptized into one body. Thus, all the body follows the head, Christ is the head of the church and God's army.

Which explain Jesus Christ is the Head of the Christian congregation, which is His body. The Christian body of people has no division racially, nationally, or otherwise. Jesus and people of all races (Gentiles) of all nations being represented in it. By his death on the cross Jesus united all races into one body.

Any person that think highly of their denomination and denominational views and who believe your denominational congregation is above other denomination or nondenominational congregation, thus being teach that your denomination is the only denomination God and the Lord Jesus Christ recognized, brother you are being erroneously teach false doctrine.

If God was a denominational God, Satan would not have created division among denominational congregations. If God was a denominational God, Jesus could not have died on the cross removing the law of Moses which separated the Jews and Gentiles. If God was a denominational God, the Holy Spirit would not have told and directed me to a nondenomination congregation performing healing miracles and miraculous works through me.

The Holy Spirit is my witness of this truth. God spoke to me audibly several times, thus saying, "If you love Me, tell the truth." God also spoke to me standing in the presence of Jesus, thus said God, "That's Jesus whom I was in the presence of God also said to me in Spirit. I give you My Spirit."

Had God whom I serve in Spirit and in truth was a denomination God, I don't believe God would have said to me a nondenominational member of the body of Christ. I give you My Spirit. Yes, I'm nondenominational and sometimes Pentecostal whom He gave His Spirit to and spoken audible to and through.

What I'm explaining is the body itself is not made up of only one part of denomination but of many. Remember what Jesus explained to the Samaritan woman. But the time is coming and is already here when by the power of God's Spirit people will worship the Father as he really is offing Him the true worship that He wants. God is Spirit and only by the power of his Spirit can people worship him as he really is. God is worship in Spirit and in truth.

Therefore, if the Methodist were to say because I am not Church of Christ, I don't belong to the body or if the Baptist would say because I'm not Jewish I don't belong to the body or a denominational congregation would say because you are a nondenominational congregation you don't belong to the Body of Christ.

Brethren, should any person whether Jew or Gentile, denominational or nondenominational preach division in the body of Christ is being expose to false doctrine and is the work of the devil. Satan is not a nondenominational devil nor his demons. He nor his demons are neither bias nor unbiased. They treat all human beings equal through division of serving Christ Jesus.

However, it is written, whether Jews or Gentiles, whether slaves or free denominational or nondenominational all are baptized into the one body by the same Spirit and we have all been given the one Spirit to drink.

It took Golgotha to universalize Christ mission on the cross to bring all mankind to God. What greater proof in there than this that it was not until after Jesus's resurrection and the moment of His ascension that the mission mandate was given. "You, therefore, must go out making disciples of all nations."

Yes, Christ is like a single body that has many parts. However, it is still one body even though it is made up of different parts. But what the ear, eye, nose does not recognize as body parts. They aren't parts of the Body of Christ nor the army of God.

The Blood and the Cross of Jesus Christ Sermon

I

Note: Congregation, it is a sad and growing reality that the Gospel of the Cross with Christ crucified is not preached in many churches. The message many are preaching has nothing to do with the Blood of Christ or repentance for sin or the fear of Almighty God.

Note: Many preached a gospel that speak of self-reliance, how to beautify self; how to build self or how to enrich self and succeed in business. Which is the reason it is so important that we go with the Gospel of Jesus Christ as it was revealed to the Apostle Paul. (The Gospel is the power of God unto salvation for all.)

Note: Brothers and sisters, if we ever move away from the simplicity of the Gospel of Jesus Christ (which is the Blood and the Cross) there is no hope for neither the Church or America.

Read 1 Corinthians 1:18. "For the message about Christ's death on the cross is nonsense to those who are being lost, but for us who are being saved it is God's power."

Note: Mankind must remember on the Cross his work of love, compassion, his death of suffering, his burial, his glorious, resurrection and his triumphant ascension to glory are all designed to lead us to the Cross which cause us to give our all.

Note: We must also remember, man cannot preach the Gospel of Jesus Christ without preaching the Blood and the Cross of Christ. Whereby we are crucified, washed, purified, sanctified, perfected in Christ, and raised up in newness of life to serve God.

Note: Since we're crucified with Jesus, buried with him, resurrected with him, ascended with him, and seated with him in heavenly places. We shall go forth and do the work of God upon the Earth offering ourselves a human sacrifice to God dedicated to His service.

Note: Mankind (*ascended*) understand, "BEFORE WE CAN BE SEATED WITH JESUS IN HEAVENLY PLACES, MANKIND MUST BE BORN AGAIN SPIRITUALLY FROM ABOVE!"

Note: Congregation, it must be preached, the death, burial, and resurrection of Jesus Christ as the wisdom and power of God to free mankind from sin and Birth them into the Kingdom of God. (The new birth, born again.)

Read John 3:3, 5–7.

> Jesus answered, "I am telling you the truth, No one can see the Kingdom of God without being born again."
>
> I am telling you the truth replied Jesus, "that no one can enter the Kingdom of God without being born of water and the Spirit."
>
> A person is born physically of human parents, but is born spiritually of the Spirit.
>
> Do not be surprised because I tell you that you must all be born again.

"Nothing short of this Gospel will work!"

Note: Children of God, this spiritual birth come from above, it supernaturally take's place internally and is spiritually tangible to the spiritual discerned. (This is the new birth.) Therefore, if any man be in Christ, he is a New Creature Old Things are passed away, behold all things are become new.

Read 2 Corinthians 5:17. "Anyone who is joined to Christ is a new being, the old is gone, the new has come."

Note: Brothers and sisters, the person and work of Christ, God made peace through his Son's Blood on the Cross and so brought back to himself all things on Earth and in heaven.

Note: Congregation, It's at the Cross that we are reconciled to God in the body of Jesus Christ through death. Mankind must understand that the one body is not the many membered body of the church but rather the body of flesh that hung on the Cross.

Read Colossians 1:21–22.

> At one time you were far away, from God and were his enemies because of the evil things you did and thought.
>
> But now by means of the physical death of his Son, God has made you his friends, in order to bring you holy, pure, and faultless, into his presence.

Note: The Cross and the Blood of Christ made it possible for all mankind to come into the one body of God.

The "Cross" or torture stake is used in such a way as to represent Jesus's death upon the Cross by means of which redemption from sin and reconciliation with God are made possible.

Read Ephesians 2:14–16.

> For Christ himself has brought us peace by making Jesus and Gentiles one people. With his own body he broke down the wall that separated them and kept them enemies.
>
> He abolished the Jewish Law with its commandments and rules, in order to create out of the two races one new people in union with himself, in this way making peace.
>
> By his death on the cross Christ destroyed their enmity, by means of the cross he united both races into one body and brought them back to God.

Note: Also Jesus death on the Cross or Torture stake was also the basic for removing the law which had separated the Jews from the non-Jews, "Gentiles." *Gentile, a person who is not a Jew.*

Therefore, by accepting the reconciliation made possible by Jesus's death, both Jews and non-Jews (Gentiles) could become "one body" to God by way of the Cross or torture stake.

Note: Congregation, because of the Cross and the Blood.
Read Ephesians 4:4–6.

> There is one body and one Spirit, just as there is one hope to which God has called you.
> There is one Lord, one faith, one baptism.
> there is one God and Father of all people who is Lord of all, works through all, and is in all.

II

THE BLOOD OF CHRIST AND ITS BENEFITS

Note: The Apostle Paul said, "The Gospel of Jesus Christ is the power of God unto salvation." Therefore, it is imperative to remember the gospel cannot be preached or teach unless the Blood and the Cross of Christ is preached.

(9) The Blood of Christ redeems.

The word *redeem* mean to buy back.

(2) The Blood of Christ washes away sins. The sinner is defiled.

Read Titus 1:15; Isaiah 1:16; Revelation 1:5–6, 7:14; Zechariah 13:1. Therefore, man is in need of being washed and it is the blood of Christ that will wash away man sins. "However, man sins are forgiven" in the Name of Jesus.

(3) The Blood of Christ justifies.

Read Romans 5:9. "By his blood we now put right with God; how much more then, will we be saved by him from God's anger!"

Note: The sinner is condemned (Jn. 3:18; 1 Tim. 3:6). He bears the guilt of having transgressed God's law. He stands in need of justification and it is the blood of Christ that does it.

(4) The Blood of Christ sanctifies; the word *sanctify* mean to set apart to a holy and divine purpose.

Read Hebrews 10:29. "What, then of those who despise the Son of God? Who treat as a cheap thing the blood of God's covenant which purified them from sin?" Also read Hebrews 13:12. "For this reason Jesus also died outside the city, in order to purify the people from sin with his own blood."

(5) The Blood of Christ reconciles. The sinner is estranged from God; the sinner is spoken of as being alienated from God. Therefore, the sinner is in need of being reconcile to God.

Read Ephesians 2:13. "But now, in union with Christ Jesus you, who used to be far away, have been brought near by the blood of Christ."

Also read Colossians 1:20: "Through the Son, then God decided to bring the whole universe back to himself. God made peace through his Son's blood on the cross and so brought to himself all things, both on Earth and in heaven."

(6) The Blood of Christ cleanses. The sinner is in need of being cleaned and the blood of Christ fulfill this need.

Read 1 John 1:7. "But if we live in the light, just as he is in the light, then we have fellowship with one another and the blood of Jesus, his Son, purifies us from every sin." (Also read James 1:27, Ephesians 5:25–27.)

(7) The Blood of Christ remit. The word "remit" means to absolve a debt. Sin is spoken of as a debt. The blood of Christ remits that debt.

Read Matthew 26:28. "Jesus said, 'This is my blood, which seals God's covenant, my blood poured out for many for the forgiveness of sins.'"

Also read Hebrews 9:22, "Indeed, according to the law almost everything is purified by blood, and sins are forgiven only if blood is poured out."

(8) The Blood of Christ purges the conscience. The sinner's conscience is defiled. This result in the need of having his conscience purged. It is the blood of Christ that does such.

Read Hebrews 10:22. "So let us come near to God with a sincere heart and a sure faith, with hearts that have been purifies from a guilty conscience and with bodies washed with clean water."

Also read 1 John 3:20, "If our conscience condemns us, we know that God is greater than our conscience and that he knows everything."

(9) The Blood of Christ purchased the Church. In Order for the church to become a reality Jesus had to shed His blood.

Read Acts 20:28. "So keep watch over yourselves and over all the flock which the Holy Spirit has placed in your care. Be shepherds of the church of God. Which he made his own through the blood of his Son."

Also read Ephesians 5:25–27.

> Husbands, love your wives just as Christ loved the church and gave his life for it.
>
> He did this to dedicate the church to God by his word, after making it clean by washing it in water.
>
> In order to present the church to himself in all its beauty, pure and faultless, without spot or wrinkle or any other imperfection.

(10) Deduction: All our hope is built on the blood of Christ and the blood of Christ alone will redeem, wash away sin, justify, sanctify, reconcile, cleanse, remit, purge the conscience, and made the Church a reality.

The Blood

The question is asked, "How does a person contact the blood of Christ?"

Answer: The Bible unequivocally affirm that the sinner come in contact with the blood of Christ in the act of being baptized.

Note: Christ shed His Blood in His death.

Read John 19:34. "One of the soldiers, however, plunged his spear into Jesus side and at once blood and water poured out."

Also read Romans 6:3. We are baptized into His death. "For surely you know that when that when we were baptized into union with Christ Jesus, we were baptized into union with his death."

Note: Therefore in baptism, we contact the blood of Christ.

Note: Congregation, the "Gospel" of Jesus Christ, death, burial, and resurrection leads to eternal salvation. Salvation is a finish work at the Cross of Calvary for all that believe the Gospel.

Note: Salvation is a finish work at the Cross of Calvary for all that believe the gospel. Our salvation (mankind) is by means of receiving sanctification of the spirit and belief of the truth.

For God hath from the beginning chosen us for eternal salvation by way of the spirit not of the flesh and truth.

God hath from the beginning chosen us to salvation through sanctification of the spirit and belief of the truth.

Read 2 Thessalonians 2:13. "We must thank God at all times for you, friends, you whom the Lord loves. For God chose you as the first to be saved by the Spirit's power to make you his holy people and by your faith in the truth."

Note: Therefore, "Ye all must be born again from above the Spirit of God."

Note: Children of God without the Shed of Blood of Christ and the Cross salvation cannot be accomplished. In baptism we contact the blood of Christ or come into union with Christ. However, without the blood, salvation cannot be accomplished.

(1) There could not be union with Christ or being united with Christ.
(2) Mankind (we) could not contact the blood of Christ.
(3) We could not be joint heirs with Christ nor heirs of God.
(4) We could not be in the Body of Jesus Christ.
(5) We believers could not be children of God, that walk holy and up right in the presence of Jehovah God without fault.
(6) We could not be crucified with Christ.
(7) We could not be wash by the blood of Christ.
(8) We could not be reconciled with God.
(9) Without the Blood and the Cross, we could not be Christians of Jehovah God nor our sin be forgiven. Sins are forgiven in the "name" of Jesus Christ!

Note: I speak of everyone that is in Christ, if you didn't come in through His death, you didn't come into Jesus Christ. If you weren't baptized into His death you weren't baptized into Christ.

Note: Congregation, water baptism is essential, it is a requirement of God, which was approved on the Day of Pentecost which was the beginning of the New Testament Church.

"Water baptism is the only baptism approved of Jehovah God."

Note: Congregation, we must preach the Gospel, the death, burial, and resurrection of Jesus Christ as it is. We must stand up and preach it, talk it, testify it, tell it, proclaim it on the job, on street corners and in the Church. "It works for all that believe it. The Gospel is the power of God unto salvation to everyone that believe it."

Amen.

I

A Living Testimony! I, an Eyewitness of Satan the Devil!

"No human being have or can or ever will see Satan on the Earth as he was in heaven as a cherub, an angelic creature who became Lucifer, Satan the angelic being also named devil! Lucifer, a name given him for leading the revolt of angels or angelic sons of God. His appearance on the Earth is Satan the Devil in transition as a person, a physical human being, but yet spirit.

Also, no human being on the Earth in the past or present nor the future have, can or ever will distinguish Satan appearance as a physical born human person from his transition human person physical appearance.

Children of Jehovah God, it is "totally" impossible, human impossibly to distinguish his Earthly appearance as a Spirit Being. Impossible!

Only God can open up one's mind and witness through the vision of the Holy Spirit to see him as a spirit being in transition as a human being.

There he stood beside me in the supermarket whom I thought was another person, a human being; however, Satan cannot, I reiterate, cannot transition in the person of the "dead," deceased loved ones as living persons.

However, he and the fallen angels, who joined Satan in rebellion against God who became demons or wicked spirits on the Earth can, however, pretend or masquerade in spirit to be persons who have died. Which is to advance the idea that the dead are still living.

Demons or wicked spirits have led many to believe the "lie" that death is only a change to another life on the "Earth."

Read Ecclesiastes 9:5–6.

> Yes, the living know they are going to die, but the dead know nothing. They have no further reward; they are completely forgotten.
>
> Their loves, their hates, their passions, all died with them. They will never again take part in anything that happens in this world!

Scripture tells, Satan appeared as an angel of light which he can appear as light in the presence of us; however, it is a light of deception in deceiving the world, the whole world as light walking and performing among us "people," the world population, as a human being, a person.

The angel of light is not only in the physical realm which can be seen and even felt. But also, an angel of light may also come as a false perception of thought which feel or look good in thy sight.

Not all mankind acknowledges Satan the Devil is on the Earth. While other ignore his or his demon's presence because their mind is occupied on or by worldly things. The world in general does not discuss the devil even though he has his spirit hand in everything mankind does, "Everything!"

Note: The question is, how does Satan appear? "As a spirit person in a human body, like you and I are spirit persons in a human body" or a demonic thought or perception is all it takes and by way of that perception, the angel of Light appears which most people does not recognize including some Christian believers.

Congregation of God, do you know most Christian believers does not take Satan to be all that he is? When the Bible clearly says, read 1 Peter 5:8, "Be alert, be on watch, your enemy the Devil, roam around like a roaring lion, looking for someone to devour."

Note: Which mean you and me, whom he's looking for to devour as he did when he appeared to me at both Supermarkets but at different locations.

Believers of God have read 1 Peter 5:8: "Now received it. Do not take it for granted. Believers are the very ones Satan want to devour."

He even began in the early stage of human lives; age is no exception nor gender. He appeared to me in transparent form at the age of five or six, which he commands me to curse God. Why at such an early age because he knows the potential which all human beings God Holds before them.

Amen.

Note: Don't ever forget. "Satan deceives the entire world appearing as a real human being of any nationality he so desires!"

II
A Living Testimony! I Am an Eyewitness of Satan the Devil!

Note: Children of God, believers and nonbelievers, I truthfully testify, I had the opportunity to ask this man, "Satan the Devil" in this life on this date, March 16, 2018, in a supermarket. Without dying but alive as the Scriptures are read in past tense of our eternal future, I had the opportunity in this life which is of the future to question and ask this man, Satan the Devil who had transition himself into human form as a person which mean from spiritual existence to human existence.

In other words, he materialized from a spirit being to a person in human form. Jehovah God is my Witness who open up my mind, not at that present time but after returning home. God allow me to see plain and clear of whom I was in the presence of!

Again, God open up my mind. Several months ago, I was grocery shopping at another supermarket at a different location but under the same name.

As I stood in the "check-out" line, I notice a gentleman standing several feet from me to my right wearing super dark lens glasses, not dark shades but regular glasses. You could not see his eyes.

He stood motionless as a statue, which caught my attention. As shoppers walk past him of being another person grocery shopping.

He stood staring at me or in my direction. He never moved, he just stood and stared in my direction.

I assumed he was staring at me, now I know he was. When God open up my mind, it was as though a light turned on in my head.

The gentleman that stood next to me in this supermarket, were the same height, same weight, same complexion and wearing similar and same color of clothing, also the same "nationality."

Note: "Wherever Satan's purpose leads him, he'll appear as a person of that nationality, which ever nationality is greater during his presences."

The identity which Satan transition for his purpose, makes him appear as an ordinary and normal person.

Note: You wouldn't attend a costume ball without wearing a costume? Why? Because you would look out of place or out of the ordinary.

Note: "I've discovered one of many of Satan's machinations he uses for the accomplishment of his sinister plans!"

Note: Children of Jehovah God (Isa. 14:13–17). This is my account of which took place March 16, 2018.

I had a biblical opportunity to ask Satan the Devil standing next to me transitioned as a person of that which Scripture says of him. "You said, you would climb to the tops of the clouds and be like the Almighty. But instead you have been brought down to the deepest part of the world of the dead."

Are you the man who shook the Earth and made kingdoms tremble? Are you the man who destroyed cities and turned the world into a desert?

Are you the man who never freed his prisoners or let them go home? These are Scripture questions being ask of Satan in the Bible. "This is my account, the other day, my daughter drove me to the supermarket. She remained in the car as I went grocery shopping at my favorite supermarket."

I had a few items, as I stood in front of the tuna fish shelf looking while checking tuna can labels. I saw a new label I had never saw before, I pick up a can which read in "oil." I like tuna in water, there I pick up another can which also read in "oil," while I stood there with both cans of tuna in my hand. A gentleman walked up and stood by of my left side as though he was looking or pretending as though reading labels.

He moved closer to me or closer to left side. I was assuming he would say, excuse me, you mine! No, however, he never spoke nor did we make eye contact.

Note: I notice he got closer to me as he looks or pretend to look at the can tuna. Then he finally moved around back of me at my right side, still pretending, just touching cans at this point.

The two cans I placed back on the shelf; he began to touch and fumble with as though he was going to buy tuna fish.

The size cans of tuna I was looking for weren't on the shelf, at this time. The man never picks up any cans, he just moved cans about as though toying with them. In reality he acted strange, abnormal, which given me the opportunity to ask, "What is it you're looking for?" However, I didn't ask! Because he never said nor spoke a word and neither did I. He did stop me by interfering with my shopping by getting so close to where I stood, yet he never made eye contact. When he should have said, "Excuse me, which he didn't which was strange!

I moved farther to my left because he moved closer to my right which was not normal and because of that movement. I just reach and grabbed a large can of tuna as quick as I could and moved away. He then stood right where I had stood when I moved away!

Note: I moved several yards down farther, occasionally I would look in his direction; however, he never made eye contact with me nor look in my direction. I said after he leave, I'll go back to get another can of tuna. I continue with my grocery shopping, never to see him again in the supermarket, "By the way, I forgot the tuna."

It appeared to me that the man wanted while waiting for me to say some unkind words because of the closeness we stood of each other. Ordinarily, I would've said, "Don't you see me shopping here which could have started and escalate into an altercation." Which I knew because of the strange way he performed in such close proximity.

But God was in the "plan," which I didn't know at that time. It was the day after, God open up my mind, that was the devil, Satan himself who had transitioned into human form as a person as he did at the other supermarket to cause trouble for me that day!

Note: Satan's plan and presence, there was for a purpose and reason, which was to get me into an altercation with store management through him. Remember, Satan is here in the world to steal, kill, or destroy by any means! But God shut my mouth while protecting me at the same time!

No other real person could perform as did the transitioned person Satan the Devil performed the way he was trying to provoke me into an altercation by way of his closeness!

Had the man been real human, God would allow me to ask whether or not he needed assistance to find what he was looking for.

Note: Even I was fooled by Satan human appearance, as well as I know of the spiritual realm and is capable of performing but not of this degree.

The way the man, whom I thought was just a man, a human I saw what he was attempting performing so methodically moving about in plain view to drew-me into an altercation using a heinous scheme to draw me in conclusion of his plan. You would not believe unless it was you, this happen to!

Note: Had Satan drawn me into his plan, others would have assumed I was just another lunatic because they would not have known nor whom I was quarrelling with because we both appeared human (men). I would not have known had not God open up my mind who the "man," gentleman was; however, I knew he was strange the way and how methodically he moved about.

Note: "Store management would have thought I was fighting another person because no human being can nor never will distinct nor distinguish the devil, Satan in transitioned as a person (human being) is Satan the Devil himself.

No one or no human being could distinguish I was in conflict with the man, Satan, no, not even me, until Jehovah God opened up my mind the next day!

Note: Congregation of God, the world population need acknowledgment, the devil, Satan walks among us today as he did in the days of Job as a transitioned person, human being. The Lord asked him, "What have you been doing?" Satan answered in Job 1:7, "I have been walking here and there, roaming around the Earth."

Children of God, the devil, Satan presences is on the Earth today and he walks among us every day. I am called to make his presences known not in spirit but as a transitioned person in human form walks among us today seeking whom he can devour.

Note: Satan had the same profile and agenda he had at the other supermarket. He can transition himself as a person, a human being of any nationality.

I reiterate, the devil approached me for a reason and purpose to "steal, kill, or destroy" me in open view as a person in human form! "But God was in the plan!"

Thank You, Father!

Amen.

Note: Don't ever forget. Satan deceives the entire world appearing as a real human being of any nationality he so desires!"

III

ANSWER TO THE QUESTION HOW DOES SATAN DECEIVE THE ENTIRE WORLD? MESSAGE

Note: By deception of the mind. "Yes" and by perceiving directly by sight or hearing. Both coincide together. However, it is by sight Satan the Devil deceives the whole world, by appearing as a human being, a real person as he did during the days of Job.

Over the years, the past, present, and in the future, ever since Satan was cast out of heaven, he has walked the Earth as a real person, human being, yet spirit.

His human appearance then and still today, walk's the Earth as a real human (person) deceiving all he encounters or encounters him until Jesus Christ return.

All who encountered him was and still deceived without acknowledging their deception of Satan or the devil's appearance.

Note: Today the world (people) think or believe the word deception is use as a figure of speech of the devil's way of deceiving the whole world which is true in some cases. Because persons believe they are deceived by way of a thought or deception in one's mind.

Deception is only a word which the world use to indicate or describe the works of the devil. Deception is only a word that goes no farther than just a word.

Eve, the first woman on the Earth was deceived with words spoken by the devil, Satan through a serpent, snake. Eve, the first woman and the last reported of God's Earthly creative works.

One day, Eve found herself near the tree of knowledge of good and bad when a serpent seeming innocence ask Eve, "Is it really so that God said you must not eat from every tree of the garden?"

Definition of *deception*: The woman replied correctly, but the serpent contradicted God.

God had stated that violating God's Command would result in being like God, knowing good and bad. Deceived by the serpent and with a strong desire for the fruit, "ate the forbidden fruit."

Note: Scripture says, read Revelation 12:9: "The huge dragon was thrown out-that ancient serpent, named the devil, or Satan that deceived the whole world. He was thrown down to Earth, and all his angels with him."

Note: Children of Jehovah, God's congregation, Satan walked the Earth before he went into the presences of God.

The Scriptures indicate that the creature known as Satan did not always have that name. Rather, it was given to him because of his taking a course of opposition and resistance to God.

Read Job 1:6–7.

> When the day came for the heavenly beings to appear before the Lord, Satan was there among them.
> The Lord asked him, "What have you been doing?" Satan answered, "I have been walking here and there, roaming around the Earth.

Also, read 1 Peter 5:8: "Be alert, be on watch! Your enemy the Devil roams around like a roaring lion, looking for someone to devour."

Satan is a spirit person, for he appeared in heaven in the presence of God. It is clear that the Jews and Jesus and his disciples knew that Satan existed as a person.

Note: The definitive answer to "How did Satan deceive the whole world?" It is by sense of sight; he deceives the whole world. Not by mind of deception but appearing on the Earth or world transition from spirit to a spirit person, a human being just as we human are spirit persons in a body.

Satan is two, an invisible spirit not seen by human eyes or natural vision; secondly, Satan is a spirit person transition as a visible spirit person that can be seen with natural human vision.

Satan spirit represent two realms, the invisible spiritual realm and the visible physical realm, transition into a visible spirit person in human form or human body.

Its imperative mankind acknowledge the devil is in the world to steal, kill, or destroy, "age nor gender" is no exception, whether as spirit or appearing as a spirit person.

Appearing as spirit, in humankind he's invisible to human eyes. A person can't see his spirit approach but must listen for his approach by way of mouth, words, tongue. All three reveal the manifestation of his invisible presences in humankind.

Note: Secondly, the devil appearing as a visible transitional person or human being by sight which can be seen with human natural vision (eyes); however, human beings cannot distinguish Satan transitional human body from that of a real human being or person. That's how the devil, Satan, deceives the whole world, transition from spirit to a spirit person who walks among us daily 24-7, looking for whom he can devour.

Read 1 Peter 5:8: "Be alert, be on watch! Your enemy, the Devil roams around like a roaring lion, looking for someone to devour."

Note: Church, children of Jehovah God, only God can open one's eyes and mind to recognize Satan the Devil as a transitional human being who walk among us daily not being recognize of who he is. Only God can reveal his identity as a spirit person that roam the Earth.

Note: While Jesus was in the world, Jesus made it clear, Satan was a spirit person, Jesus Christ said of him. That one was a manslayer, when he began, and he did not stand fast in the truth because the truth is not in him.

Satan is also an invisible spirit, appearing in spirit by mind of deception but not of sight. Which mean a person receive a thought or perception which is perceived in one's mind as their own thinking or thought to act or perform accordingly by their action or words by mouth, speaking.

Note: Jesus speak of His suffering and death, which Peter spoke the perception that Satan's spirit perceive in and throughout him.

Read Matthew 16:21–23.

> From that time on Jesus began to say plainly to his disciples. I must go to Jerusalem and suffer much from the elders, the chief priests and the teachers of the Law. I will be put to death, but three days later I will be raised to life.
>
> Peter took him aside and began to rebuke him. God forbid it, Lord! He said, "That must never happen to you!"
>
> Jesus turned around and said to Peter, "Get away from me Satan! You are an obstacle in my way, because these thoughts of yours don't come from God, but from human nature."

Note: Which means Satan possesses power to control human nature, the other spirit. That which you (we) have no control over! Scripture says, "The flesh is weak, but the Spirit is willing."

Throughout Scriptures, the qualities and actions attributed to him, Satan could be attributed only to a person, not an abstract or principle of evil.

It is clear that the Jews and Jesus and his disciples knew that Satan existed as a person. So from a righteous perfect start this spirit person deviated into sin and degradation.

Note: The question and the ultimate answer. How does Satan deceive the entire whole world?

The identity that Satan transition for his purpose makes him appear as an ordinary and normal person or human being to accomplish his plans. Not as an invisible spirit but as a spirit person with a human body just as we humans are spirit persons with human bodies.

Satan the Devil deceives the whole world as he walks among us today as he did in the day of Job as a transitional person, a human being in the form of a human body.

Scripture say Satan is a spirit person, appearing in heaven and on the Earth as a transitional Spirit person.

A spirit person are visible just as we human beings are visible with human bodies; however, Satan possess transitional power to transition to human form and transition back to an invisible spirit being, that which I've witnessed.

Child of God, the devil, Satan presences is here on the Earth today. He walks and talk with mankind.

Satan dialogue verbally to communicate with mankind throughout the land or four corners of the world. He dialogued with me, not knowing who he was, not until later after he walked off, then God open my eyes and mind after he dialogued with me.

Note: Satan has the same profile and agenda he had when God ask him, where he had been, Satan reply was, "I have been walking here and there roaming around the Earth." Satan's agenda is still the same, to steal, kill, or destroy by any means.

Note: Apostle Peter confirmed Satan's answer and reply. Therefore, Peter tells the world.

Read 1 Peter 5:8. "Be alert, be on watch! Your enemy, the devil roams around like a roaring lion, looking for someone to devour."

Satan's agenda is to steal, kill, or destroy human livelihoods by any means.

Satan is performing year around the agenda he had when God ask him, "Where had he been. His reply was, "Walking here and there roaming around the Earth."

He is here today on the Earth, walking among us in a provocative manner tending to provoke, to incite anger or resentment among human races.

Note: Children of Jehovah God, no human being can distinguish Satan of being a human being or spirit person, just as we are human beings and spirit persons.

No one not even I, until later God open my mind and eyes who it was roaming around me in the supermarket one day pretending to be grocery shopping.

Congregation of God, the whole world population need acknowledgment, the devil, Satan walks among us today as he did in the days of Job as a transitional person appearing as a human being, a spirit person like ourselves.

Satan has the same profile and agenda transition as a person, a human being of any nationality. Deceiving the whole world as a living human being which only God can open the human mind and eyes of mankind to distinguish the two. Man, a spirit person or Satan as a spirit person, "Only God can distinguish the two."

"The devil, Satan approached and stood staring at me, as a human being, a person in human form for a reason and purpose which was to attempt to destroy me by any means in open view of other people, but God was in the plan!"

Thank You, Father, amen.

Note: Don't ever forget. Satan deceives the entire world appearing as a real human being of any nationality he so desires!

Satan Is on the Earth as a Person-Man What You Should Know

The hidden enemy walks among us today somewhere, someplace as a human being, a man appearing to be human, yet spirit. This man is Satan the Devil. Walk the entire Earth disguised as a person just as you or I, deceiving the whole world.

No one throughout on the entire Earth know Satan's identity but God, Jesus Christ, and the Holy Spirit. Satan transitional purpose is to deceive the world. The Bible says so all nations were deceived (Rev. 18:23). No nation knows nor recognize the devil, Satan identity nor identities. He has deceived all nations and still deceiving nations as he walks and talks among us appearing human, a human person yet a spirit person looking for whom he can devour.

The entire world should acknowledge the creature known as Satan did not always have that name. Rather it was given to him because of his taking a course of opposition and resistance to God.

God is the Only Creator and his creation and activity is perfect, with no injustice or unrighteousness.

Read Deuteronomy 32:4. "The Lord is your mighty defender, perfect and just in all his ways, your God is faithful and true, he does what is right and fair."

Note: Therefore the one becoming Satan was when created, a perfect, righteous creature of God. Note: *He is a spirit person*, for he appeared in heaven in the presence of God.

Note: People of Jehovah God, Satan, the Devil, is today on the Earth, just as Jesus said of him then. Satan is that of today on the Earth.

Read John 8:44. "From the very beginning he was a murderer and has never been on the side of truth because there is not truth in him. When he tells a lie, he is only doing what is natural to him, because he is a liar and the father of all lies."

Note: Satan was once in the truth, but forsook it, beginning with his first overt act in turning Adam and Eve away from God. He was a manslayer, for he thereby brought about the death of Adam and Eve, which in turn brought sin and death to their "us" offspring.

Note: The question how is it, sin and death brought to us offspring.

As help in your understanding the situation, think of what happens when a baker bakes bread in a pan that has a dent in it. A mark will show on all the bread that is baked in that pan. Adam became like that pan and we are like the bread.

He became imperfect when he broke God's law. It was as if he received a dent or a bad mark. So when he had children all of them received a dent or a bad mark. So when he had children all of them received this same mark of sin or imperfection.

Note: Throughout the Scriptures, the qualities and action attributed to Satan. Attributed only to a person not an abstract of evil. It is clear that the Jews and Jesus and his disciples knew that Satan existed as a person.

From a righteous, perfect start this spirit person deviated into sin and degradation, bringing about James 1:14–15. "But we are tempted when we are drawn away and trapped by our own evil desires. Then our evil desires conceive and give birth to sin, and sin, when it is full-grown, give birth to death."

Note: Satan also became the tempter and a liar, the father of the lie and by his wicked action Satan has brought men, women, and children under his leadership and control, standing up in opposition to God, as a rival god.

Note: When Jesus was on the Earth or in the world, it was clear then that the Jews and Jesus and his disciples knew that Satan existed as a person.

Note: The Scripture account, therefore, makes it plain that it was Satan who spoke as a medium of a serpent, seducing Eve into disobedience to God's command.

In turn, Eve induced Adam to take the same rebellious course. "Human disobedience."

Read Genesis 3:1–7.

> Now the snake was the most cunning animal that the Lord God had made. The snake asked the woman, "Did God really tell you not to eat fruit from any tree in the garden?"

"We may eat the fruit of any tree in the garden." The woman answered.

> except the tree in the middle of it. God told us not to eat the fruit of that tree or even touch it, if we do, we will die.
>
> The snake replied, "That's not true, you will not die."
>
> God said that because he knows that when you eat it, you will be like God and know what is good and what is bad.

Note: For this reason, the Bible give Satan the title "serpent," which as a consequence of Satan's use of the serpent which came to signify "deceiver," he also became the tempter. Thereby tempting Jesus in the wilderness. "A liar, the father of the lie."

Note: Jehovah's Word, the Bible reveals Satan appearing before Jehovah God in heaven as a spirit person as a human being challenging Jehovah to His face, saying that he could turn God's servant Job away from him, which Satan still attempting today to turn mankind away from God as a spirit person in human form.

The spirit person Satan reveal the might and power this spirit person or creature has over the entire human race along with his vicious murderous attitude.

Note: To remember Satan does not challenge God himself nor God's power and authority, he does his action against God Word through mankind.

By his challenge of God's Word and his charging God's people with lack of integrity, Satan lives up to his title devil, which means "accuser, slanderer," which he deserved.

The Apostle Paul associates Satan with the wicked spirit forces in the heavenly places and speaks of them as the world rulers of this darkness.

Read Ephesians 6:11–12.

> Put on all the armor that God gives you, so that you will be able to stand up against the devil's evil tricks.
>
> For we are not fighting against human beings but against the wicked spiritual forces in the heavenly world, the rulers, authorities and cosmic powers of this dark age.

Note: As a governing force in the physical and spiritual realm, Satan appears in both realms, transition in the physical realm as a spirit person as a human being "Man" just as you and I are spirit persons in a human body. And also appear as a spirit, invisible to the human eye. Note: Satan is two, a spirit person and a spirit.

Children of God, in Revelations he is shown to be the one misleading the entire inhabited Earth. The Apostle John said that the whole world is lying in the power of the wicked one.

Read 1 John 5:19. "We know that we belong to God even though the whole world is under the rule of the evil one."

Note: He is, therefore, the ruler of this world. That is why James wrote that the friendship with the world is enmity with God.

Read James 4:4. "Unfaithful people! Don't you know that to be the world friend means to be God's enemy? If you want to be the world's friend, you make yourself God's enemy."

What the people should know, Satan is on the Earth as a person, walking the Earth appearing as a real person like you and I, deceiving the world, even appearing as an angel of light through his supposed-to-be good deeds but deadly to all human beings.

It is written Satan continue to wage war all over the world against Christians and all Christ followers, even waging war against Holy Spirit in man. His objective is to destroy Christians spiritual integrity.

Note: The Apostle Paul said, "But to keep me from being puffed up with pride because of the many wonderful things I saw, I was given a painful physical ailment, which acts as Satan's messenger to beat me and keep me from being proud" (2 Cor. 12:7).

Note: All Christians must fight to do what's right. Although it's a spiritual battle, it has been won through Jesus Christ, our Lord and Savior, the Righteous One who appeared before the person of God in our behalf.

Also, God's Word Christians must realize Satan's existence, his power, his designs, and his purposes so that they can fight this spiritual foe with the spiritual weapons God provide.

Read Ephesians 6:13–17.

> So put on God's armor now. Then when the evil day comes, you will be able to resist the enemy's attacks, and after fighting to the end, you will still hold your ground.
>
> So stand ready, with truth as a belt tight around your waist with righteous as your breastplate.
>
> And as your shoes the readiness to announce the Good News of peace.
>
> At All time carry faith as a shield for with it you will be able to put out all the burning arrows shot by the Evil One.

And accept salvation as a helmet, and the Word of God as the sword which the Spirit gives you.

Do all this in prayer asking for God's help. Pray on every occasion, as the spirit leads. For this reason, keep alert and never give up, pray always for all God's people.

Amen.

Satan: An Enemy of Everlasting Life Sermon and Message

I

Note: Congregation, nearly everyone on Earth seek happiness. Then why are so many unhappy? What is wrong? Since almost everybody wants peace, why do nations go to war and why do people hate one another? Is there some guiding force that moves them to do these bad things? Could it be that a common invisible power control the nations?

Note: Many have wondered about how terrible cruelty mankind really is. Just think the fearful gases uses in warfare to choke and burn persons to death and the napalm bombs and the atomic bombs. Also, the flame throws, the concentration camps, the mass murder of millions of helpless people.

Do you think that all these evils simply happen by chance? When you see the gross wickedness of these acts, does it not seem that man has been influence by an evil, invisible power?

Note: Congregation, there is no need to guess at the matter. The Bible clearly shows that an intelligent unseen person has been controlling both men and nations.

In the Bible, Jesus Christ calls this powerful one, the ruler of this world.

Read John 12:31. "Now is the time for this world to be judged, now the ruler of this world will be over thrown." Jesus also says in

John 14:30, "I cannot talk with you much longer, because the ruler of this world is coming. He has no power over me."

Note: Well, who is he? Allow me to help you to find out who he is. At the beginning of Jesus ministry here on Earth, the Bible tells us that after Jesus was baptized, he went into the wilderness where he was tempted by an unseen creature called Satan the Devil.

Definition: *Adversary.* An aggressor, a competitor, an enemy. The name Satan means "adversary and devil, the personified spirit of evil, a candidate of hell and foe of God and mankind." (His angels became demons.)

Note: Part of that tempting is described in Matthew 4:8–9. "Then the Devil took Jesus to a very high mountain and showed him all the Kingdoms of the world in all their greatness. All this, I will give you, the Devil said, 'If you kneel down and worship me.'"

Note: Think about what the devil offered Jesus Christ. It was all the Kingdoms of the world.

Congregation, so you think all these worldly governments really belong to the devil? Yes, for how else could he have offered them to Jesus?

Jesus did not deny that they were Satan's which he would have done of Satan did not own them. Church, Satan is really the unseen ruler of all the nations of the world.

Note: The Bible plainly says, "The whole world is lying in the power of the Wicked One."

Read 1 John 5:19. "We know that we belong to God even though the whole world is under the rule of the evil one."

Note: Congregation, in fact God's Word calls Satan, the god of this system of things.

Read 2 Corinthians 4:4. "They do not believe, because their minds have been kept in the dark by the evil god of this world. He helps them from seeing the light that comes from the Good News about the glory of Christ, who is the exact likeness of God."

Note: I want you to understand, congregation, who Satan the Devil really is and understand why nations hate and try to destroy one another, when it is the desire of all normal persons to live at peace. Yes, Satan is misleading the entire inhabited Earth.

Read Revelations 12:9: "The huge dragon was thrown out, that ancient serpent named the Devil, or Satan that that deceived the whole world. He was thrown down to Earth, and all his angels (demons) with him."

Note: Satan misleading multitudes in false religions and false worshipping. He does not want us to receive God's gift of everlasting life. Therefore, we Christians must fight to keep to from being influenced by this spirit creature.

Read Ephesians 6:12. "For we are not fighting against human beings but against the wicked spiritual forces in the heavenly world, the rulers, authorities, and cosmic powers of this dark age."

Congregation, you need to know about Satan and how manipulative he is in order to resist his efforts to mislead us.

II

Who the Devil Is?

Note: Satan the Devil is a real person. He is not merely the evil in all mankind, as some person may believe. We human cannot see the devil for the same reason that we cannot see God. Both God and the devil are spirit person forms, of life higher than humans and unseen to our eyes.

Note: Congregation, this is a short descriptive testimony of how I saw Satan. God is my witness of this truth and testimony. I've encountered many spirit confrontations with the devil.

I've seen Satan the Devil at three different times but in two different forms, once in a transparent form, when the telepathy commanded me to curse God and twice as a person in whom I dialogued with as a person in a materialize human body and dematerialize back into spirit.

I did not comprehend how could I have seen the devil, until later it was revealed to me how I saw into the spiritual realm, it was through the vision of the Holy Spirit at the time Satan telepathy command me to curse God, this occurred at the age of six. Which the Holy Spirit did not allow that to happen.

On those other occasions, I had become an adult, when I witnessed and saw him as a human being with my natural vision whom I dialogued with in a materialized body and then dematerialized back to spirit in my presence.

Note: The question, but if God is love, why did he make the devil?

Read 1 John 4:8. "Whoever does not love does not know God, for God is love."

Note: Congregation, the fact is, God did not create the devil, if God did not create the devil. Where did the devil come from?

Note: The Bible explains that God created many, many spirit persons similar to himself. In the Bible, these spirits are called angels. Also, they are called "sons of God."

Read Job 38:7. "When the morning stars sang together, and all the sons of God shouted for joy?"

Note: God created them all perfect. Not one of them was a devil or a Satan. The word "devil" means *slanderer* and the word "Satan" means *opposer*.

The time came, however, when one of those spirit sons of God made himself the devil that is a hateful liar who speaks bad things about another. He also made himself Satan, that is an opposer of God. He was not created that way but later became that kind of person.

Note: The angel that became the devil was present when God created the Earth and later the first human couple, Adam and Eve. So he would have heard God tell them to have children.

Read Genesis 1:27–28.

> So God created human beings, making them to be like himself. He created them male and female,
> blessed them, and said, "Have many children, so that your descendants will live all over the Earth and bring it under their control. I am putting you in charge of the fish, the birds, and all the wild animals.

Note: Satan knew that after a while the whole Earth would be filled with righteous people worshipping God. That was God's purpose. However, this angel though a great deal of his own beauty and intelligence and wanted to receive for himself the worship that would be given to God.

Note: "This is what God says to the angel, who became the devil."

Read Ezekiel 28:13–15.

> You lived in Eden, the garden of God, and wore gems of every kind; rubies, and diamonds, topaz, beryl, carnelian, and jasper, sapphires, emerald, and garnets. You had ornaments of Gold. They were made for you on the day you were created.
>
> I put a terrifying angel there to guard you. You lived on my holy mountain and walked among sparkling gems.
>
> your conduct was perfect from the day you were created until you began to do evil.

Note: Instead of putting this wrong desire out of his mind, it led to his rebellious attack, taking action to obtain the honor and importance be desired and so does man.

Read James 1:14–15. "We are tempted when we are drawn away and trapped by our own evil desires. Then our evil desires conceive and give birth to sin, and sin, when it is full grown, gives birth to death."

Note: On Satan's attack of taking action. This rebellious angel used a lowly serpent to speak to the first woman, Eve. He did this much as a skilled person can make it seem as if a nearby animal was speaking. But it was really this rebellious angel, the one called in the Bible "the original serpent," who was speaking to Eve.

Read Revelation 12:9. "The huge dragon was thrown out, that ancient serpent, named the devil, or Satan, that deceived the whole world. He was thrown down to Earth, and all his angels with him."

Note: But Before He was cast down, the serpent lied to Eve. Read Genesis 3:1–5.

> The snake was the most cunning animal that the Lord God had made. The snake asked the woman, "Did God really tell you not to eat fruit from any tree in the garden?"
> We may eat the fruit of any tree in the garden, the woman answered,
> except the tree in the middle of it. God told us not to eat the fruit of that tree or even touch it, if we do, we will die.
> The snake replied, "That's not true, you will not die."
> God said that because he knows that when you eat it, you will be like God and know what is good and what is bad.

Note: This was a hateful lie and it made him a devil. He also became an opposer of God or a Satan. Congregation as you can see, it is wrong to think of the devil as a creature with horns and a pitchfork. He is really a very powerful but wicked and evil spirt person on the Earth along with fallen angels that became demons.

Note: The lie the devil told Eve worked just as he planned. She believed it and so disobeyed God. And she was able to get her husband to break God's law also.

Read Genesis 3:6. "The woman saw how beautiful the tree was and how good it's fruit would be to eat, and she thought how wonderful it would be to become wise. So she took some of the fruit and ate it. Then she gave some to her husband, and he also ate it."

Note: The devil's claim was that humans can get along without God. He argued that people can rule themselves successfully without God's help and he also challenge God that he could turn away from God all those who would be offspring of Adam and Eve.

Remember, Satan's fight or challenge against God is through mankind and Christians are no exception, matter of fact it is

Christians whom he uses the most to oppose or challenge God and his word and works.

Christians, yes Christians believe they are free of Satan's attacks. I like you to know, Christians are more vulnerable of the devil's attack today more than never before.

Majority of Christians does not acknowledge he or she are under the attacks of the devil because the Church or the Body of Christ aren't teaching nor preaching spiritual attacks or spiritual warfare as it should from the pulpits and evil are simply normal conditions that will always be.

Satan created "spiritual challenges" or "spiritual warfare" upon the Earth forever lasting to oppose God, until the return of Jesus Christ, then they will cease.

A spiritual challenge began with Job. The devil claim that he could turn away from God all those who would be the offspring of Adam and Eve.

Job didn't have the fainted belief or thought that he was under the attack of Satan the Devil.

The challenge was raised when Satan appeared before Jehovah in the courts of heaven.

III

His Method of Misleading the World (Person) Is by Deceptions

Congregation, do not think that Satan's methods of getting people to follow him are always easy to see. He is a master at fooling people. His methods over the thousands of years have, in fact, been so clever that today many people do not even believe that he exists.

Note: Now it came to be the day when the sons of the true God entered to take their station before Jehovah, and even Satan proceed to enter right among them, Jehovah God said to Satan, "Where do you come from?" Satan answered Jehovah and said, "From roving about in the Earth and from walking about in it." God asked, "Have you set your heart upon my servant Job, that there is no one like him in the Earth?"

Read Job 1:1–8.

Jehovah went on to say to Satan, there is no one like him in the Earth. Jehovah went on to say to Satan, there is no one like him in all the Earth, a man blameless and upright, fearing God and turning aside from bad.

Read Job 1:9–12.

> At that, Satan answer Jehovah and said, have not you yourself put up a hedge about him, and about everything that he has all around. The work of his hands you have blessed, and his livestock itself has spread abroad in the Earth. But for a change thrust out your hand, and touch everything he has and see whether he will not curse you to your very face. Satan was making an excuse for Job's faithfulness to God. Job serves you because of the things you give him, not because he loves you.
>
> Jehovah answered him, "Everything that he has, is in your hand, but you must not hurt Job himself."

Note: Job's children and wealth are destroyed.

Right away, Satan begun causing trouble for Job. He had all of Job's livestock either killed or stolen. Then he saw to it that Job's ten children were killed. Job lost almost everything, yet he remains faithful to Jehovah.

Read Job 1:22. "In spite of everything that Job had, Job did not sin by blaming God."

Note: Satan again appeared with the other angels before Jehovah. Once again, Jehovah asked Satan if he had seen the faithfulness of Job.

"At that, Satan answered, Skin in behalf of skin and everything that a man has he will give in behalf of his soul. For a change, thrust

out your hand, and touch as far as is bone and his flesh as see whether he will not curse you to your face."
Note: Satan tests Job again.
Read Job 2:1–5.

> Satan again appear with the other angels before Jehovah. Once again Jehovah asked Satan, "Where have you been?" Satan answered, "I've been walking here and there, roaming around the Earth."
> Did you notice my servant Job? The Lord asked. "There is no one on Earth as faithful and good as he is. He worships me and is careful not to do anything evil. You persuaded me to let you attack him for no reason at all but Job is still as faithful as ever."
> Satan replied, "A person will give up everything in order to stay alive. But now suppose you hurt his body, he will curse you to your face."

Read Job 2:6–7, 9.

> So the Lord said to Satan, "Alright, he is in your power, but you are not to kill him."
> Then Satan left the Lord's presence and made sores break out all over Job's body.
> His wife said to him, "You are still as faithful as ever, aren't you? Why don't you curse God and die?"

Note: But Job refuse to do that, even in all his suffering Job said nothing against God. Job said, "Until I expire, I shall not take away my integrity from myself."

Note: Congregation, Job remained faithful to God. So it was proved that Satan was wrong in his challenge that he can turn persons away from God. By the way, that challenge still stand until Christ return.

Note: Job gave God an answer to Satan challenge that humans would not serve Him under test.

Note: Of course, God could have destroyed Satan right away. But that would not have answered the challenge that Satan raised. So God allowed time for Satan to try to prove his claim, "with no results."

Note: The Bible tells us Satan himself can transform himself into an angel of light appear as a person, a real live human being to you, me, and the entire world. Thus, we can expect that his schemes for misleading people would often appear innocent, even beneficial.

Read 2 Corinthians 11:14. "Well, no wonder! Even Satan can disguise himself to look like an angel of light, a real person! A human being."

Note: Remember Satan posed as a friend to Eve. Then he tricked her into doing what she thought would be for her own good.

Read Genesis 3:4–6.

> The snake [Satan] replied, "That's not true, you will not die."
>
> God said that because he knows that when you eat it, you will be like God, and know what is good and what is bad.
>
> The woman saw how beautiful the tree was and how good it's fruit would be to eat, and she thought how wonderful it would be to become wise. So she took some of the fruit and ate it. Then she gave some to her husband and he also ate it.

Note: Congregation, Satan still deceiving the world through his human representation Satan cunning by deception and encouraging people to put human interests and affairs above their service to God.

Whether you know it or not, Satan chief aim is to get persons to break God's govern laws, laws that require us, mankind to live by.

Note: If we are to receive "everlasting life" we need accurate knowledge of Jesus, God, and God Kingdom.

Read John 17:3. "And eternal life means to know you, the only true God, and to know Jesus Christ, whom you sent."

Note: Congregation, you can be sure that Satan the Devil does not want you to have this knowledge and that he will do all in his power to stop (us) you from getting it.

Question: How does Satan do this?

Answer: Through opposition. All those desiring to live with godly devotion in and with Jesus Christ will be persecuted.

Read 2 Timothy 3:11–12. "My persecution, and my sufferings. You know all that happen to me in Antioch, Iconium and Lystra, the terrible persecution I endured! But the Lord rescued me from them all. Everyone who wants to live a godly life in union with Christ Jesus will be persecuted."

Note: A family member, friend or relative may try to discourage you doing so in all sincerity because they do not know the "truth" found in the Bible.

Note: On the other hand, Satan may tempt you to share in some immoral activity which is displeasing to God.

Read 1 Corinthians 6:9–11.

> Surely you know that the wicked will not possess God's Kingdom. Do not fool yourselves, people who are immoral or who worship idols or are adulterers or homosexuals' pervert.
>
> Or who steal or are greedy or are drunkards or who slander other or are thieves, none of these will possess God's Kingdom.

Note: Congregation, the Bible urges, "Oppose the devil. If you do this, Satan will flee from you."

Read James 4:7. "So then, submit yourselves to God. Resist the devil, and he will run away from you."

Question: Does this mean that if you resist Satan's attack he will give up and no longer cause you trouble?

Answer: No! He will try over and over again to get you to do what he wants. But if you keep opposing him, he will "never" be able to get you to take a course in opposition to God.

Amen.

Mankind Should Know and Acknowledge the Spirit World

We live in a world more spiritual than physical in which we are being more observe by evil and wicked Spirit beings, demons than we are of our human neighbors. Unfortunately, some people under the assumption taking the spirit world for granted, big mistake. While others fail to believe that the spirit world exist.

Some believers believe the spirits of deceased loved ones does return to haunt the living. Something that is far from the truth. The truth is demon spirits are the culprits pretending to be spirits of the dead, demons are impersonating and disguising themselves as spirits of deceased loved ones.

They can disguise to take the identity of any person deceased or alive. Demons can also speak through the demon-possessed and demonized individuals without their knowledge is well as imitate or mimic the voice of the deceased.

Evil spirits or demons are the same culprits roaming the Earth seeking human bodies to enter as their own. Possessing a person mind, body, and soul to bring under their evil control. Under such control, the person become demon-possessed or demonized. In today's time, more human beings than ever before are either demonized or under some kind of demonic control influence. "Age is no exception."

The spiritual realm of Satan is to cause possession by way of deception, oppression, and depression in the lives of mankind. I reiterate, age or gender is no exception, demons are entering all ages by deception through the work of Satan.

Observe today's societies and adolescences they are the evidence of this truth. Evil spirits (demons) are at work and performing through them the work and plans of the devil without their knowledge of detection. Which is something that should not be ignored nor swept under the rug.

Thereby, it's imperative that all nations be educated that we live in a hostile spiritual environment control by evil spirits seeking whom they can destroy. Not only human beings but nations throughout the world.

Nations are in spiritual warfare with spirit enemies seeking whom they can destroy by any means of aggression, oppression, depression, or demon possession of the mind, body, and soul. Many nations are serving and entertaining the same evil spirits as though they are gods here to help. Not acknowledging Satan and demon spirits are strategically and geographically position throughout this nation and the world to steal, kill, or destroy mankind through mankind.

The evidence is present throughout the four corners of the Earth, nations fighting against nations. Wars that appear to be ordinary wars are really spiritual wars demonically motivated and control by demonic forces.

No nation is exempt from spiritual warfare. Demonic forces exist over the entire Earth provoking aggression, violence among nations and family members. Every person, age is no exception is vulnerable of their attack in the home and abroad.

I'm a victim of such attacks in my home and in public places. I've been in spiritual conflicts my entire life and which this nation of people is in but yet appear to have gone unrecognized. Which mean demonization by demon possession is condemning this nation of people.

I've been victimized, but now I'm a witness of this truth and the war. People tend to ignore the existence of the spirit world in order to satisfy their human desire. People are lovers of pleasure rather than lovers of God. They are lovers of money.

Wherever you look you see acts of greed. Many will do practically anything for money. People will steal or even kill. It is not unusual for greedy person to produce products that are known in one way or another to make others sick or even kill.

More people are demonized or under demonic influences than ever before. People are possessed or act as if by a demon spirit that represent evilness or diabolic intent which is motivated by a demonic force greater than their natural spirit.

Children are more criminally active than ever before. Because today's parents have little or no control over their children. Every country on Earth is affected by the plague of youth crimes. More than half of all serious crimes in some countries are committed by children ten to seventeen years of age. Murder, rape, assault, robbery, burglary, and car theft—all these things children are doing. Never in history has disobedience to parents been so common.

Fear is now probably the biggest single emotion in people's lives today. People fear crime, disease and many other things that threaten their security and their very lives. Yet most people or the world still think only of doing what pleases them or their families, not what pleases God. They do and love what God condemns, including fornication, adultery drunkenness, drug abuse and other so-called pleasures all demonic related or motivated.

World leaders are well as common people alike often make an outward show of being godly. They may attend church service and make contributions to religious causes. Those in government may put their hand on a Bible when they take office. But often it is simply a form of godly devotion.

Brethren, demonization has entered the country by way of demonized foreigners who worship other gods rather than the true God Jehovah. Who are now in government working as government officials of all levels. Demons have infiltrated our government and the governments of all nations and majority of the nation's inhabitants.

Because Satan has pulled the cover over the eyes of the educated and uneducated, the civilize and uncivilized, throughout this nation and world. Countries that claim to acknowledge God as well as countries that worship false gods, idols are being defeated right before their eyes but, yet they still do not recognize they are in spiritual warfare.

What is spiritual warfare? Spiritual warfare is fighting against demonic forces, demon spirit, the unseen enemy of mankind and the enemy of God in the spiritual realm and in the bodies of humankind. Man, spirit enemies are demon spirit, persons without bodies and not made of flesh and blood possessed or demonized individuals under demonic influences.

Victory over demonization, Satan, or demonic forces. The world's spiritual enemies are accomplished only by way of Jesus Christ and the "Word" of God, mankind spiritual weapons. To fight spiritual enemies, man must have spiritual weapons, which is the "Word" of God.

People, demonic forces are at war with the world which our eyes are too blind to recognize and our minds are too dull to understand. The world needs the "Word" of God and the Authority of Jesus Christ name to overthrow the forces of evil in one's life and the world.

Demonic forces have family members fighting against one another. The Bible speak of the devil coming to steal, kill, or destroy human lives, that which he is doing and accomplishing at an alarming rate even though Jesus defeated Satan and demon forces nearly two thousand years earlier.

However, the world does not recognize their defeat, because the world does not recognize Jesus. Therefore, the "Gospel" must be taught and preached throughout the four corners of the globe to every living creature.

But through spiritual warfare, the devil and demonic forces are attempting to prevent it from happening. And the only way to abstain that goal is by way of spiritual warfare against mankind.

Brethren, I'm a victim but now I'm witnessing a spirit war in the lives of all humankind ("age is no exception"), which take the Spirit of Christ in you, mankind to see to acknowledge the war in which man is engaged in.

The flesh is of no use, the flesh is weak but the Spirit is willing to give all who has accepted Jesus Christ as Lord and Savior victory over death, sin, Satan, and all demonic forces that inhabit the Earth.

I was in spiritual conflicts with demons internally in my body for over forty years. I was demon-possessed and heard demonic voices in my head for as many years until Jesus Christ and the Word cured me.

However, I'm currently in external conflicts with demonic forces of the world, people. Which is forever and Jesus Christ is the world only hope.

Thereby, I know what it is like to be control by forces internally and externally that man has no control over. There was a period in my life I wanted to destroy myself, not knowing why I felt this way. I never heard nor my parents speak of demon possession nor the existence of demonic spirits that are real and alive in the Earth atmosphere and living in human bodies as their own.

I now have children which I've informed them we live in a spirit world coexisting with spirit beings in the Earth atmosphere and in the body of persons. They now know demon spirits are real and alive in the atmosphere seeking human bodies to enter to possess as their own.

A person does not have to be demon-possessed, to be demonized; a person is operating under the perception and influence of the devil's spirit and control. Several occasions I've detected demonic presence in one of my daughter's physical ways and attitude, even in the tone of her voice.

She doesn't recognize her condition, but I do from self-experience. This child was raised in a Christian environment, sung in the youth choir, and is currently singing with young adult choir. Thereby, she is capable of distinguishing right and wrong or obedience and disobedience but yet she believes she is right when she is actually wrong. However, when you distinguish right and wrong to children and some adults, they look at you as though something is wrong with you.

As parents it is imperative to pray and cast out in the Name of Jesus any demonic activities or conflicts that may occur in family members. If Satan or demons get control of the mind, they can and will destroy you or cause you to harm or destroy yourself or others. It is the mind the devil want to control. Once he captures the mind, he uses it for a stronghold. Their power is in the mind.

The devil realizes the mind is the most powerful organ in human anatomy. It is the mind they use to articulate to influence humankind. Their strength and power of influence is in the mind of every creature.

But I will not through prayers and Jesus Christ allow the devil or demons destroy the lives of my children nor my neighbors. Parent stand in the gap of your lost child, pray because without prayers of Christians, I believe this nation and the world would condemn itself.

Our nation is built on Christianity and Christian values and it will forever stand until Jesus returns because of our prayers. Brethren, Satan, along with his demonic hosts, are trying their very best to bring condemnation up this nation inhabitants by way of spiritual warfare that begin in homes through family members or loved ones.

The devil and demons are more visible than ever before. They are exposing their spirit's presence in the atmosphere and their work in humans without our detection. Because Satan have our eyes fix on worldly things that are seen but not on spiritual things that are not seen with eyes but can be seen with the mind and ears. Even evil spirits in the midst and at work in the living can be seen with the mind and ears of others without visual visible sight (eyes).

Mankind must be receptive of the Holy Spirit to recognize the spirit of the devil or demon approach and manifestation in man's counterpart and the atmosphere. Man must be receptive to hear the devil's approach in man's speech (words). Thus, the manifestation of his spirit is through man's tongue.

You recall Matthew 16:22–23. Jesus rebuke Peter as Peter spoke the perception that which he perceived of the devil's spirit being. Jesus rebuked the devil. He said speaking to Peter, "Get behind me, Satan." Your thoughts did not come from God, but from man, which is confirmation the devil is a spirit person that use mankind as instruments to represent his spirit being. Age nor gender is no exception.

Brethren, the Holy Spirit is my witness, I have seen Satan the Devil in human bodily form as person and which I spoke to as a person without reply. I've also had physical encounters with demon spirits in the atmosphere of my home and in public places.

I have acknowledged to the spirit world I possess authority over Satan and demonic forces in the Name of Jesus Christ. Jesus Spirit, the same Spirit that defeated them, now lives in my body, which means I'll forever live in victory over Satan and all demonic forces.

Friends, there is no other way to victory over the devil and his agents, demons, but through Jesus Christ. The spirit realm acknowledge Jesus Christ has authority over death, sin, Satan, and all demonic forces on Earth and the universe.

Amen.

Questions and Answers of the Spiritual Realm

Satan the Devil, the chief adversary of God, was when created a perfect, righteous creature of God. He is a spirit person, for he appeared in heaven in the presence of God, Jesus Christ said of him, "That one was a manslayer when he began and did not stand fast in the truth because truth is not in him."

The truth was Jesus and the liar was Satan. It's the beginning of spiritual warfare with Satan the Liar challenging the integrity of Job. God permitted Satan to test Job's integrity to the limit but not allowing Satan to kill Job.

God said concerning Job, "There is no one like him in the Earth, a man blameless and up right, fearing God and turning aside from evil."

Satan spoke that Job served God primarily for selfish consideration. Satan made this point of his statement clear when he said, "Skin in behalf of skin and everything that a man has he will give in behalf of his soul." Try striking Job's own body with pain and he will curse you to your face.

Satan said in effect that no man could be put on Earth that would maintain integrity to God's sovereignty if Satan was allowed to put him to the test. This I believe was the beginning of spiritual warfare.

God permitted the testing not because he was unsure of the righteousness of his own sovereignty. He needed nothing proved to himself. It was out of love for his intelligent creatures that he allowed time for the testing out of the matter.

As it remains today, God permit mankind to undergo a test under Satan before all the universe. Which he gives his creatures the privilege of proving the devil, a liar.

However, it does not stop with Satan alone. Satan has spirit followers, demon spirits, persons without bodies and not made of flesh and blood. They are invisible wicked spirit creatures, sometimes called fallen angels, having superhuman power and speak in their own language.

These demons as such were not created by God. They were angels, angelic sons of God that conspired will Satan made themselves demons. The first to make himself one was Satan the Devil who became the ruler of demons. Demons now like Satan possess great power of influence over the minds and lives of humankind of all ages even possessing the ability to enter by the power of Satan into and possess human beings and animals as well.

Their purpose as well as all such demonic activity is that of Satan is to turn people against God and the pure worship of God. Therefore, the faithful must put a hand, spiritual fight through Jesus Christ against the devil and his followers against the world rulers of this darkness against wicked spirit forces in heavenly places. "Such fight is called spiritual warfare."

Man's fight against spiritual forces are not carnal but spiritual; therefore, man need spiritual weapons to combat spiritual forces. As believers in Jesus Christ, man need the Word of God which is the whole armor of God to combat the invisible enemy forces. But man must acknowledge we live in a spirit world.

Here are some questions that has been answered in the spirit world. What are Satan and demons' purpose and objective here in Earth? They are on a mission to turn people against God and the pure worship of God, as well as to steal, kill, and destroy human lives. Also, in today's world God is allowing Satan to test mankind as when he challenged God in testing Job's integrity in his attempt to turn mankind against God and the pure worship of God.

Who orchestrate their purpose and mission? The chief of demons, Satan the devil, God's adversary. Which is to bring condemnation upon the human race.

Where and how does demon spirits operate? They operate both in the spiritual and physical realms. They operate supernaturally in spirit; in the spirit realm and physically through the demon-possessed in the physical realm. Evil spirits or demons are real; they are persons without bodies. They speak in their own language through the demon-possessed or supernaturally in the spirit realm. I've heard my name called audibly in the atmosphere several times.

Why did the fallen angels which are now evil spirits or demons come here and where do they dwell? Demons are Satan followers called minions who conspired with him against God in heaven and are now his agents on Earth still in an attempt to conspire against God and mankind throughout the nations and the world.

What power does demons possess over man and where they get such power from Satan or mankind? Both, through the possessed and the power of influence Satan's spirit possess over mankind of all levels of societies. However, demon possession and demonically controlled persons are greatest among the gay population. It's power of influences to control are over homosexuals, lesbians, female homosexuals, bisexuals, transsexuals, transvestites, and pedophilia.

Homosexuals relating to or having a sexual orientation to persons of the same sex. Lesbianism, sexual orientation of women to other women. Bisexual, relating to or having a sexual orientation to persons of either sex. Transsexual, one whose primary, sexual identification is with the opposite sex. Transvestite, a person who dresses and acts in a style or manner traditionally associated with the opposite sex. Pedophilia, sexual attraction felt by an adult toward a child. And nymphomania, excessive sexual desire in a female. All those demonically control societies are demonically overtone and motivated.

Demon possession has culminated among nonbelievers and unbelievers of all human races. The infidel, an unbeliever who has no religious beliefs or one who doubts or rejects a particular doctrine. Atheism, disbelief in or denial of the existence of God. Agnostic, one who believes that there is no proof of the existence of God but does not deny the possibility that God exists.

Categorically speaking, without exception, all those societies and the division of non- and unbelievers are under the power of influence or controlled by a spirit or spirits greater than their natural spirit. They are either demonize or under demon possession by one or more evil spirits dwelling in their body.

How do demon spirits enter people's body, mind and why? First of all, do not be misled by hearsay. Demons cannot enter or possess a person's body or mind unless such a person is in agreement with the spirit realm and have given demons permission to enter to possess their body as their own. The person's body become and perform as its spirit body and the mind perform as it spirit being.

However, demons cannot enter or possess a person's body under their own power. It is the spirit of Satan that possess such power to enter demons into people's body and mind by creating false perception for individuals to perceive as their own thoughts of the senses, but in reality, it is the thought or perception of Satan's spirit in a person that create habits or other uncontrollable urges in a person that become avenues or accesses that allows Satan to enter evil spirits into the mind and body of people.

Their purpose of entering is to turn mankind away from God and to accomplish the task or challenge Satan's attempt he made against the integrity of Job through man throughout the Earth.

Satan know the spirit realm is powerless against man in the spiritual world alone; therefore, it is imperative demons or evil spirits enter human bodies to be effective in and against all human races in the spiritual and physical realms.

Does the spirit realm discriminate in the possession of human beings? No, the spirit world has no respectful person nor race of people to demonize. However, demons prefer to possess the bodies of nonbelievers but Christians are vulnerable to demon possession as well.

Does a person know whether or not he or she is demon-possessed or under the influence of demonic power? A small percentage recognize something is wrong with them hearing voices in their head but does not recognize their condition is demon possession while others go undetected with hidden demon or evil spirits disguised in them.

I was demon-possessed for over forty years without any knowledge of my condition. I heard voices in my head for over thirty years. Ten years of forty hidden demons disguise themselves in my body without my knowledge. I knew something was wrong with me but I didn't recognize the state of my condition because no one never told me nor explain to me the realization and the existence of demon spirits nor demon possession of human bodies.

After thirty-six years, God cured me of alcohol demons. After I was cured the voices, I had heard of thirty years left as well.

What is the duration of a demon-possessed person? As I've stated, hidden demons can possess a person's body until that person die or dwell in a person a lifetime undetected. Therefore, it's imperative to be specific when expelling demon spirits out of people. All demons are cast out in the Name of Jesus. But man must be a believer in God and Jesus Christ to cast out demons.

Can any person cast out demons? No. Only believers in God and Jesus Christ.

Are we under observance by the spirit world? Yes. In which demons in the atmosphere know us by name. They see and hear every word spoken and see everything we do or perform in the physical realm.

After an evil spirit or demon is cast out of a person where does it dwell? It's spirit dwell in the atmosphere of homes, public places, school buildings and among other shelters. Demons do not like wondering. Thus, it stays around for the right or another opportunity to enter another person or the same person by the power of influence of Satan or by the power of Satan's new creation of avenues or habits in man's false perception which allow demon spirits accesses to reenter.

Are demons more prevalent among the gay population? Yes. However, they are all in spiritual warfare individually and collectively. Also, demonic activity is more prevalent throughout the gay population, demon spirits have taken on the character and characteristics of the possessed speaking to and through the mouth of those that believe or wish to be the opposite sex. They are out shouting, "We are out and we are proud."

Spiritually speaking, no human being in their rightful mind and natural spirit would biologically be in denial of his or her biological sexual gender. Only a spirit or spirits greater than one's own natural spirit can make such proclamation.

What can they do or perform without the assistance of mankind? Demon spirits perform in many ways supernaturally in the spirit world. They can physical harm as well as frighten a person to death by moving objects that appear to move by themselves. However, their power in the supernatural is limited. They are characterized as persons without bodies and possessing similar characteristics as human beings and perform in human beings as human beings in the bodies of those whom their spirit possesses.

Can Satan or demon spirits speak? Yes. They speak in their own language, which meant demons can speak the language of all nationalities that they exist and dwell in. They also speak by proxy in and through the demon-possessed.

What are their destiny? The Lake of Fire. Hell, the abode of condemned souls, a place of eternal punishment for the wicked after death presided over by Satan.

How and why do demons disguise themselves? In the flesh of the wicked. Why? As a spirit of deception. They master the art of deceptions and disguises. All in and through the flesh of mankind, age is no exception.

Where do they reside? They reside in the possessed and around us in the Earth's atmosphere, in our homes, public places and school buildings. They even make their homes in sanctuaries. However, demons are more effective dwelling in the body of the wicked and demon-possessed. They are comfortable residing in physical bodies to cause person to steal, kill, and destroy others or even whom they in.

What is the duration of demon possession? I reiterate to stress the answer of this question. Some persons are demonized or demon-possessed their entire lives or until they die with or without ever knowing their condition. Others are possessed until demons are expel or cast out of them in the name above all Names Jesus Christ. There is no other Name but Jesus, demons will obey. But a person must be a believer in God and Jesus Christ in order to expel demons. Brethren, believe in me, the spirit realm know the believers in God and Christ. Nonbelievers are asking for trouble in attempting to expel evil spirits. The spirit world knows who we are in Christ, demon or evil spirits know who's hot and who's not.

Will the spirit realm perform for mankind? Yes, and it is currently in the process of performing for those who are in agreement with the spirit realm. However, it is forbidden, it is against God's will to worship or seek evil spirits or demons or be in agreement with. Such demonism activity turns people against God. Therefore, God forbids demonism in any form.

But there are those who seek and worship demons for power, prestige and authority in agreement or exchange for the use and purpose of their body and mind. Which then they, too, along with Satan and wicked spirits become condemned for hell, the lake of fire that which was created for the devil and demons.

Who has power over wicked spirits? All believers in God and Jesus Christ. Satan and demons are defeated foes but they do not accept defeat in mankind because their physical power is in the carnality or the mind and body of the human race of all nationalities. Therefore, man's lack of knowledge of their defeat give demons power over nonbelievers and some believers as well.

However, believers who acknowledge their defeat has power and authority in the Name of Jesus Christ to expel demons and the Word of God as spiritual weapons. Man need spiritual weapons to combat spiritual enemies. I reiterate. Nonbelievers are asking for trouble attempting to expel demons or evil spirits out of man.

Where does Satan and his followers get their power? Even though they acknowledge they are defeated foes in which their power exists in man's lack of knowledge and intellectual perception of how and what he perceives through the senses give the devil power to oppose man perception because the devil knows the thoughts of man in the carnality realm but not of the spirit.

Can demon spirits physically harm people? Yes, they can physically harm a person by way of the demon-possessed and supernaturally harm a person in the atmosphere of the spirit realm. I've been physically abused and attacked by evil forces in the atmosphere of my home and on the job. I've been slapped several times by an unseen force and as an adult demon forces punch on me several times while striking me on the leg. I've also had numerous physical encounters with demons in my home on the job and in public places and in the sanctuary.

I've experienced many encounters with demon-possessed people provoke to harm me but only two stand out from the others because my life was threatened. The first gentleman that I knew approached me as I was getting out from my truck asking for a loan of three dollars. I told him I would loan him a dollar, but first, I must get change. As we approach the store, he said to himself, "You better leave me alone before you make me hurt somebody," which got my attention, so I stopped to pause to see who he was talking to. I know I had not spoken which there were not anyone to be seen. As we proceeded, he spoke out again stressing. "I told you, you better leave me alone before you make me hurt somebody." It was then I knew who was trying to provoke him into harming me. It was a demon or demons in him that spoke to provoke him to say, "You better leave me alone before you make me hurt somebody." Well, needless to say, several years later, he was killed.

The second demon-possessed gentleman rode up to me riding a bicycle. I smelled his approach by the scent of alcohol and alcohol demons in him. He rode up to me with eyes bucked, rolling around in his head and said, "I'm going to kill you."

I asked him, "What did you say?"

He said, "I'm going to kill you."

I asked him, "Are you crazy?" I knew then who I was confronting.

He looked at me eyes still bucked this time I had prepared myself to handle him when he said, "Loan me a quarter."

I didn't ask any questions. I gave him a quarter in which he pedaled off. Since then, I've seen the gentleman several times but missing his right leg. He had been run over by an automobile.

There you have it: demon spirits are wicked. They can provoke the possessed into harming people while getting the possessed kill or injured.

What geographical area are demons most prevalent? Evil spirits or demons are most prevalent in non-Christian countries and uncivilized lands. Geographically speaking they exist throughout nations and the Earth manifestation through the carnality of whom their spirit possesses, that is the demon-possessed.

In some countries, including this nation, "incubus" an evil spirit or demon believe to descend upon and have sexual intercourse with women as they sleep. Evidence of this demonic act take place throughout the Earth; however, "incubus" is most prevalent in third-world countries because of ungodliness, nonbelievers, not revering God, impious and wickedness all associated with evil spirits. Therefore, do not be astonished or amazed of the wickedness and deception in today's world between mankind and is or her decisiveness of their gender, the demon-possessed nor the spirit realm.

Why cannot human beings visually see demon spirits in the atmosphere around us or in the demon-possessed? The answer of this question was revealed to me one day as I was writing eight years ago by the Holy Spirit after witnessing, two angels that stood at my door. "Flesh and blood cannot enter the Kingdom of Heaven." The Kingdom of Heaven is the spiritual realm. But God make it possible for whom he chooses in the physical realm to witness in the spiritual through the vision of the Holy Spirit. He that is in man.

Remember, "Greater is he in you, than he that is in the world." Therefore, a person witness through the vision of the Holy Spirit. He that dwells in believers. That's how I see demon spirits and the angels when no one else saw them. I witnessed through the vision of the Holy Spirit.

"Thank You, Jesus."

How does mankind combat against invisible enemies and the spirit realm of Satan and demons? First and far most have Jesus Christ as Lord and Savior over your life. Also, believing in God and possessing the knowledge of His Word by wearing the whole armor of God's Word.

The Bible says, "For we are not fighting against people made of flesh and blood but against persons without bodies, the evil rulers of the unseen world, those mighty satanic beings and great evil princes of darkness who rule this world and against huge numbers of wicked spirits in the spirits world."

In every battle, you will need faith as your shield to stop the fiery arrows aimed at you by Satan. And you will need the helmet of salvation and the sword of the Spirit which is the Word of God. So use every piece of God's armor to resist the enemy whenever he attacks and when it is all over, you will still be standing up. And remember, "pray" in the Spirit all the time.

Mankind in Spiritual Warfare

We live in a spiritual realm of good and evil. The spiritual realm of evil is the enemy of humankind, not just man. However, mankind is whom the spirit realm uses to spread evilness among the human race throughout the Earth.

But many of us have defeated the spirit world, the invisible enemy of mankind. We didn't defeat it but the Lord Jesus Christ defeated the invisible, Satan and demons through us in which he uses as vessels.

My revelation is that I've been face-to-face and spirit to spirit in spiritual warfare in which I defeated demon spirits and the devil in the Earth's atmosphere of the world.

Demons exist in the Earth atmosphere in the millions waiting to enter and possess human bodies. However, several times as many are now possessing and dwelling in the minds of humankind throughout the four corners of the Earth which mean no matter where mankind travel, he or she is in spiritual warfare even in the home.

All human beings including Christians are in some kind of spiritual warfare or conflict with demon spirits of the atmosphere or in the flesh of humankind, including family members.

Therefore, every man, woman and child should know the devil and demon spirits are real and alive living in the Earth's atmosphere and dwelling in the flesh of humankind of all ages. Which mean mankind is in spiritual warfare with himself, the flesh but does not realize it.

I'm a living witness of the truth and the Holy Spirit is my witness. People, the spiritual realm of evil is here to destroy all human lives by any means possible, age is no exception. Demons are here to take us (you) out any way possible.

They are person without bodies, not made of flesh and blood. However, they need human bodies to enter to be effective in and against humankind, age is no exception. So don't be misled nor fool by a person's age or appearance, that can be deceiving.

The spirit realm uses many disguises to fool and deceive the world, which this nation and the world is now living in deception. Does this nation realize it? I don't think so. And those that do the devil and demons has cause this nation to ignore their cries?

Which mean spiritual warfare start in the flesh, the body and mind of man, which mankind is in war with the flesh and demons. The flesh is a tool that demon spirits use to harm, steal, kill, and destroy lives, age is no exception.

I've been in spiritual warfare my entire life with the flesh while under the power of demonization. I was demon-possessed well over forty years. I was motivated by demonic powers, not only power but by the demon spirit itself.

Demons spoke to me audible in the atmosphere, and I've heard voices in my head that no one could hear but me. Voices told me to kill myself and to do things unimaginable to humankind. Friend spiritual warfare isn't a game, it's real in all human lives of all ages. But people take spiritual warfare for granted. Big mistake.

People are in spiritual warfare with their minds that are controlled by demon spirits that are much stronger than their natural spirit which keep them in bondage and in conflict with their flesh. Which mean multitudes of people aren't in their right mind. I weren't in my right mind for over forty years, yet I appeared normal.

But today, I'm in my right mind. God cured me of demon possession and now I'm witnessing how real and physical spiritual warfare really is and without Jesus Christ in one's life as Lord and Savior there isn't hope nor salvation.

God cured me of a legion of demons. Now I acknowledge I possess the spiritual mind of Jesus that no demon nor devil can get access to. Which mean no demonic power ever again prevail in nor against me.

I've physically had encounters with demon spirits of the atmosphere. I've supernaturally fought the spirit realm with spiritual words of God as spiritual weapons and the Name of Jesus Christ. The power is in the Name of Jesus Christ for believers and spiritual weapons of mankind is the Word of God.

I've literally witnessed demons in the atmosphere and in the flesh of mankind obey the Name of Jesus Christ and the Word of God. God's glory is seen, heard, and felt in the spirit world as well as the physical world.

I'm a living witness and testimony of God's glory in the spirit realm. All of God's glory are in the Name of Jesus Christ and His Word. God's glory is seen in spiritual warfare when the devil and demons glorify God in their obedience of hearing the Name of Jesus.

People, no other Name nor power can form against the Name of our Lord. Man's strength and power over the devil, demons, and the entire spiritual realm is in the Name of Jesus Christ.

As I've said, I'm a living witness and testimony of the power in the Name of Jesus and God's word. Believe me mankind cannot survive in this life without Jesus Christ as Lord and Savior.

People, we live in a demonically control society and a supernatural environment. People have turned away from God and ignored Jesus Christ to seek help in the spiritual realm, the spiritual realm of Satan and demons. Which mean spiritual warfare is more rampant today than ever before.

Spiritual warfare is at its highest level as godly people and some Christians ignores its presence. People of all nations throughout the world are consulting demons in the atmosphere to help fight against Christians and Christian's way of living.

They are using demonic power as bodyguards throughout the world and communicating with the devil as he consults people to spread and perform evil and wickedness throughout the four corners of the Earth against Christians and even those whom his spirit use to aid and represent him.

We, mankind, are in the midst of a war where only victory is through Jesus Christ. The spirit realm realize mankind is lost and defenseless without Jesus Christ in their lives as Lord and Savior. Brothers and sisters, you need Jesus in your life and every word proceeded out of the mouth of God. That's why it's imperative all mankind invite Jesus Christ into their heart as Lord and Savior.

We have supernatural enemies' mankind cannot see but God and Jesus do. Jesus reveal their presence in mankind and in the midst of the atmosphere. He also showed and displayed his power of authority over the spirit realm.

And now the power which Jesus displayed is now given to us believers in his Name. Now believers' power and authority over the spirit realm is in the Name of Jesus Christ, which the devil and every demon is in obedience of, "I'm a witness."

Spiritual warfare is real. It is effective against mankind only through mankind, the flesh of human being. The devil and demon spirits use human bodies for manifestation of their spirit to use in and against the world. The world is people.

Through demon possession of human beings, the spirit realm is fighting against the population of the world through the population of the world which the world does not acknowledge nor accept. Because it is supernaturally being fought in and by way of the flesh.

Only a few detect and acknowledge spiritual warfare in the midst. I say a few because multitudes ignore the conflicts, they are in. The devil and demons have dulled their minds and blind their eyes.

Therefore, spiritual warfare does not exist as far as they are concern. But friend, spiritual warfare is real, very real which mankind of all ages should be concern. Because in the end, spiritual warfare will ultimately bring destruction to mankind through mankind.

Multitudes are in spiritual battle with Satan and demons, evil spirits throughout the Earth but does not realize who or what they are up against. I believe I've experienced every demonic tactic formed in and against the flesh and weapons the spirit realm have in its arsenal.

I was in spiritual warfare which millions are now in for over forty years but did not recognize it. Matter of fact I was unaware of the existence of a spirit realm, a realm of demons, evil and wicked spirits roaming the Earth and in the Earth's, atmosphere seeking human bodies to take up residency in.

People, age is no exception are in conflict with themselves and the world never realizing it isn't themselves responsible or causing conflicts in their lives but a spirit or spirits greater than their natural spirit in spiritual warfare in their minds and bodies.

The Holy Spirit is my witness of the spiritual battle I was in which my most difficult battle was with alcohol demons that controlled my life and lives of millions and my way of living for over forty years as well as other controlling demons that attempted to condemn me for life.

But God cured me of demon possession through Jesus Christ. It was the supernatural power of Jesu Christ that freed me of demon possession and demon bondage. Through Jesus Christ, I've won the battle I was in over forty years, which the spirit realm acknowledges. People, there is no greater victory acknowledging you've defeated the enemies of Jesus and the invisible enemies of the human race throughout the world.

Spirits of the Unseen

The exploitation of television shows on drug abuse, alcoholism, homosexuality, lesbianism, incest, nymphomania, pedophilia, and pederasty in which sodomy is perform between males as practiced by a man with a boy or any kind of pervasiveness or unnatural sex acts are all exploited but never the demonic forces that are responsible for such unnatural practices.

The truth is, there aren't medical treatment for neither of them. Because they are all demonically motivated and demonically control. The time is now to focus on the issues and realize we live in a spiritual realm that is more spiritual than physical.

There are millions of spirits habituating the spiritual realm which we, mankind share. Some spirit demons possess life-form. They are persons with bodies under the control and command of Satan the Devil. While other spiritual sons of God, angels operate and perform by the command of God.

Which means it is two sides of the spiritual realm in which mankind share both. There is a light side and a dark side; therefore, do not be deceived, both mankind and demons play a major role in. We aren't free because we live among evil and wicked spirits that use human bodies by way of possession to live in and operate as though as their own body.

Human bodies are their homes, shield as well as representatives of their spirit being. And as a result, demon bring condemnation through deception on human beings of all ages. They possess human bodies for use by proxy to deceive man himself and to steal, kill, or destroy other human lives.

The time is here for this nation of people and people throughout the world to be inform of the realization of demonic spirits, demon possession dwell among us and that the world population is under attack. It's imperative that man realize demons are the culprits that are responsible for mankind pervasiveness, inhuman behavior, or any kind of unnatural sexual acts.

If a person cannot control him or herself to act as their natural self—something is extremely wrong or cannot control their emotions that determine whether he or she as being the opposite sex rather than their biological sex indicate the presence of demons in their body stronger and more powerful than their natural spirit.

Even though mankind does not see them, their work of performance in the physical realm are seen, heard, and felt. Yet the manifestation of their spirit aren't seen nor is it tangible in the physical realm still they exist around is habituating in human bodies of all ages. So do not be deceived by people appearance. They are here in spirit and in the body of humankind. Everywhere man exist their invisible presence are there is well.

I reiterate there are two sides of the spiritual world. A dark and light side of the physical and spiritual world. Both of which manifest in one's life. One side brings eternal destruction, the other everlasting life in the presences of God to those who have faith and belief in Jesus Christ. Some that Satan is trying to prevent in all human lives.

I cannot stress strong enough the realization of their attack on human lives. They are real in spirit in which life in the spirit world is alive and what makes it even more prevalent they are alive in bodily form in human bodies, in the physical realm as well as in the spiritual realm. Thereby, the manifestation of their presence through their effectiveness can be seen and felt in the physical realm.

I've witnessed many times manifestations of evil spirit in people. I've heard demons answer me through people, in which many of them did not recognize who had spoken through them. I've heard demons speak in the atmosphere in their own language.

People, demon spirits and demon possession are presence among us and it must be address to the nation and the world. Mankind must take upon himself just as I am to expose the manifestation of the spirit realm that is present around us.

Demon spirits in the atmosphere has harassed and physically attacked me. Thereby, in my experience, I discovered mankind is fearful of the world of the unseen and afraid of the unknown or something that is alive but intangible.

However, man must first acknowledge the spirit realm of the unseen is real and alive, then expose demon possession is prevalent among this nation of people to bring to the light for the good of the world population and for the world to witness the realization and manifestation of demon spirits come out of individuals right in the presences of the world. Then loved ones will discover fathers, mothers, daughters, and sons weren't responsible for their pervasiveness nor their unnatural behavior nor their inhuman and uncontrollable habits or alternate lifestyles.

Any human being who says they cannot contain nor control themselves. Their natural spirit is revealing something to them and loved ones something is terribly wrong in their body and is more powerful than their own natural spirit. Which indicate he or she need spiritual help.

Spirit enemies, spiritual weapons. Spiritual weapons are God's spiritual Words spoken through his Son Jesus Christ and apostles. An enemy of God is an enemy of believers. Which mean it's imperative that mankind and believers possess spiritual weapons, God's Words against spirit enemies.

I believe God realize mankind would be in a fight for his spiritual life after the cherub who became angel, Lucifer was cast down from heaven along with one third of God spiritual sons, angels that conspired against God. They become demons or evil spirits habituating the Earth and Earth atmosphere seeking human bodies to enter to possess. Obviously, many has already entered. Once a demon or demons enter a body, it won't leave until cast out in the Name and Authority of Jesus Christ. You must be a believer in Jesus Christ in order to expel demons.

Our enemies aren't man himself but evil and wicked spirits that dwell in body and minds of mankind. They are the culprits to reckon with. Yes, they are person but without bodies performing through the body of mankind thereby functioning as human beings with all human characteristics of human beings. But yet invisible to human eyes and goes undetected in man himself.

Man must focus on unseen things rather than things that are seen in the physical realm. Because we aren't fighting against flesh and blood but against invisible enemies in the physical and spiritual realm through the four corners of the Earth.

In which they are well disguise and conceal particularly in the presence of people or an audience. What the world witness is that which the spirit realm let it witness. Its spirits are well camouflage in the world's population but the world isn't aware of who's who in the body of whom.

Because what is unnatural is natural and that which is natural is unnatural in the eyes of the world. If a person, ask him or herself, if what the other person does is normal, why is it abnormal or unnatural for me or what is natural for me is unnatural or abnormal for others. It is because man cannot see the invisible force that is responsible for the world false perception.

Even though a person appears normal in every aspect of life, he may not be in his right mind. Remember, appearances can be deceiving and friend there is plenty deception in this evil and wicked world.

I served in the world for over forty years, I thought I was normal in every aspect of life until God cured me of many kinds of possessive demons. Alcohol demons was most prevalent in my life for over thirty years. I also heard demonic voices in my head speak to me over forty years. Therefore, I confirm and testify demon spirit are real and alive in human beings' disguise in human bodies, human abilities, and characteristics. They speak in their own language through whom their spirit dwell's in.

They are here for several purposes first to steal, kill, and destroy human lives, secondly to seek vengeance against God through the world and thirdly to perform vengeance through the flesh of mankind on the human race.

That mean the world is in spiritual warfare with every kind of demon and demonic force imaginable to mankind but does not recognize its war and those that do demons has cause them to be in such condition that they've lost credibility and self-esteem in life.

It imperative that the world's population be educated of themselves as being under the influence of demonic powers and demon spirits that are alive in their body, which is necessary to expose to the world that demons are stronger in a person's body than a person natural spirit and is responsible for the world's abnormal behavior and alternate lifestyles.

They are habituating the Earth and it's atmosphere by the millions seeking human bodies to enter and use as their own. It is obvious multitudes have already entered human bodies. Once demons enter it will not leave until cast out in the Name and Authority of Jesus Christ.

I've been demon-possessed, victimize, and tested by many kinds of demon spirits in the physical and spiritual realms beyond any humans being imagination. But today, I'm a witness of demon possession among the young generation taking control of young minds and bodies and some adults as well through creative habits.

The spirit realm is superhuman intelligent and intellectual. It acknowledges there isn't anything of God's creation that a human being could drink or smoke just once and become addictive of. I reiterate, there isn't anything.

However, God has in man's heart and on his mind that the spirit of Satan can indeed enter into man, woman, or child to possess power to control mankind intellectually and physically. Thereby, after a person consume into their system a kind of drug or alcoholic beverage it opens up avenues and creative habits for Satan to enter demon spirits of all kinds into the body and mind. The mind is Satan's access of entering controlling spirits by way of evil and wicked resources or power of influences. By way of his power of influence, Satan can control intellectually all five senses, the entire human mind and body.

Thereby, I'm implying categorically that people be told of demonic possession existence throughout the world's population.

But demons or evil spirits can be expelled or driven out in the Name and Authority of Jesus Christ by mankind who believe and has faith in God and Jesus Christ. Someday, the world will acknowledge God's Spirit is greater than the spirit and evil spirits in those who belong to the world. Also, children of the devil those who have sold or given their soul to the devil in agreement for prestige, power, and wealth over the flesh of the physical world.

There is something else that are imperative the world should acknowledge as well which is to recognize the presence of evil and wicked spirits in its midst and in the appearance of humankind. Multitudes of evil spirits, demons that possess human bodies can in fact give simultaneously mankind multiple intellectual personalities. Therefore, expelling out demon believers must be specific.

There are many spiritual elements existing in the physical world and Earth atmosphere. There are persons without bodies functioning as human beings in human bodies as human beings. Which explain our enemies aren't flesh and blood but persons without bodies.

Mankind need to know how to recognize the devil and demonic spirits in the body of mankind, even in his own physical body. Because their spiritual characteristics are similar to man physical characteristics that is applied in the physical realm against man himself.

Man cannot see the devil in its natural spirit form; however, I did at the young age of six when he command me to curse God. I didn't know any better but the Holy Spirit led me not to. I imagine you like to know how I saw into the spiritual realm. I witnessed through the vision of the Holy Spirit. He that dwell in me. "He that is in me is greater than he that is in the atmosphere and in those who belong to the world."

There isn't anything demon spirits perform in the physical realm is supernatural to me in the spiritual realm. I see into the spiritual realm as well as I see into the physical realm. The supernatural is natural to me, as is the spiritual realm is physical for me.

Therefore, the devil is two persons, first he's a spirit person in the spiritual realm. Secondly, he's a person appearing as a person or human being in the physical realm. His spirit is the representative of two lives, a spirit in the supernatural realm and as a person who has manifest or transition his spirit being in the physical realm that appears as a person who roams the Earth seeking whom he can devour or use to steal, kill, or destroy human lives.

But mankind did not choose to be a representative of the devil's spirit. But unfortunately, some of us did and became "children of the devil." Remember his approach is through mankind. But man does not see himself as the devil's spirit being. But you, mankind can hear his spirit approach by way of man's words (mouth) or speech. But you must listen for his approach through the mouth of man that which reveals his spirit presences.

So pay attention when a person speaks because the manifestation of the devil or demons are in the tongue. "Don't ever forget it." The manifestation of either spirit is transformed into the spirit of that of a human being male or female, child, or an adult, "age is no exception" to accomplish their efforts in the natural against mankind.

But stand your ground and always remember, "He that is in you is greater than he that is in whom is speaking to you and also in those who are in the world." I've acknowledged their presence around me in bodily form and in the atmosphere. Their work of performance that is supernatural to the world is natural to me. Because greater is he in me, than he that is in the world.

Therefore, I do not fear evil nor do I fear demon, because Christ lives in my heart, and it is through Christ whom I've defeated every kind of demon and devil on and in the Earth's atmosphere. The Good News is that Satan and demons realize that I know as well as they acknowledge I've defeated as well as proclaimed to the spirit realm of my victories over death, sin, the devil, and demons through Jesus Christ, my Lord and Savior.

I've made it plain and clear to Satan and the spirit world, there isn't a demonic force I will not confront in private nor in the presence of mankind for which I will expose their presence in the flesh and bodies of mankind and in the Earth atmosphere wherever the Holy Spirit lead me. The Holy Spirit is my witness of this truth and proclamation.

Amen.

Are you ready for this? "The devil and man's perception." The power and control of Satan is in man's own perception. Satan and the power of demon spirits in one's life is their ability to intellectual perceive to intercede mankind perception as their own to act on.

God did not put the devil nor demons over mankind. Man give the devil authority over himself. Had God given his spirit over man? God would've given authority over himself because "He is in man and man's body is God's temple."

Man allow his intellectual perception put Satan over himself to rule and control all those who allow him to control their thought pattern. Thereby, allowing his spirit to intercede into man intellect in which cause man to perform his will.

The devil looks upon his spirit being to rule man when he chose an as representative of his spirit by grasping man intellect to adversely use against man himself. Which explain his power to control exist in mankind intellectual perception. Man's perception is the devil's ability to know his thoughts which he perceives in mankind of his own perceptions but not of the spirit. He can only perceive man's natural or thoughts of the flesh but not man's spiritual thoughts that which is perceived by the mind of Jesus. We believers possess the mind of Jesus.

Man's intellectual mind of the flesh inform the devil's spirit to know when, where and how to perform against mankind and man himself. He knows whom his spirit can or cannot manifest in. "Believe me, he knows."

Do not forget the power to control you is in your perception and his spirit ability to know when, where and how depend on your way of thinking. However, Jesus Christ had given believers victory and authority over the devil and spirit realm, over demons on Earth and of the universe.

I reiterate, Jesus has given believers authority over the devil and every kind of demon spirit that inhabit the world. Satan is a defeated foe but he does not accept defeat because his presence in mankind is essential to accomplish that which he is here for, that is to steal, kill, or destroy human lives. Which his power is in man's carnal perception. Without an intellectual perception, the devil's spirit is powerless.

However, Satan and his followers recognize the authority of believers in the Name above all Names, Jesus Christ. Jesus know it is man intellectual perception that Satan use to control and speak through mankind. Thereby, we believers possess the spiritual mind of Jesus Christ but not of the flesh.

Satan and demons speak in spirit, still their spirit is present in the mouth of man. And because of their ability to speak and perceive man's intellectual perception man is responsible for the commitment of their evilness and wickedness among the human race.

But we believers possess the spiritual mind of Jesus Christ but not of the flesh. Therefore, brethren, be vigilant also remember the manifestation of Satan or demonic spirits presence manifest through the tongues of mankind.

Prophecy

I proclaim this decade will become the realization and the exposure of demon spirits and demonic activity throughout the nation and the world. It'll be the exposure of demons in our everyday lives and in our homes. More people than ever before will be delivered of demonic bondage, demon possession, oppression, and depression.

Through realization and exposure of demonic forces, parents will reunite as husbands and wives again, boys and girls will reunite as sons and daughters again. Husbands and wives will reunite as fathers and mothers again, sons and daughters will reunite as brothers and sisters again. And all will unite in the presences of God as families again. May we all be in agreement for this is what the Lord want.

Amen.

Invisible Enemies in Our Government Demonization by Proxy!

I

Satan the Devil, the prince of the air, is an enemy of God, and mankind has strategically established his invisible government in and among our nation's government and governments of every nation.

Scripture says Satan is prince of the air, which means his spirit being is omnipresent, present everywhere simultaneously. Air is throughout the world which mean the devil and demons exist throughout the world.

The devil s established government is governed by several sources himself as a spirit person, demons, and mankind. His government in the spiritual realm is govern by himself and high demonic officials, demons. His spiritual government is set up in our physical or natural government and is set up in our physical or natural government and is in our natural government as government officials.

Without human government officials his physical government could not exist. Mankind human power is essential in his evil and wicked deeds in the world.

Thereby, governments throughout the Earth must acknowledge we are in spiritual warfare with invisible enemies in every level of government principalities and homes. This nation and the entire world are in spiritual warfare with unseen enemies but does not recognize the invisible foes in the government because Satan physical government even though in spirit is operated and control by human sources with or with his or her knowledge.

The devil and demons are spirit persons without bodies. Only the devil's spirit possess power to visibly manifest himself as a visible person. Demons does not possess such power they lost their materialization power when they forsook their own proper dwelling place in heaven to come to Earth. However, they possess supernatural powers in the spiritual and physical realm.

But demons need bodies, human bodies to perform by proxy physically in the government which Satan has established in our government. Therefore, demon possession is essential among government officials throughout the country and world. Demon spirits need to enter human bodies to be effective in all levels of government all levels of governments.

However, demons cannot enter human bodies under their own power. They either enter upon individuals request (children of the devil) or consent or Satan's spirit being create habits for individuals which open up avenues or the accessibility to enter demonic spirits into the lives of the world.

"Human beings do not acknowledge demon possession of their own bodies unless under their given consent of demon possession."

The world must acknowledge, there are two kinds of children. Children of God and children of the devil. Demon possession is greatest among children of the devil can bear only evil and wickedness in the world. Children of the devil is against everything Jesus Christ teaches. Read 1 John 3:10. However, here is the clear difference between God's children and the devil's children, those who do not what is right or do not love others are not God's children. That's how you distinguish the two groups of children in the world.

Through children of Satan, demons are attempting to remove Jesus Christ name and teachings from government. However, the "gates of hell will not prevail" now or ever. Yet he is in the process of giving all he has to remove God and the Name of Jesus Christ from his established government in our nation's government. In third world non-Christian countries, he has been successful to some degree.

It isn't a game but an insidious plan to destroy the works of God and Jesus Christ through mankind. And because of such operation. More people has become influence of the devil, demonized, or demon-possessed to perform the works of Satan and demons more than ever before, "Age is no exception."

This nation and the world are at war and under attack with invisible enemies the devil and demons. Without Jesus Christ mankind cannot do anything for him or herself nor against enemies he or her cannot see.

Demons who has entered human bodies are the culprits performing such evilness and hideous acts through humankind. They are culprits causing nations to fight against nations and family against family. I reiterate, "The works of the devil or demons aren't effective in the physical realm without the aid of humankind."

It is all about Jesus, a Name above all names. The world has invisible enemies thereby the world needs invisible weapons which is the "Word of God" in the Name of Jesus Christ. Jesus's Name saves lives and nations. There is power in the Name Jesus, a Name above all Names in all the Earth and the universe. Satan and demons obeys the Name of Jesus. There is more power in Jesus Christ Name than there is in all the Earth and the universe.

No demonic force in humankind or in the spiritual realm can come against the Name of Jesus. Wherever Jesus's Name permitted in public or public places, the presence of demonic forces isn't in force. Wherever the Name of Jesus Christ is not permitted demonic forces are in possession of humankind and are at liberty committing evil and hideous acts.

Wherever Jesus is not welcome, God, the Father isn't welcome. Thereby, mankind cannot worship God without worshipping Jesus Christ. Satan and demon rather mankind to worship God than Jesus because there is all power over the spiritual realm in the Name of Jesus Christ. Demons tremble just hearing Jesus's Name. Just imagine if Jesus Christ name was permitted in all public and government buildings. There would be no demonic activity present. Jesus says, "Where two or three are gather in my name there I am in the midst."

The nation is under attack against Satan invisible government in us, through us and against us and mankind through the four corners of the Earth. Age is no exception or nation.

This nation and nations throughout the world must wake up and recognize Satan established spirit government within the world's government. Which has declared war on the innocents and Christians throughout the world because of Jesus Christ.

The spirit realm (Satan and demons) fought against Jesus through mankind and his government when Jesus walk the Earth. But today they are more prevalent against mankind and the world than ever before since Jesus's ascension into heaven.

Therefore, it's essential that our government and mankind recognize the power of influence and freedom demonic forces has over our government without Jesus Christ in their lives.

I know beyond a shadow of doubt, the government nor mankind cannot over throw the evils of the world without Jesus Christ and the Word of God in man's heart, which the devil and demons acknowledge.

I've been in spiritual warfare with demonic force my entire life. I'm currently in spiritual conflict with the devil. It's real even though it's not visible to man's sight. It's a spirit war against demons in the body of man and demonic forces in the body of mankind and the Earth atmosphere.

The greatest war ever to be fought are personally being spiritually fought against the innocent through demonic forces within our own government and governments of all nations. "I reiterate, demonic forces aren't effective without the aid and possession of human bodies."

Wake up America repent, permit God and Jesus Christ back into public schools, places, and government.

It is this nation Christian values that hold this nation together as a people. Regardless of denomination, we all accept and teach Jesus Christ is Lord and Savior. Now the world over must accept

Jesus Christ is Lord and Savior to possess authority over Satan and demonic forces.

Satan acknowledges Christians possess authority over him and demonic forces. It's the Christians and believers of Jesus Christ that has power in the Name of Jesus that control the works of evilness over this nation and abroad.

No nation or government can win the battle against the devil's established government within our government without Jesus Christ as Lord and Savior.

I reiterate, the world is in spiritual warfare within the body of its people. Satan realize any nation that does not recognize God Jehovah or Jesus Christ as God and Lord he has control over such nations and its people.

Beyond a showdown of doubt his government is in control of such nation. There are no exceptions among the devil-established government.

We are a Christian nation, a nation who has blasphemously turned away from God, Jesus Christ, and Christian values. The nation is in a state of denial, a condition which Satan and demonic forces are in control of. Even though we are a Christian nation, no nation or country without God or Jesus Christ can stand nor stay united against the attacks of the devil or demonic forces.

Repent, turn back to God. Terrorism is rampant throughout the political world. Turn back and believe in His Word and Son, Jesus Christ.

Believe me, there are demonic forces sweeping the nations not only through the Earth's atmosphere but through people human sources all over the world as well. Human source is the invisible working power of these demonic forces.

These demonic forces are governmental power over nations and its residents. Even though it's not seen the results of it evidence and its effect is seen and felt. The devil's demonic forces has invisible moved its human power and presence into mankind everyday of life. Age is no exception.

Demon spirits are possessing human beings at an alarming rate of all ages to move and work comfortably into homes and strategically in all levels of governmental positions, local, state, and through the world. Because of such mammoth move the nations are in for a great shock.

Spiritually, this nation has diminished from the nation it once was. It has turned away from God and Jesus Christ to open its doors to alternate lifestyles to homosexuality, lesbianism, same-sex marriage, pornography, and vice which are all demonically control. Which mean demonization has brought condemnation upon this nation and its government.

Some fact and evidence the government officials of all levels of government act as though they are blind to this fact and evidence that Satan and demonic forces are at this time working continually in and through them as elective government officials or state representatives.

However, the question is, "Why is it so difficult for our government to comprehend that the god of this world system of things is trying to destroy or condemn the nation and the world through government and political powers?"

The nation acknowledge Satan is called the "god of this world's system of things." He is the invisible spirit ruler who rules influence and sways this world's society, educational and religious system, and government. Which confirm, we the nations is in spiritual warfare with demonic forces that are attempting to stop all who truly seek to know to serve and obey the Creator God.

Spiritual warfare is real. We, mankind needs to acknowledge it is not; the "works of God" man must take in our own self-defense. Scripture says, "We need to put on the whole armor of God to withstand the wiles of the devil." For we aren't fighting against flesh and blood but against person without bodies, demons, the evil rulers of the unseen world, those mighty satanic beings and great evil princes of darkness who rule this world and against huge numbers wicked spirits in the spirit world.

People, Satan's established government is real and active in our everyday lives. In the beginning God placed a great cherub an angelic creature of high rank who became Lucifer, the devil to carry out His government on the Earth but Lucifer refused to carry out God's will, God's commands, and God's government. He wanted to substitute his own. That he has done in the spiritual realm and by way of proxy in the physical realm of this nation government officials and governments throughout the world.

Adam had the chance to supplant him. However, by way of his disobedience Adam failed instead he obeyed the devil and man became the property of the devil and the whole human race been held captive by the devil's works ever since.

Therefore, man, this nation must return to God and Jesus Christ as Lord and Savior over this nation, the world, and lives. Allow God to restore law and order to lands throughout the nations.

I wonder how can America sing "God Bless America" when America refuse to allow God or Jesus Christ into its buildings and prayers into public places? I wonder and so does God.

This nation nor no nation can survive rejecting God's Word while Satan and demonic forces through mankind continue to keep God's commandments and the testimony of Jesus Christ out of government.

II

Demonization by Proxy

As we, mankind, knows Satan the Devil is an adversary of God and is attempting to demonize this nation and world to bring it under the influence power of demonic spirits. Also, as you well know more human beings are under demonic influence that ever before. That explain demonization is more prevalent in all ages than ever before.

I acknowledge demonization has already cause this nation of people to live immoral lives and be disobedient of God's Word. The devil is systematically and strategically working demonic spirit into the body of mankind that represent all levels of government.

The works of demons are clearly visible in our nation population performance especially in the gay population. Demonic spirits are speaking out throughout the world by proxy for the demon-possessed and people under demonic influence.

The devil and demons are demanding government benefits for same-sex marriages as oppose to heterosexual marriages I know is well is anyone in their right mind, a person that profess to be the opposite sex to marriage the same biological sex aren't in their right mind, neither the person who pass or upheld such a law. A person that prefer to marry or anyone who support same-sex marriages are under demonic influence of a demon spirit greater than their natural spirit. But the secular world does not recognize the problem nor it's condition because the devil has blinded the minds of this nation.

It's imperative that the nation and throughout the four corners of the globe acknowledge we mankind live in a spirit world and a demonized society. There is evidence all around us, in the homes, public places and schools in government facilities. Wherever mankind dwell's there is a demonic society and an evil and wicked environment.

Brothers and sisters demonic spirits by proxy are representing people throughout the world. It is no fairy tale; demons are performing through people of all levels and ages of life without their knowledge. That explain why demon possession of human beings are so vital and important to the spiritual realm of Satan.

If the devil tried to get Jesus Christ to perform for him, you can imagine what he is doing to mankind. Similar temptations he tried with Jesus, he's using to this day on mankind to perform his work and plan. However, these temptations are in disguise as oppose to Jesus's temptations.

However, some compromise has been and still being use in the livelihood of many. Promising great wealth and prestige for them who comply. It isn't secret any longer, the devil and his agents, demons are trying to gain influence over the secular world to bring the world under their authority and power.

Today's people act and perform differently than when I was an adolescent even though they appear normal in their physical being and appearance and all aspect of life. But there is a dark side of more people today than ever before which they aren't afraid nor ashamed to expose nor express.

People of this generation displays more evilness and wickedness than ever before. Performing the right thing is wrong to the secular world. And to do that which is right is wrong in the world's sight and mind.

People are also more aggressively evil and wicked than ever before because the devil has programed their secular minds. Thereby causing the righteous to think or believe something wrong with them. This demonic output is occurring throughout the four corners of the world. Man cannot get away from the evil and wicked displays of mankind. Because whenever man dwell's both Satan and demons are present in the atmosphere and the demon-possessed.

Which explain demonization by proxy is occurring all over the world starting in the homes. Yes, demonic possession originates in the home, believe it or not in toddlers, adolescents, and adults of all ages. There aren't exceptions; all mankind are vulnerable.

However, the percentage rate of demonic possession is higher among younger people because vulnerability of alcohol and drugs are greater and easy to abstain access to than ever before. Therefore, younger people are more susceptible to comply to what the devil or demons command. And because lack of knowledge of the spirit world we live in.

Young people as well as some adults do not acknowledge we live in a spiritual environment and an evil and wicked society. Satan has blinded the minds of this nations need for spiritual education of demonization and demonology. The need is urgently in demand because the nation and the world are overly populated with demonic spirits taking up residency as their homes in human bodies without knowledge of their presence.

The mystery is that people does not realize their demonized condition, nor do they acknowledge we live in a world that is more spiritual than physical. But those that do acknowledge does not acknowledge demonic activity in themselves nor the condition of others.

The purpose of all demonic activities are to turn people against God and reject the pure worship of God and Jesus Christ. No human being in their right mind would turn away from God or reject Jesus

Christ as Lord and Savior. Only persons under demonic influences turn from God or the Lord Jesus Christ to live a life contrary of God's Word.

Only the devil's spirit or demons possess such power that cause mankind made in the likeness of the Creator to turn away from the Creator is well as demonic influences in human affairs throughout the Earth is attempting to bring all God's creation under the influence, power, and control of Satan.

I know of experience what cause a person to reject God and the Lord Jesus Christ. I was under demonic influence and demon-possessed for over forty years. I did not like to hear God's name nor the Name, Jesus Christ. But it wasn't me who did not like to hear their names. It was the demons that held residency in my body for over forty years which there was many that did not like the name of God nor hear the Name of Jesus.

The secular world may wonder what it's like to be demonized, under the influence of the devil or be completely demon-possessed. A person demonized has literally turn into or as if into a demon, befilling a demon, an evil, and a wicked supernatural being. And demon possession is the captive and influence of a person by an invisible wicked spirit, a demon.

I remember when I could not pray in the Name of Jesus because demon possession was so great through my body that it prevented me. During this long period of time demons knew something I did not know. There is power and authority over the spirit world in the Name of Jesus. And whenever Jesus's Name is spoken the spirit world glorifies God in obedience of His name.

It's imperative the secular world acknowledge when Jesus Christ walked the Earth demonic influence was very prevalent and some of his greatest miracles consisted of expelling them from victimized persons. The secular world must realize demons exist and possess great power and influence over the mind and lives of men having the ability to enter into and possess human beings by the power and influence of the devil.

Satan is very smooth, shrewd, and manipulative that mankind never realizes he or she is victimized under demonization nor the power of demonic influence. For over forty years, I was under demonic possession which I never had known had not God cured me.

People under such condition does not acknowledge demonic conditions nor the condition of other demonized persons. Because demon spirit is represented as speaking in their own person with superhuman knowledge through the mouth whom the demon spirit possesses.

Thereby, the faithful must put up a hard fight against the devil and his agents, against the world rulers of darkness, against the wicked spirits forces that are deceiving the world. However, it is clear Jesus know Satan's spirit and the spirits of demons exist as a person by proxy in the flesh of human beings. Which makes them two, first a spirit person and secondly a person by manifestation of their spirit in bodily form a human.

Manifestation create evil and wicked person; all evilness and wickedness are related with demonic possession. Throughout Scriptures the qualities and actions of wicked spirits are attributed through persons. Persons either demonized, demon-possessed or under the influence of the devil.

Satan the Devil is a spirit person male or female manifested by wither sex and so does demons. Age is no exception. Remember the devil's spirit being is the representative of two as are demons, they represent themselves in spirit and through the flesh of man in bodily form as a person. So don't be misled nor deceived by a person's outward appearance. It is that which you cannot see that is deceptive.

But I've discovered by experience God knows the thoughts, perception, and deceptions of the devil or demon spirits in man even before materialization in the mind or manifestation in the physical world.

Therefore, it is imperative for all mankind know God, the Holy Spirit and acknowledge Jesus Christ as Lord and Savior. There is no other name throughout the four corners of the globe demons will obey. Just to name a few such as Buddha, Mohammed, or Allah, and there are others cannot protect humankind of demon possession nor cure humankind of demonic possession. They only assist in false beliefs and make believe. Which explain how demonic forces possess power and control over non-Christians.

The Name of Jesus is the only name the devil or demonic forces obey. Had it not been for his Name, I could not daily face demon spirits face-to-face in the atmosphere or if I was on my own, I could not stand against the evilness or wickedness I encounter in bodily form of man.

Oh yes, I've been tested beyond anyone's imagination of all kinds of demon spirits that inhabit the Earth. Several times I believe every evil spirit or demonic force on Earth came against me in my home and public places from all directions in spirit and through persons not acknowledging his or her demonic condition.

It's imperative that the entire world acknowledge to be save in this evil and wicked world the full gospel must be taught and preached throughout the four corners of the Earth. Its imperative other countries hear the Good News of Jesus Christ, our Lord and Savior.

The world must acknowledge that Jesus Christ has defeated the world and its invisible inhabitants, the devil and demons, the invisible enemies of God and mankind throughout the world.

How to Recognize Satan the Devil's Spirit Message and Sermon

Note: Congregation of God, Satan will use any person or any means to stop or prevent Jehovah God will and purpose in one's life. Servants, preachers, teachers, apostles, prophets, or evangelist or anyone.

Our lives are based on Jehovah God, "will and purpose," which some Christians and the world does not know. But the devil, Satan know and as long as he can prevent mankind from knowing their purpose in life, he will do whatever he can by placing obstacles in one's path.

Note: When man was created and woman, God created them (us) for His will and purpose.

Jehovah spoke of His "will and purpose" in the Garden of Eden.

Read Genesis 2:15. "Then the Lord placed the man in the Garden of Eden to cultivate it and guard it."

Note: God's will for Adam and Eve whom He placed in the Garden was to "cultivate it" and were there to "guard it." Jehovah God has a will and purpose for all mankind.

Jehovah's will and purpose in one's life has already been establish. Therefore, one cannot trust himself nor trust not even others.

Note: Satan, also has a will and purpose for mankind, which is to cause mankind to bring condemnation upon him or herself by any means.

To cause mankind to disobey God is Satan number one priority in man's life. Disobedience cover a broad area in human being lives.

Note: Scripture says, "Obedience is better than sacrifice in God sight." Disobedience shorten one's life" and is an act of aggression of behavior toward God and God's will and purpose in one's life.

Note: Then come a day when the woman while not in the company of her husband, found herself near the tree of knowledge of Good and Bad. There a serpent (*snake*) seeming innocent appeared. Read Genesis 3:1–5.

> Now the snake [serpent] was the most cunning animal that the Lord God had made. The snake asked the woman, "Did God really tell you not to eat fruit from any tree in the garden?
>
> "We may eat the fruit of any tree in the garden," the woman answered.
>
> Except the tree in the middle of it. God told us not to eat the fruit of that tree or even touch it, if we do we will die.
>
> The snake replied, "That's not true, you will not die."
>
> God said that because he knows that when you eat it, you will be like God, and know what is good and what is bad.

Note: The woman and man ate the fruit thereof and was deceived through hearing the voice of Satan the Devil, which he is still deceiving but through humankind. People are being deceived throughout the entire world even of his human appearance.

Children of Jehovah God, "Adam and Eve" distinctively discover that which was Good and that which was Bad in the Garden of Eden. Satan's spirit approached and appeared to Eve, through a serpent (*snake*).

Today Satan's appearance and approach before the human race as flesh as a human being, a person and demon spirits appear as well in fleshly bodies of individuals but cannot transform nor materialize as flesh of a human being. There is no exception, of gender nor age of whom they appear through.

Note: Congregation, you mankind can't see Satan approach nor recognize him as flesh nor demon's approach. One must listen for their approach by mouth and tongue, "articulation" of a person vocal expression or utterance (*speech*).

Satan the Devil is representative of two realms, one is the spiritual realm or atmosphere and the other as a human being as flesh as a person in a materialize physical body.

Short Testimony

Note: My brother in Christ, I am revealing to you and the congregation, that which you never heard nor witness or spoke to anyone of what you are about to read or hear from some other source.

The devil, Satan walk the street in the flesh, disguised as a real person not as a female but as a man in the flesh.

He possesses the ability to appear all across the Earth as a human being in the flesh, devouring lives and livelihoods wherever he appears.

Note: Some persons have even spoke to him walking in opposite directions or have dialogue with him walking in the same direction. Not to know it was Satan the Devil disguised as a real person and which he is real just as real as you or I but yet spirit.

Note: Servant of God, "Jehovah God is my witness," not mankind; God is. "I dialogued with Satan in flesh as a man in a yard, I didn't know who he was, "he walked off into the midst."

Satan the Devil appeared in my home. This time I knew who he was then he transformed back into spirit.

Read 1 Peter 5:8. "Be alert, be on watch! Your enemy, the devil roams around like a roaring loin, looking for someone to devour."

Note: Congregation, remember, the devil is here to steal, kill, or destroy human life and livelihoods. He and demons are adversaries (enemies) of the entire world.

Note: My testimony of Satan being two, a spirit and a supernatural spirit being. To this day and over the years, I've experienced many encounters with the devil, Satan, and demon forces in the physical and spiritual realm.

I am a "spirit-filled witness" of Satan materialized presences as a human being whom I dialogued without knowing who he was until he vanished, "never to be seen again until he appeared in my home. I stopped and paused, I said to him, "I see you." As I stood across from where he transformed back into a spirit being and called him a defeated "foe" and that I possess authority and power over him in the Name of Jesus Christ.

Note: Congregation, you (mankind) can't see Satan approach nor recognize him as or in the flesh. One must listen for his approach by way of mouth and tongue, "articulation" of a person vocal expression or utterance (*speech*).

Brothers and sisters, this you must remember: How to recognize who the devil, Satan is. His spirit may manifest through father, mother, son, daughter, brother, sister, relative, friend, associate, even yourself or animals.

Note: Children of Jehovah God, "this is how to recognize representatives of Satan Spirit. Remember, Satan represent two realms, one as a spirit and the other as a person transform or transition into flesh but yet a spirit person.

Jesus Christ gave a clear and comprehension example of Satan the Devil's spirit when he spoke to Jesus through the "articulation" of the "vocal" expression of Peter which Jesus knew and recognize his spirit by addressing him while he make it known to the other disciples that Satan can and will use anyone as representative of his spirit being and demonic works.

Note: Example, Jesus spoke to his disciples about his suffering and death.

Read Mark 8:32–33.

> He made this very clear to them. So, Peter took him aside and began to rebuke him.
> But Jesus turned around, look at his disciples and rebuked Peter. "Get away from me

> Satan, he said, "Your thoughts don't come from God, but from human nature."

It may be noted, that Jesus looked at the other disciples when doing this, likely indicating that he knew Peter spoke sentiments shared by the others.

Note: Church, humankind didn't choose to represent Satan nor his devious work. He chose (man) humankind so do demons delegate human representatives for their demonic work and activities.

However, there are children of the devil.

Read 1 John 3: 9–10.

> Those who are children of God do not continue to sin, for God's very nature is in them and because God is their Father, they cannot continue to sin.
>
> Here is the clear difference between God's children and the devil's children, those who do not do what is right or do not love others are not God's children.

Note: I believe mankind unknowingly and some knowingly represented some form of demonic behavior or activities at some point in one's life.

However, we must not forget their approach is in the flesh as a person which can't be seen with natural vision, therefore, one must listen for their invisible spirit approach in and through the mouth of a person "words," you must listen for their approach in and through the tongue that which reveal the "manifestation" of the spirit or spirits presences through vocal expression and "speech" articulation.

Congregation, because of Jehovah God's will and purpose in one's life. Satan the Devil has assigned demonic forces all across the Earth to stop or prevent that which God have plan in One's (our) life.

These demonic forces exist externally in high places and internally in human form in human beings fighting against God's will and purpose for mankind.

One period of my life, I was a victim but now I'm a conqueror over the spiritual realm of Satan and demonic forces through Jesus Christ who brought me through many impossibilities. Impossibilities that defies the human mind.

Man must realize if Satan appear to you as a person in the flesh and transform back to spirit, he appeared for a purpose that is to stop you by any means from accomplishing God's will and purpose in your life but stand your ground.

By the eternal "Word of God," Christians should be enlightened to know that Satan and demons existence their powers, designs and purpose are defeated with the spiritual weapons which Jehovah God provides.

Read Ephesians 6:13–18.

> So put on God's armor now. Then when the evil day comes you will be able to resist the enemy's attacks, and after fighting to the end. You will hold your ground.
> So stand ready, with the truth as a belt tight around your waist, with righteousness as your breast plate.
> and as your shoes the readiness to announce the Good News of peace,
> at all times carry faith as a shield, for with it you will be able to put out all the burning arrows shot by the Evil One.
> Do all this in prayer asking for God's help.
> Pray on every occasion, as the Spirit leads.

Note: Congregation, remain vigilant in the world. Wear at all times, "The whole armor of God and remember, He is in you is greater than he is in whom is speaking to or coming against you!"

Amen.

Servants of Jehovah God, I'm not here for notoriety nor popularity. I'm here to hear the message, the Good News, Jesus brought of his Father and the full Gospel of truth of Jesus Christ.

Long as you preach the truth, you won't to be popular. Only when a lie of the devil come from the mouth of man is when you gain popularity in this world and in some Christian's world.

The Other Spirit

Note: Children of Jehovah God, the other Spirit enter into the flesh of the human race "mind" as a thought of entertaining itself eventually manifesting into sin, which bring both physical and spiritual death.

Any perception or thought which created or bring entertainment and the results are potential death is not a perception of the Spirit of him or herself but a spirit at the time of the perception or thought is the spirit of an entity, something considered apart from its properties. Which means not a part of you spiritually but physically in the flesh.

Note: The devil, Satan is capable of transcending beyond the limit of mankind human perception or thought to prevail and be greater in and effective in whatever motive his spirit influences a person to succumb to which is to give up spiritually and give in or succumb to the flesh!

The other Spirit continuously at work throughout the land (Earth) twenty-four hours a day without rest. Sin is always at work and active in and through human personnel. Christians believers, nonbelievers, denominations, religions, age, male or female genders is no exception. We are all vulnerable of entering sinful thoughts.

Note: No human being is immune or exempt of a sin perception or thought that leads to physical or spiritual death.

I'm a servant of Jehovah God, called by the audible voice of God to perform His will and purpose in my life. Yet I stay in conflict to do that which is right in God sight, which isn't easy for anyone to control those sinful thoughts of influences to entertain because it's not a human perception but an entity perception performing that which it was created to do 24-7, which cause human personnel to entertain. Which bring sin and sin brings potential death, not only physical death but spiritual as well.

Sin purpose is to cause spiritual death, a death that can cause an eternal separation from God.

The only entity that cause this heinous evil wicked act is Satan the Devil himself. Don't be fool brothers and sisters, this spirit is continuously at work throughout the land.

Entertaining a sinful thought is not a perception or thought of your own, it's the work of a spirit rather than your own that cause death, hardship or suffering in one's life.

Note: The entity, spirit's perceptions or thought, is demonic; however, it is not to be seen as demonic but a natural nature's perception not of one's own. Which can give access to "live" demon spirits to enter the human (person) mind and Body as their own to influence, possess, and control which lead to sin.

"Mankind can control of what he thinks but cannot control thoughts or perceptions other than his own. Therefore, he must cast them out in the Name of Jesus Christ."

Note: Once that thought or perception enter the mind, that spirit of deception, sin become alive and active ready to perform that which it was placed in the person's mind for.

It's imperative that mankind stay alert at all time because that spirit of deception roam continuously to devour anyone by any means.

Children of Jehovah God, sin is alive in humankind. Man does not activate sin. Sin activate man, although man control's himself, the activation of sin may control man into performing sinful acts.

Note: "I reiterate, sin is alive in humankind. Sin activates itself by means of the flesh, mind, and body."

I a servant of God, called by God, yet sin activated itself in and through the flesh and mind producing all kinds of worldly and pornographic thoughts. Which I knew wasn't me. Not even the perceptions I perceived, which was for me to entertain. I didn't entertain them, I immediately cast them out!

Suddenly those worldly perceptions left sin came alive in me. My mind and body without any doubt. Sin is alive, which takes a thought or perception to activate it; however, all five senses can also activate sin, the other spirit.

The world does not acknowledge sin is alive, not only throughout the world but many Christians do not acknowledge sin is alive even in themselves.

Sin put man out of harmony with God, the Creator. It thereby damages man own self, his mind, heart, and body. It brought consequences of enormous evil upon the human race.

Note: This sin also, mars man's reflection of God's likeness and glory, it makes man unholy, that is, unclean, impure tarnished in a spiritual and moral sense. Scripture says about the sense of sight, which activate sin.

Read Matthew 5:27–30.

> You have heard that it was said, "Do not commit adultery."
>
> But now I tell you, anyone who looks [sight] at a woman and wants to possess her is guilty of committing adultery with her in his heart.
>
> So if your right eye cause you to sin, take it out and throw it away! It is much better for you to lose a part of your body than to have your whole body thrown into hell.
>
> If your right hand [feel] cause you to sin, cut it off and throw it away! It is much better for you to lose one of your limbs than to have your whole body go off to hell.

A Physical and Spiritual Conflict in Mankind

Sin is alive; however, God set a law against sin. Sin may give its orders in different ways to different persons and at different times, internally or externally.

Note: (Internally.) The anger of Adam's first son Cain against his brother. God warned Cain that if he did not turn to doing good (externally) there is sin crouching at the entrance and is craving with envy and hatred to lead him to murder his brother Able.

The Apostle Paul says read Romans 7:15–21:

> I do not understand what I do, for I don't do what I would like to do, but instead I do what I hate.
>
> Since what I do is what I don't want to do, this shows that I agree that the Law is right.
>
> So I am not really the one who does this thing, rather it is the Sin that lives in me.
>
> I don't do the good I want to do, instead, I do the evil that I do not want to do.
>
> If I do what I don't want to do, this means that I am no longer the one who does it, instead, it is the Sin that lives in me.

Note: The Apostle Paul makes it clear. Sin is alive in us mankind, which has its own agenda. Which means the mind senses can activate sin or sin can activate any one of the five senses of a human being.

Note: The Lord's Prayer cover's all the ingredient sin has to offer. There isn't an external nor internal sin, the Lord's Prayer does not cover. Yet many take the Lord's Prayer for granted. Not in general but some does literally; therefore, sin abound with them. I was once literally among such group where sin abounded.

Note: I was a victim (sinner) but now a believer and a servant of the Most High, Almighty God. I can testify, sin was at one time alive and active in my body. And in fact, any one of my mind senses could and would activate sin, which was already alive in my body and discovered sin does activate the mind five senses!

Once sin is activated, the flesh become weak nor has control. Scripture says, "The Spirit is willing, but flesh is weak."

Note: Desires of the Flesh

Satan can use desires of the flesh to activate sin which he used to tempt Eve. We possess victory through Jesus Christ over desires of the flesh. It was temptation that influence Eve, the desires of the flesh, which led to her demise.

Read 1 John 2:16. "Everything that belong to the world that people are so proud of, none of this comes from the Father, it all comes from the world."

The devil used desires of the flesh against Christ but fail and Jesus followers too. By Jehovah's underserved kindness, defeated the sinful flesh.

Read "The Temptation of Jesus" (Luke 4:1–12).

> Jesus returned from the Jordan full of the Holy Spirit and was led by the Spirit into the desert.
> Where he was tempted by the devil for forty days. In all that time he ate nothing, so that he was hungry when it was over.

> The devil said to him, "If you are God's Son, order this stone to turn into bread."
>
> Then the devil took him up and showed him in a Second all the kingdoms of the world.
>
> I will give you all this power and all this wealth, the devil told him. It has all been handed over to me, and I can give it to anyone I choose.

Note: In the Lord's Prayer, we ask Jehovah, "And lead us not into temptation and forgive us of our sin!"

All flesh that exercise faith will became perfect, it is not fleshly reasoning but Jehovah's Spirit that reveal God's purposes to men of faith, which guides us.

We trust not in the arm of flesh but in Jehovah. We strive with God's help to cleanse ourselves of every defilement of flesh.

Amen.

Demons: Evil Spirits in the Homes

All homes that I stress in this nation and throughout the four corners of the world are occupied with demon spirits dwelling in the midst. There aren't no exceptions regardless of race, religion, or age. We are constantly in the presence of demon spirits twenty-four hours a day.

Their purpose of residency is to demonize the occupants or bring a person under the power influence of its spirit or possess the body of the occupants. We eat, sleep, and perform in their midst in which we have conversation in their presence. Therefore, they see everything mankind does and hear every word mankind speak. Demons, evil spirits are the invisible enemies of humankind.

Brothers and sisters, they inhabit the Earth in the millions. Persons without bodies seeking whom body their spirit may enter to possess to bring under their demonic power and control.

Evil spirits (demons) will cause a person to perform it's will of evil and wickedness or either by demon possession perform through a person. Their plan is to possess human bodies to perform the will of Satan through mankind.

And mankind wonder what's wrong or gotten into the generation of today or people in general. The world is living in a demonize and demon-possessed society in which it does not acknowledge its presence nor it's protocol it's plan nor course. Which is to steal, kill, and destroy human lives.

People, demonic powers in the flesh of mankind is more prevalent and occurring today than ever before and its steadily progressing. And as I've stated, their protocol is to possess human bodies to perform the will of Satan through mankind.

Therefore, remember we are never home alone, demon spirits are ghosts of the atmosphere throughout the world. Demons are the ghost in homes that goes bump, hit, or knock against something in the night or day. Not a deceased person's spirit that people falsely accuse them to be. They are responsible for bumps and knocks in the day or night of one's home.

I've been writing well over thirty years and each day of those years. I've written in the midst and presence of demon spirits in the atmosphere of my home. They displayed their presence supernaturally by moving objects on my desk. They supernaturally do things to me unimaginable to stop or prevent me from exposing their existence and presences in the homes.

Had it not been for the Holy Spirit, I could not expose their ghostly presence. Because Satan, the chief of demons, personally sent demons, evil spirits to physically harass me, which they did but to no avail. "For greater is He in me, than he that is in the atmosphere and the world."

Many times, I've been physically touched while writing, objects literally moved on my desk, as well as hearing footsteps throughout my home and hearing heavy breathing in my ears. I've suffered and been physically abuse by the hands of demons. Several times I've been slapped and pounced on by demons in my home. I've been physically harassed on my job, in other homes and supermarkets as well.

The Holy Spirit is a witness of the truth. People they have done it all to spook and drive me out of my home. Somethings are too difficult to explain or describe how and what demon spirits performed in my presence. Thus, you won't believe what I've seen and experienced in the spirit realm. It is beyond man's belief.

People of this world, "Lord Jesus Christ," the Son of the Living God is the main source in everyone's life against Satan and demons. Without Christ in your life as Lord and Savior, you are lost in an evil spirit realm. You are a candidate for demon possession and demonic harassment.

The spirit realm tested me beyond mankind imagination, which I endured spiritually and physically. No way I could've witness what I've seen and physically experience the demonic activity in my home and remain here to write as demon spirits display their presence without Jesus Christ as my Lord and Savior.

I've witnessed the power in the Name of our Lord, I've also witnessed the spirit realm obedience when the Name Jesus is used to stop its spiritual and physical harassment. I know what the Name Jesus Christ can and will supernaturally do. The power is in the name which Satan and every demon spirit that inhabit the Earth obeys. And as a believer, I've defeated Satan, demons, and the spirit realm through Christ Jesus.

That's right, demons, I said, "I've defeated you and your chief, Satan through Jesus Christ my Lord and Savior." Now you are a witness of your defeat in the Name of Jesus Christ as I write to acknowledge my victory over the spirit realm in your presence.

I reiterate, we are not home alone, demons are constantly with us in our homes. We are surround by the spirit realm of evil and wickedness. Demons manipulating by way of the flesh of family members and others in the atmosphere.

I'm a retired welder, and now I do carpentry work that allows me to enter homes which I've encountered demons in each home. I've experienced some kind of demonic activity in the home's atmosphere, the homeowner or both. However, the homeowners do not realize their presence in their home.

I've told homeowners of their presence and why they are there which is to steal, kill, and destroy human lives by any means possible. And demon possession of humankind bodies is their main objective.

I've told several homeowners; demon spirits inhabit their homes. One homeowner replied, "I'm the only demon lives here." I laugh. He was serious; he could've very well spoke the truth about himself. "Remember demon spirits does speak by way of human voices." Age is no exception.

Demons does not want the world to know they are here and they don't want to be expose. However, this generation does not believe in demons and those that do, does not take the spirit realm serious while mankind does not acknowledge their presence. Big mistake.

Young and old people should realize there's a devil and demons roaming the Earth seeking whom they can destroy. For we live in a demonically control environment and society, which people does not realize because the devil's spirit has dulled their minds and blind their eyes.

My entire adolescent life and part of my adulthood was control by the spirit realm; I was demon-possessed. I lived under the influence and power of the devil and demons for over forty years not knowing as many of you not knowing we live in an evil, wicked world and a demonically spirit control society, a society I now spiritually see into.

Demon spirits dwell throughout the world in homes, sanctuaries the atmosphere and most of all in the body of humankind performing whatever task they are assign to. However, their main object is to steal, kill, and destroy as many human lives as possible. Age is no exception.

Demons in the body of mankind cause people to kill and be kill. Look, the world today, people of this generation which age is no exception are committing hideous acts never before committed. Children are killing children and adults without remorse because they are demoniacally control and live in a demoniacally control society.

Some adolescents, children, and adults believe to have imaginary friends that no one sees nor hear except themselves. They are aware something or someone are in them and in the atmosphere of the world but does not comprehend who or what are speaking to and through them.

Therefore, they believe in imaginary friends because the spirit realm is invisible to them. Which there are not imaginary friends but invisible enemies of the spirit realm, demons. Person without bodies not made of flesh and blood are speaking to and through them.

And children of all ages are their objective to enter the body there of to possess and dwell in them until death. As I've said, children and adults' imaginary friends are demons. They are real and alive in the atmosphere of the Earth and in the body of mankind.

I'm a victim of demons' supernatural work and power over one's life; however, I am now witnessing the work of demons in the spirit. My purpose now is to expose the spirit realm of evil that plague this nation and the world.

The spirit realm does not discriminate in age, gender, or race. It is at work in and against all humankind. Which mean vulnerability of becoming demon-possessed, demonize, or influence by demon spirits are great.

Therefore, it is imperative people of all ages throughout the world realize we live in an evil spirit world and a demonically control, a society that is attempting to condemn Christians and Christian nations.

They are indiscriminately at work performing by way of the flesh which no carnal weapon cannot prevail against.

Only the Name and power of Jesus Christ and the Word of God is mankind defense against the spirit realm.

Friend, the spiritual realm knows Jesus Christ. Evil spirits acknowledge Jesus Christ's power and authority over them; however, not all mankind and as long as mankind does not acknowledge Jesus Christ as Lord and Savior of their lives, mankind is in trouble.

Without Jesus Christ in our lives as Lord and Savior, we cannot live in accord to God's will and purpose. We have supernatural enemies; therefore, we must possess supernatural power. The Name Jesus gives us believers such power and authority over all supernatural enemies.

However, you must be a believer in God and Jesus Christ. Nonbelievers possess no such power, even those believe in God and not Jesus Christ. I'm a witness of this truth. It is impossible for nonbelievers to possess such power. Christians does not resort to weapons of carnal warfare but to the Word of God in the Name of Jesus Christ.

The Reality Is, We Live in a Spirit World

We live in a world inhabited and control by unknown and unseen demonic forces that are real and alive. Some of which live among us and even dwell in the bodies of the majority of us without us acknowledging their existence.

Their existence and power are phenomenal and far beyond mankind physical power and knowledge. Which mean man think of the world "the people" only as physical and natural but in reality, we live in a spiritual world shared with millions of evil spirits, demons in search of human bodies whom their spirit can enter.

And from my observation of the world demon spirits has enter the body of multitudes of all ethnic groups with and without their knowledge. It appears the world "the people" has accepted demon spirits into its livelihood and humanism way of living.

If the world could see into the spirit realm it would recognize what each person individually is up against. Every man, woman, and child regardless of age are involve in some kind of spiritual warfare which no person can fight and have victory without Jesus Christ as Lord and Savior.

The Name Jesus is whom Satan the Devil and demons are obedient to. Therefore, they glorify God in their obedience hearing the Name of Jesus. We share in existence with unseen forces and supernatural beings, demons, millions of demons in the Earth's atmosphere.

Therefore, knowing Jesus and who he is in man's life is the only hope mankind has to live the life God like for us to live. Jesus Christ is our only protection living in the spiritual world.

Before I became a witness, I was victimized in the spiritual realm before I realize I was in the midst of spiritual warfare alone with multitudes of others. I did not realize it was reality until I began witnessing.

During that period, I did not acknowledge Jesus Christ as my Lord and Savior. I was alcoholic possessed with many kinds of demons, alcohol demons being the most prevalent. Demons become fearless in my life that they had the audacity to literally say to me in spirit, "Here we are, what can you do?"

I was witnessing, I did not know Jesus Christ. I was alcoholic demons possessed and I was lost in the world. The spirit realm knew I was lost without knowledge and under its control like multitudes of others.

I've also witnessed some awesome demonic displays and encountered demon spirits, which many perform in my home as well as in public places. I've had demon spirits to physically punch and pounce on me as I laid in bed. Not knowing their motive, I called out to Jesus. When I called out to Jesus, they got off me but then got back on me in a matter of seconds, more forceful than the first time. I called out to Jesus a second time, they got off me; however, this time I was struck on the leg as they got off.

I've witnessed manifestation of demon spirits that the world cannot comprehend unless the Holy Spirit reveals such things to the world. We live in a spirit world, real to some, imaginary to others.

I cannot stress strong enough that we, mankind throughout the world are in spiritual warfare, spiritually and physically in which demonic forces are taking charge of human lives in every aspect. Age isn't an exception. And what so amazing is that the world is unaware or ignoring their existence.

The devil, Satan and all the demon spirits that inhabit the universe, the Earth and the Earth atmosphere know the assignments given to mankind, an assignment I delight in. That is to expose the spiritual realm that Satan and demon control. But mankind as believers has power through Jesus Christ to control the spiritual realm.

However, many believers lack knowledge of spiritual power that lives in them. They either lack both, spiritual power or forgot

"Greater is He in them than he that is in the world and the world's atmosphere."

Church, we as believers possess power through Jesus Christ over every demonic spirit that inhabit the entire Earth and universe. Do you comprehend? I and you as believers has power over Satan and every demon in the spiritual realm.

Even though I cannot visually see the invisible realm when I like; however, I do witness through the vision of the Holy Spirit and witness their obedience when I use the Name above all names, Jesus Christ against the manifestation of their evil and wicked manipulations in the things they perform in my presence.

I've witnessed things in the spiritual realm that man define as paranormal, "something beyond the range of normal experience or scientific explanation." However, it was supernatural but I witness demon spirits perform in the natural which man define as the supernatural. I've encountered many demonic displays that are incomprehensible or imaginary to the eyes and senses.

Church, I've been associated with the spiritual realm my entire life. But for the last twelve years, not a single day pass that I do not experience dramatic encounters with demons in the atmosphere of my home or in public places.

The spirit realm acknowledges who's hot and who's not of the Word of God. It also recognizes its own demon-possessed wolves in sheep clothing. Those who pretend to be what they aren't in the Word of God.

The spirit realm has test me numerous times on the Word of God beyond man's imagination in every inconceivable way through mankind and by way of demonic spirits in the atmosphere's spiritual realm.

The spiritual realm I'm preferring to is Satan and demon spirits that inhabit the bodies of mankind and the Earth's atmosphere in an attempt to destroy me to prevent me from accomplishing that which God has ordain me to do. Which is to expose and challenge the spirit realm to bring to the attention of mankind we live in a spirit world control by a spirit realm.

Therefore, mankind should focus on the invisible things in the world rather than the visible things. Thus, if mankind focus on the unseen I believe it will bring about repentance and change man's immoral ways of living and turn him in the direction of God.

There is a great need for mankind throughout this nation and the world to acknowledge the realization of the devil and the spirit world and to know God did not place the devil or demons over mankind. Man allowed his intellectual perception to place the devil's spirit and his minions over himself to rule and control those who lack knowledge of the Word of God. There is a vast number that allow this evil spirit to intervene intellectually into their perception to cause man to perform his spirit physical will.

It is very easy for his spirit to enter a person and change the intent of good to the intent of committing evil. He does not need an invitation to enter a person. His spirit is so accustomed of entering a person unknowingly allow him to enter undetected.

Therefore, it's imperative that man remember the devil is two, a spirit and a person. He is a spirit person in the spiritual world and a spirit in a person's body in the physical world in which his spirit manifest as a person. His spirit is the representative of two manifestations.

Satan is the supreme evil spirit and the prince of darkness. He is the god of this world and the enemy of the world here to steal, kill, and destroy. That is the manifestation of his spirit that appear as a person who roams the Earth seeking whom he can devour.

You cannot see him, so pay attention of what I'm explaining. The devil's spirit or demons approach in or against mankind is in the flesh as a person to devour by mouth or speech to steal, kill, or destroy.

However, you (mankind) can hear his spirit's approach by way of man's words (mouth), but you must listen for his words, mouth and speech or intellect that which reveals his spirit presence. Man cannot see him as his natural self, therefore, pay attention Satan and demons approach are heard by their words and the manifestation of their spirit is through man's tongue.

But man did not choose to represent the devil, he chose man to represent him. But unfortunately, some of us do and they are called children of the devil. So remember the devil is two, a spirit person in the spiritual realm and a person transition into the body of a person in the physical realm.

He is the enemy of all human races with evil words that taste so good to him that he keeps them in his mouth to enjoy its flavor. His words are venomous to the bone even to whom he chooses to manifest through.

Which mean his spirit transform into the spirit of such person male or female to accomplish his mission in the physical realm against mankind. Satan's power of influence and strength to control man is in man own intellectual perception. His power lies in his ability to spiritually intervene intellectually into the perception of humankind.

Now you know what makes him powerful in the lives of mankind. Why did God give him power? God did not give Satan power over man. Man gives his spirit being power over himself. Had God given the devil power over man, God would have given power over Himself. "God is in man, and man's body is God's temple which the Holy Spirit dwells."

Satan took upon his spirit being to rule mankind as he chose man as representative of his spirit being by manipulation to control man's intellect, the ability to learn and reason to use adversely against mankind. And the ability to think abstractly or profoundly through speech such as the lips and tongue which is a sign of his spirit manifestation. Which allow him to perceive man's thoughts.

Even though he perceives man's thoughts, he can only perceive man's natural thoughts, which he places in man to perceive as his own, but not thoughts of the Spirit. However, because greater is He in you than he that is in the world. But you must remember his power lies in your perception which he does not want mankind to acknowledge. Now you know it is man's own intellectual perception that Satan abstain his power.

Power to know whom his spirit can or cannot manifest into accomplish his missions in one's life. Believe me, he knows man perception of when, where, and how to perform in or against mankind.

Remember his power and strength exist in your perception of how you think and his ability to know where and how to perform in or against you depend on your perception.

However, I've got "good news" to tell you, even though we live in a spirit world Jesus Christ has given us, mankind authority over the devil, the spiritual realm of demons on Earth of the universe.

But unfortunately, those who lack knowledge of the Word of God does not know of Jesus defeat over Satan when He died on the cross for mankind transgressions and was raised to life by the power of God's Spirit and now Jesus is in heaven where he sits at the right side of God with the keys of hell and of death where angels, authorities and powers are under his control.

Which mean Jesus defeated death and the world of the dead so now believes through Jesus has authority over the devil, demons, and death that which the devil once held over both man and death. But now is a defeated foe as well as every demon spirit that inhabit the Earth and the universe.

Even though Satan is a defeated foe, he does not accept defeat in mankind believers nor nonbelievers. Because his manifestation as well as demons are essential because without the use of human bodies, they could not accomplish their mission which is to steal, kill, and destroy.

That's why its imperative man learn to recognize Satan approach. Man must listen to man's word to hear his spirit approach. It is man's words and tongue that reveal his spirit manifestation.

Jesus did after He spoke of his death, and Peter rebuked Him. Peter said, God would never let this happen to you Lord. Jesus turn to Peter and replied, "Satan get away from me! You're in my way, you think like everyone else and not like God."

Jesus know it is man's intellectual perception that Satan use to speak through and he spoke through Peter. The manifestation of his spirit being was through Peter's tongue. That's why Jesus replied, "Get away from me, Satan." Satan manifest himself through the tongue of Peter like he does through all human beings.

But man cannot visually see him; however, I saw Satan transparent spirit at the age of six. He telepathically communicated with me commanding me to curse God. I didn't know any better, but the Holy Spirit led me not to.

I imagine you like to know how I saw Satan's spirit? I witnessed through the vision of the Holy Spirit. He that dwell's in me dwelled in Jesus as well. Jesus witnessed through the vision of the Holy Spirit when he replied to Peter, "Get away from me, Satan."

You see, Satan's spirit manifest in Christians as well. Peter, the disciple was a Christian even a disciple can be in the world for a period of time when his or her thoughts become of the world.

There you have the reality of a spiritual world we live in which Satan; the devil is a representative of the two. He's spirits in the spiritual realm and a person in the manifestation of his spirit being in the physical realm, the world. Which Jesus knew as he replied to Peter, "Satan, get away from me! Your thoughts don't come from God but from man." That confirm Satan is a spirit person.

His manifestation in humankind is essential because his power exist in the perception of man. Which speech, tongue, and venomous words are used to destroy man and all three manifests through the tongue and mouth of a person by way of that spirit being.

However, you can resist him but you must stand firm don't give in to his thoughts nor intellectual perceptions that spirit being will attempt to perceive through you. No perception, no power. Not only in yourself but also in those whom his spirit use to come against you.

Therefore, it's imperative to always wear the whole armor of God, which is the Word of God. Stay vigilant and remember the tongue and words of humankind reveal the presences and manifestation of Satan's spirit being or demons in the spiritual world we live in.

I Speak to Them That Are Not Seen

I truthfully say Jehovah God made it so that I can speak to what is not seen in our midst. I am now in my seventies, I've never heard of anyone to truthfully make such broad statement, a biblical statement because it concerns the spirit realm in which we live.

However, I can say such a statement, a true statement, which Jehovah God is my witness with proof of his Son Jesus Christ and the Holy Spirit as witnesses.

No other human being of my knowledge can make or state such a statement and to have the Father, Almighty God, the Son, and the Holy Spirit as witnesses.

The results are 100 percent pure of obedience of that which I speak to in an invisible realm which we live. The obedience is performed or carry out in the spiritual realm which manifest in the physical world for me to see and witness the obeying of God's Word and the Great Commission of that which Jesus authorized. Which gives us, believers, power to enforce a law in the spiritual realm and witness evidence of such power in the Name of Jesus Christ is amazing.

The opposition I face in the spirit realm that manifest in the physical realm and sometimes in Spirit while other times in and through the flesh of persons either way, I receive manifestation of obedience in the physical realm yet in spirit which no one else sees but me and the spirit world.

"I am Blessed and Elated to be among a chosen few to Witness and speak to that which is not seen with physical eyes."

Note: Scripture says, "So that, they may look and look yet not see, they may listen and listen, yet not understand" (Mark 4:12).

I visionally see with the eyes, but I can see farther with the mind. I can see with the spiritual mind that which the physical eyes cannot see nor the physical mind.

But the Spirit sees what both the physical eyes and mind can't see. What is amazing, "the Spirit sees all!"

Short Testimony Story

I was a demon-possessed alcoholic—I reiterate, a demon-possessed alcoholic for over thirty years. In March of 1984, Jehovah God sent two messengers, angelic beings with His Word, the Holy Bible to present to me.

Yes, two angels were sent with the Word of God from heaven to give me, then vanished, disappeared right before me. The angelic beings were dressed in black priestly garments.

I could see them but no one else. Why no one could? Later, I was told by the Holy Spirit, "I saw and witnessed through the vision of the Holy Spirit during the spiritual event!" Neither my physical mind nor my physical eyes were involved. When the event ended, it was later revealed to me, God open up my mind to see, to understand that which I experienced. Shortly thereafter, God cured and delivered me of demon possession of over thirty years!

Amen.

Congregation, What Satan Does Not Want You (Us) to Know Sermon

I

Note: Children of God, it's imperative, that it be preached and taught in pulpits across this nation and the entire Earth, the spirit enemy Satan the Devil is the least enemy you ever hear spoken of in and out of Christian sanctuaries or the house of worship.

"Yet he's glorified in the secular world, all over people of all nations portraying to be and look like him and what they believe the devil resemble."

Note: Congregation, as impressive he is in every human life, you must never forget the spirit person Satan approach is in the flesh of humankind as a spirit person, manifest by mouth and tongue as an angel of light to steal, kill, or destroy you, mankind!

Note: Children of God, you must know who the devil, Satan is and how to recognize him in spirit in the flesh of humankind. Those who he manifests in spirit become his human representation with and without some knowledge. Therefore, he is spirit and a person.

Never forget he is two, a spirit and person.

Note: Human beings can't see him as he is in spirit; however, I saw him at the age of six. He commanded me to curse God! I didn't know not, the Holy Spirit led me not to.

I imagine you like to know how I saw the spirit Satan? I witness this spirit enemy of Jehovah God and mankind through the vision of the Holy Spirit.

Note: Brothers and sisters, no person is exempt from the works of Satan in the past, present or future. All human being is susceptible or vulnerable of the work of the devil at some point and time in one's life.

Note: Several years ago a co-worker and I was in a discussion of the spirit world, "I mentioned Satan which insulted him. He said, in profanity, "I do not discuss nor speak of the devil," and then left.

At that time, to my belief, he was under demonic influences or under control of this spirit creature, Satan.

The Temptation of Jesus

Note: The Spirit led Jesus into the desert to be tempted by the devil. Then the devil came to him and said, "If you are God's Son, order these stones to turn into bread." Read Matthew 4:1–11.

But Jesus answered, "The Scripture says, Human beings cannot live on bread alone, but need every word that God speaks."

Satan took Jesus to Jerusalem, set him on the highest point and said to him, "If you are God's Son throw yourself down for the scripture says, God will give orders to his angels about you, they will hold you up with their hands so that not even your feet will be hurt on the stones.

Jesus answered, "But the scripture also says, "Do not put the Lord you God to the test."

Then the devil took Jesus and showed him all the kingdoms of the world. All this I will give you, the devil said, if you kneel down and worship me.

Then Jesus answered, Go away Satan! The scripture says, "Worship the Lord your God, and serve only him." Then the devil left Jesus.

Note: Congregation, Jesus Christ is the only person whom Satan spirit could not possess to entertain a thought nor perceive his perception. Each time Satan attempt to tempt Jesus, he quoted Scripture of the Book of Deuteronomy. Read Deuteronomy 8:3. Also read Deuteronomy 6:16 and Deuteronomy 6:13. Then the devil left him.

Note: Children of God, this is what we, mankind must do to escape Satan hideous plan against humanity. We must stay alert and vigilant at all time and quote the Word of God to him.

Thereby, it's imperative to listen for his approach even in oneself. His perception can enter man in an instant, without man's knowledge to comprehend whether it's his thought or a perception of a spirit other than man's own.

Note: Before man distinguish the thought or perception, he acts and carry out as his own perception. We all victims of the world's deception and works of the devil. "Thereby, you can literally say, "The devil made me do somethings."

Read 2 Corinthians 10:3–5.

> It is true that we live in the world, but we do not fight from worldly motives.
> The weapons we use in our fight are not the world's weapons, but God's powerful weapons, which we use to destroy strongholds. We destroy false arguments.
> We pull down every proud obstacle that is raised against the knowledge of God, we take every thought capture and make it obey Christ.

Note: Congregation, it's imperative that it be preached and taught in pulpits. God did not create a devil, God created a beautiful, perfect super angel, a cherub, an angelic creature of high rank who allowed his beauty and perfection to fill him with vanity.

The cherub who became Lucifer became envious of God's power, resented authority over him so he plotted with a third of Jehovah's angels to knocked God off the throne of the universe. The cherub who is now Lucifer was going to be God.

In his deceptive sway over God, Lucifer was no longer a light bringer but now an enemy or adversary of God and the third of the angels that united with Lucifer who is Satan in the rebellion now became demons or evil spirits of the Earth.

Note: Congregation, Jehovah's "Word" tells us demon spirits cohabitate with us, and Satan the Devil who is their Chief, rule this present Earth system of things and sway or influence its inhabitants. The Bible indicates and affirms that very fact.

Note: He is called the god of this world or system of things. He is the king or the prince of the evil world that we live in today.

Read John 12:31. "Now is the time for this world to be judge, now the ruler of this world will be overthrown."

Read James 4:4. "Unfaithful people, 'Don't you know that to be the world's friend means to be God's enemy? If you want to be the world's friend, you make yourself God's enemy.'"

Brothers and sisters, the glorious angelic cherub who became Lucifer, the devil, Satan; God originally created him, the pinnacle of God's creative power in a single being. Few today, does not realize how great is the power now turned to cunning deception, possessed by Satan which this generation must realize.

Note: To be the world's friend, means to be God's enemy or if you want to be the world's friend, you'll make yourself God's enemy.

Note: Congregation, Jesus acknowledge, Satan is a deceiver, and which he uses man's own perception or thought to deceive man himself while deceiving others and the entire world.

Read Revelation 12:9. "The huge dragon was thrown out—that ancient serpent named the devil, or Satan that deceived the whole world. He was thrown down to Earth, and all his angels with him."

Note: Therefore, it's imperative to listen, to hear his approach even in oneself because you cannot see him.

When I saw him (Satan) at the age of six, I didn't see him through my natural or physical eyes. I saw him through the vision of God's Holy Spirit.

Note: Congregation, we all are vulnerable or victims of worldly works of deception of the world. This young generation must realize…

Read James 4:4. I reiterate, unfaithful people, "Don't you know that to be the world's friend, means to be God's enemy? If you want to be the world's friend, you make yourself God's enemy."

Note: The Bible describe a true friend as one who stick's closer than a brother comes to the aid of his companions in distress and gives counsel to him in faithfulness.

Jesus himself set the example in this regard by helping spiritually those looked down upon.

Read Matthew 11:19. "When the Son of Man came, he ate and drank, and everyone said, 'Look at this man! He is a glutton and wine drinker, a friend of tax collectors and other outcasts.'"

Congregation, Jesus indicated that only those obeying his commands were his real friends. He demonstrated his love for us by surrendering his "Soul" on our behalf, encouraging us to loved one another likewise. Jesus tells us in John 15:12–14.

> My commandment is this, "loved one another, just as I love you."
> The greatest love you can have for your friends is to give your life for them.
> And you are my friends if you do what I command you.

Note: But the enemy, that old serpent, identified in the scripture as Satan the Devil, the chief enemy of God, has exercised influence over mankind and we the world yielded to that influence, thereby the whole world is lying in the power of the enemy, Satan.

Note: Congregation, we know we are children of God, for the Son of God keeps us safe; therefore, the evil one cannot harm us. But the scripture says to us. (Reiterate.)

Read James 4:4. "Unfaithful people! Don't you know that to be the world's friend, you make yourself God's enemy."

Note: Those who are enemies of God are at the same time enemies of mankind because they fight man's reconciliation with God and they oppose the truth.

II

The Enemy, Satan, and How to Recognize His Spirit

Note: Satan is the supreme adversary or enemy of Jehovah God and the world. Congregation, there is a great need for teachers and preachers to stressfully teach the realization of the devil and demonic forces are real and alive currently performing in persons livelihood.

Note: Mankind has allowed Satan intellectually place influences over himself to rule and control with demonic influences.

Read 2 Corinthians 4:4. "They do not believe, because their minds have been kept in the dark by the evil god of this world."

Note: Children of God evil wasn't in the world, not until Lucifer, the cherub made himself the devil, Satan. Jehovah God said,

> Your conduct was perfect from the day you were created, until you began to do evil.
>
> You were proud of being handsome and your fame made you act like a fool. Because of this I hurled you to the ground and left you as a warning to other kings. (Ezek. 28:11–19)

Note: Ever since Satan been cast down to Earth his wisdom became perverted. It became tricky and deceitful.

Read Revelations 12:9. "The huge dragon was thrown out—that ancient serpent named the devil, or Satan that deceived the whole world. He was thrown down to Earth, and all his angels with him."

Note: Congregation, there's a proverbial saying, "You can fool some of the people, some of the time and some of the people all of the time but you can't fool all of the people all of the time."

But Satan has done it starting with "Eve" and through her, Adam. Satan has fooled or deceived humanity in all generations.

Note: And we wonder how it is that he has such deceptive power. God didn't give Satan nor demons power over you, "You give the devil and demons power over yourself because lack of spiritual knowledge, the Word of God."

Question, how does he do this? "He doesn't appear personally to every individual and lie to each one as he did Eve. He has a more effective method, the new media, broadcasting human, "propaganda," systematically broadcasting false doctrine or information reflecting the world.

Read Ephesians 2:2. "At that time you followed the world's evil way, you obeyed the ruler of the spiritual powers in space, the spirit who now controls the people who disobey God."

He also emits or gives off an attitude of a spirit of defiance and disobedience, outright lies, information of a mixture of truth and deceit. Not only in spirit, but as a human being a person.

His works of deceiving all humanity continues, he has the Atheists in his camp as well as many tribes of people that openly claim to be devil worshipers. There are individuals in all nations who are just plain evil.

Question. Can Satan fool you? Yes. It is vital that we understand. Satan is a spirit person just as you and I are spirit persons. Be not ignorant of his devices. Here is something the devil does not want you to know. He is a compromiser, he is flexible. He will bend to give and take as long as he gets his way in the end. The devil has something for everyone.

Note: Congregation, you must remember, you belong to God.

Read 1 John 4:4. "But you belong to God, my children, and have defeated the false prophets, because the Spirit who is in you is more powerful than the spirit in those who belong to the world."

III

How to Recognize the devil, Satan Spirit

Men and women of God, it must be preached and taught in the pulpits to be heard in the "pews" across the nation and the entire world. The enemy of Jehovah God, Satan is the representative of two beings, first a spirit being, represented as a human being.

This invisible spirit person or being's approach cannot be seen with physical eyes but can be heard by way of a person (mouth) words but you must listen to a person's words in order to hear his approach, "mouth/speech," which manifest this spirit person, the devil's spirit through the tongue.

Note: "Congregation, Satan today speak or articulate to and through humankind in an audible voice and so can demons speak in audible voices. I am a victim and witness of hearing demonic voices speak out from the atmosphere."

Note: Throughout Jesus ministry, he was constantly in danger, Satan using human agents to oppose and to try either to cause him to stumble or to kill him.

Jesus was constantly harassed by those whom Satan used to try to trap him.

Read Matthew 22:15, 18.

> The Pharisees went off and made a plan to trap Jesus with questions.
> Jesus, however was aware of their evil plan, and so he said, "You hypocrites! Why are you trying to trap me?"

Note: The same method Satan use to trap Jesus, he is using today to trap mankind especially Christians. The reason is Satan know God has ordained that to break one of his commandments is to break all.

Read James 2:10–11.

> Whoever break's one Commandment is guilty of breaking them all.
> For the same one who said, "Do not commit adultery, also said, "Do not commit murder. Even if you do not commit adultery, you have become a law breaker if you commit murder.

Congregation, what Satan does not want humankind to know is that if he must. Satan is even willing to allow you, mankind to obey many of God's laws and believe in God and Christ as long as he can still control you, make you miss the mark. His goal is to keep you out of the coming Kingdom of God which will replace him and his demons by blinding you to what is really happening!

Therefore, to refuse to obey or submit to one law is to rebel against God's entire divine code of behavior. That's good enough for Satan.

Note: Children of God, this is Satan does not want you (us) to know there are those who many preach powerfully against Satan and his evil works.

But stop sort of teaching we must obey all of God's holy laws, and they say God's laws have been done away with, that they no longer binding upon people. Also, they never will tell you that Jesus directly and consistently taught obedience to all of the Ten Commandments.

Note: Listen to what Jesus taught.

Read Matthew 5:17: "Do not think that I come to destroy the law or the prophets. I did not come to destroy, but to fulfill."

Note: Children of God, in this Jesus set Christians an example that we are to follow because we are expected to fulfill the law.

Read James 2:8–12.

> You will be doing the right thing if you obey the law of the Kingdom, which is found in the scripture, "Love your neighbor as you love yourself."
>
> Whoever breaks one commandment is guilty of breaking them all.
>
> Speak and act as people who will be judged by the law that sets us free.

Note: Also brothers and sisters, Satan doesn't want you to know you can believe Jesus Christ is Lord and Savior, even worship him, all in vain.

Read Matthew 7:21–23.

> Not everyone who calls me Lord, Lord will enter the Kingdom of heaven, but only those who do what my Father in heaven wants them to do.
> When the Judgment Day comes, many will say to me, Lord, Lord! In your Name we spoke God's message, by your Name we drove out many demons and performed many miracles.
> Then, I will say to them, I never knew you. Get away from me, you wicked people!

Note: Congregation, Satan is a master in making evil appear good. His strategy is to use deceptiveness. He deceived Eve to believe that the innocent looking but forbidden fruit was good for her.

He tried to deceive Jesus to disobey God, he even quoted good valid scriptures to Jesus.

Read Matthew 4:1–10.

> Satan said to him, "If you are God's Son throw yourself down for the scripture says, "God will give orders to his angels about you, they will hold you up with their hands, so that not even your feet will be hurt on the stones."

Note: Children of God, it's obvious Satan is a deceitful and defeated foe which our hope of not being fool or deceive by him is to study and believe Jehovah God's Word and obey God's laws. Ask for God's Holy Spirit to give you light and understanding.

Also, the gift of the Spirit of discernment of inspired utterance, that will help you listen for Satan or demonic influences approach.

Note: Therefore, pay attention, their approach is heard by mankind spoken words thus, the manifestation of his spirit is in the person tongue. "DON'T EVER FORGET THAT." Satan is two, a spirit and a spirit person.

Note: Brothers and sisters, do what the devil, Satan doesn't want you to do, which is to surrender to God.

Read James 4:7. "So then, submit yourselves to God. Resist the devil, and he will run away from you."

Congregation, that's how to get rid of Satan's influences and deceptive (thoughts) perceptions of one's mind.

Amen.

Mankind Must Prove Himself in the Spirit World Realm

I

Note: I, a servant of Jehovah God's will and purpose have proven myself to the spirit realm in which We humankind live in. Christians, non-Christians, believers, and nonbelievers has something to prove of themselves in the spirit realm. Not only themselves but to the invisible enemies watching and observing everything we, mankind does while listening to every word spoken in the physical realm—world.

Something the physical world or realm (people) never given a thought of, because it's not addressed nor preached in today's pulpits, that we live in a realm that is more physical than the physical realm, which we, humankind, live in which is the spiritual realm of the devil, Satan.

Note: Congregation of Jehovah God, we are not alone, believe me. We aren't alone. It must be revealed and made known in pulpits across the nation as well as throughout the entire Earth that we mankind are cohabitants with live spirit beings as live as we humans are.

Imagine seeing into the spirit realm. What would you look for? Well, you can see into the spirit realm to some degree with the mind and ears.

The mind and ears can see much farther into the spirit realm than any human eyes; however, it's different from the spiritual realm of the devil, Satan, but just as important that serve the same purpose.

Humankind can see into the spirit realm of the devil with the assistance of the Holy Spirit. In essence, seeing and witnessing through the vision of the Holy Spirit.

I've seen angelic beings which came to visit through the vision of the Holy Spirit. I've heard Jehovah's voice in heaven with my (ears) hearing. I saw into the spirit realm with both mind and hearing (ears) on several occasions which saved my life.

Children of Jehovah God, it's the spirit world of the devil who is attempting to destroy humankind as well as human livelihood.

There aren't any exceptions nor discrimination in the spirit realm, everyone is equal even of age.

We are up against enemies like no other spiritual warfare. This war is like no other and there never will be another war in the future nor was there in the past that can compare fighting invisible Enemies on the surface of the Earth externally in the atmosphere and internally through human beings.

Child of God, this war is like none other fighting against mankind. Mankind and spirits and spirits in the Earth's atmosphere which is not preached nor taught as it should for the Kingdom of God.

Note II: True Christians

The spiritual realm of the devil know true Christians who has dedicated their lives to God, Jehovah through Jesus Christ.

The spiritual realm also acknowledge true hypocrites and nonbelievers.

The spirit realm is more interested in humankind than humankind is of the spirit realm and that is because Satan is attempting to destroy human lives by any means possible.

Note: The spirit war is like no other in the past, present nor future. It's a war fought like no other because no physical weaponry cannot be used, only the Name above all Names, Jesus Christ and the true word of the Father, Jehovah God, the Holy Bible is used to combat the invisible adversaries of mankind which aren't seen.

Also, one's faith and belief must be used to accomplish our invisible spiritual victory over the devil and demonic forces use against us, mankind.

However, Satan and demons recognize and acknowledge true Christians and believers. They know who will stand up for the Kingdom of God and who won't.

Christians, the spirit realm know us better than we know ourselves. It knows family members as well as we know them and even better. They see what we don't see and hear what we don't hear and know what we don't know of our loved ones.

Note: The spirit realm also acknowledge, it's not being expose nor investigated as it should because Satan have shut the mouth of the five-fold ministry and some men and women who were called to preach the Gospel of Jesus Christ and the Good News, which He brought of His Father into the world.

Note: Congregation of Jehovah God and the world population. Do you know, if it weren't for the Holy Spirit whom Jesus Christ sent on the Earth, mankind could not live among one another because Satan and demonic forces would rule the entire Earth with wickedness wherever man exist? "Did you know this?"

I don't think so, because it's not being preached nor taught in pulpits, nor among the world society that which we share the Earth with an unseen spirit population, which has now begun to make their visible appearance among and through the human race of people on the Earth. Which is now, no surprise because Jesus told a parable of this race of people when He told the parable about the "weeds and the wheat."

Note: Congregation of Jehovah God, that parable has come to past, which some ministers and other servants has any clue of it coming to past, the parable of the weeds and the wheat. Because Satan diverted their minds in other directions which has no bearing on human livelihood nor eternal salvation.

It's saddening to witness literally mankind in general, see the planet Earth as just a place to live and die on.

The average person sees no farther than what they hear or see which isn't far unaware they are under observation of a world which is as real as the physical world in which we live.

The spirit realm of Satan and demonic forces has a lot to do with "our" eternal salvation in heaven or eternally separated from Jehovah God in hell, which there is a hell. The Scripture that is Jehovah God's Word speaks of was created for the devil and demons of the Earth and those (mankind) that choose to follow the devil performing wicked and evil deeds.

Congregation, Satan has multitudes of followers following his direction, some knowing and not knowing they are being led by an invisible being, an adversary or adversaries, name Satan and wicked spirits, demons assigned to carry out their missions against all humanity either to kill, steal, or destroy human lives and livelihood.

Me, a young child and adolescent, I didn't know there was a devil. I thought, the name Devil was a figure of speech I heard adults speak of a devil, "Lucifer" who became Satan the Devil was real and alive on the Earth.

I had my first live encounter with the Devil Satan at the age of six, when he appeared and commanded me to curse God.

I had several more encounters with him and demon spirits before the age of ten. Apparently, he knew God had a calling of me becoming a servant, a prophet in His Kingdom and Christian congregation, something I didn't know.

Children of Jehovah God, as I grew older, I began to experience many things out of the ordinary, the supernatural in the atmosphere of the physical realm.

Note: "A white cloud in angelic form descended out of the heavens and touched my head then ascended back into the heavens and vanished. This happen in the physical!"

I saw a door to my bedroom supernaturally open and close on its own. There were times, my bed would shake uncontrollable back and forth, side to side, which I never thought was demonic activity.

I witness several times the inside lock to the passenger door of my truck to lock again, after I had unlocked it from the inside to go around to the passenger side to retrieve items, as I reached to open the door, the door lock would go down in the locking position.

I've been locked out of my house as I reached to open the door, I heard the "dead bolt," lock on the inside, which I then used the key.

I've had heavy breathing in my ear and footsteps as though someone was walking or running through the house while in the process of praying.

Note: Children of God, my entire life, I've experience encounters with the devil and demons (spirits), Jehovah God, Jesus Christ, and Holy Spirit are my witnesses.

It was God that spoke to me in the process of demonic activity which took place in the kitchen of my home to say to me, "Don't be afraid." Which I thought just for that encounter, children of God, I was in for a rude awakening for many years to come, even at my workplace (job). I've seen objects literally move in all directions.

Demon spirits performed in my office while other employees were presence attempting me to speak out or do something, I saw in the spiritual realm, which others didn't see nor had experience.

Demonic encounters become so prevalent and common in life; the Holy Spirit told me to photograph their actions. In which I did of having objects thrown across the room and at me. There were many other demonic displays against me in the spirit realm, you would have to see to believe.

Several times, I've been slapped hard in the face by an invisible force; struck hard on the leg while in bed; and pounced on while still in bed which I had to called out to the Lord Jesus Christ for help because things were beyond human control.

I've had my feet tickled which woke me up laughing. I thought it was just a dream, it was no dream; it happened on several occasions.

Children of Jehovah God, it's not mankind, man must prove his or her Christian life and values, it's the spirit realm. We must stay in the Word of Jehovah God and live the life God requires us to live.

The spirit realm see's everything and know true dedicated Christians, the spirit realm know the believer and nonbeliever.

Note: They know who has power to make or cause them, the devil and demons to obey in the Name of Jesus, the Christ.

Bible Scripture says demons tremble hearing the Name God.

Read James 2:19. "Do you believe that there is only one God? Good! The demons also believe and tremble with fear."

Note: Children of Jehovah God, there isn't no other name the devil, Satan, or demons will obey. No other Name other than Jesus Christ which you yourself must be a "believer" in Jehovah God and Jesus Christ.

I was a victim and witness in the power of Jesus's Name in the spirit world. I've been victimized my entire life while demonic action and activities was against me even today. Jehovah God is my witness of me being persistently harass by the spirit realm through the atmosphere.

Wherever I travel or visit here at home in the city or abroad, the forces of evil and wickedness is there to accommodate me in the atmosphere or come against me through individuals. People whom I've never seen or know.

Congregation, the world, people does not acknowledge Jehovah God has a will and purpose for each (mankind) of us to perform on the Earth, as is in heaven.

In our Lord's Prayer, we quote "that which is to be done on the Earth as it is in heaven, Jehovah's will."

The spiritual realm of Satan and demonic forces are defeated foes that they acknowledge however, multitudes of people or the world does not acknowledge nor even know there is a spirit world of evil and wickedness which we live in nor aware of being watch and observed of everything we do or say.

The truth must be made known in pulpits across the nation and the entire Earth through congregations of Jehovah God, the Church!

Amen.

SPIRITUAL DECEPTION

For many years, the spirit realm has deceived mankind into believing the spirits of the dead continues to live and dwell in a spiritual realm in the Earth's atmosphere. There are documents that claim loved ones of a decease to have seen their spirit or spirits of others roaming grounds or locations of their death.

During the early period of my life and even today, I still hear many ghost events by persons told of seeing the spirit of a decease loved one who return to visit or haunt or inhabit the home or place for which he or she expired or haunt the homes of those they disliked.

On the other side, I've heard of friendly ghost or spirits of the decease returning to pay friendly visits with loved ones. I've spoken with persons who claim or claim to know someone to have had visitations of decease parents of their children. I've also heard of decease loved ones returning to assist dying loved ones to meet in heaven. Something that is contrary of biblical doctrine.

> Jesus Christ says, "Let not your heart be trouble, you are trusting God, now trust in me. There are many homes up there where my Father lives and I am going to prepare them for your coming. When everything is ready, then I will come and get you so that you can always be with me where I am." (John 14:1–3)

World, I see into the spirit realm as well as anyone. However, I've never seen the spirit or ghost of any loved ones nor the spirit or an apparition of a decease person. What I have and can see are demon spirits masquerading in the atmosphere as spirits of the dead but never a spirit or ghost of a person.

The question is there a spirit world? Yes, it certainly is in which we live in but not of the dead. This world is more spiritual than it is physical. Believe me, mankind are more spirit in human form than physical form as is the spirit realm they demons are just without bodies.

Demons or evil spirits are persons without bodies but possess human beings' characteristics. They speak in their own language but still without bodies. They are the culprits that are deceiving the world of being spirits of decease loved ones.

World, I wish everyone possess the gift I'm bless with that is to see into the spirit realm in which I've never seen a decease loved one ghost or spirit. It's imperative to acknowledge Satan the Devil is the deceiver of this evil and wicked world. He is the culprit behind every evil and deceptiveness mankind encounter throughout the world. Now his demons who are his agents are deceiving the world masquerading as spirits of decease loved ones more than ever before.

Spiritual deceptiveness is rampant throughout the land, has been for years in third world countries. And now this nation is under an attack by demon spirits disguise as loved ones of the dead because mankind is more susceptible influence by the spirit realm than ever before. But why?

Because Satan and demon spirits are more visible today than ever before. Today, evil and wicked spirits like mankind to believe there is life after death on Earth in the spiritual realm regardless of how one lives their life in this lifetime. Some persons even claim to have contact spirits of the dead, seen them and even dialogue with their spirit. Which is far from the truth.

Scriptures admonish us God is against attempting to contact spirits of the decease. To be faithful no person in their rightful mind would not want to contact the dead. Persons who does anything against God's law do so under the power of influence of the devil and demon forces. They are the culprits behind all deceptiveness of the dead or otherwise.

God's law says, "Do not turn yourselves to the spirit mediums and do not consult professional foretellers." Why does God admonish his people of this? Because God knows the angels that join the cherub in rebellion against his Throne but are now wicked and evil spirit, demons pretending and masquerading as persons who has died.

It is to advance the idea that the dead is still living. Thereby, to spread this lie demon spirits provide spirit mediums, fortunetellers and others who seek spirits of the dead special knowledge that only seems to come from persons who have died.

However, the Bible is ever clear where it says, "As for the dead they know nothing." So if it is not the dead speaking, then who are? Demons masquerading as spirits of the dead. The Bible says flesh and blood will not enter the Kingdom of Heaven, which also explain human eyes of the living cannot see into the spirit world. Therefore, for human eyes to witness the spirit world man must witness through the vision of the Holy Spirit. "He that is greater in man than he that is in the world."

Which also explain no human being can witness the spirit world without the Holy Spirit dwelling in him including myself. No human being can witness spirits unless through the vision of the Holy Spirit or through the deceptive vision of the devil's spirit.

There's a different of knowing God's Spirit living in you and having the spirit of Satan dwelling in you. If man can witness through the vision of the Holy Spirit, nonbelievers and children of the devil can also witness spiritual deceptiveness through the vision of Satan spirit, that gives a spiritual perception of witnessing masquerading demon spirits disguise as spirits of the dead. "Remember the dead know nothing. They will never again take part in anything that happen in this world."

Having God's Spirit dwelling in you, you will also display the attributes of His Son, Jesus Christ. Which are the fruits of the Spirit: love, joy, peace, patience, kindness, goodness, faithfulness, humility, and self-control. You do not live as your human nature dictate you to instead you live as the Spirit show and tell you to. If in fact God's

Spirit lives in, you. Whoever does not have the Spirit of Christ does not belong to him.

If you are a child of the devil, you live as your human nature dictate you to live. Because the devil's spirit lives in you, any person that obeys their human nature isn't a child of God. Anyone who follow the world's evil and wicked ways obey the ruler of the flesh the devil's spirit that control the people that lives in disobedience of God's Word.

Humankind is more spirit than flesh. It is by God's Spirit in which we do things. Without the spirit, the flesh is useless. It isn't the flesh that God's Spirit communicate with but the spirit of man. The flesh is just a tent that which house the spirit of mankind.

When God said, "Let us make man in our image." God was referring to His Spirit being and not the physical being of man. God is Spirit for which He is worship in Spirit and in truth without or spirit being mankind could not communicate with God. It is the spirit that gives life as well is His image that gives life to all mankind.

When God said, "Let us make man in our image." God was referring to His Spirit being and not the physical being of man. God is Spirit for which He is worship in Spirit and in truth. Without our Spirit being, mankind could not communicate with God. It is the Spirit that gives life as well as His image that gives life to all mankind.

I believe if I weren't made in the image of God, I could not communicate with God through prayer, thus God could not communicate with me. Because whoever does not have the Spirit of Christ in them does not belong to him. Therefore, anyone that does not belong to Christ is a child of the devil, the devil's spirit lives in you. That explain the flesh and mind is control by the spiritual forces of Satan.

The flesh has its own spiritual elements that mankind neglect to control because of man's thoughts pattern. Man's ability to think is spirit. Man's thoughts are spirit until they manifest into physical things.

That explains the only time the flesh spiritual elements became evil or wicked or even detrimental is when man neglect to control his or her thought pattern in which allows Satan's spirit to created and control in mankind the manifestation of evilness and wickedness throughout the world.

Mankind has yet to realize the devil or demons has not anything to act on without a person's thought or perception. Acknowledging a person perception or thought they know how, when, where and whom to manipulate by way of their spirit being.

So now a person's intellectual perception now become a manifestation of a spiritual deception created and manifested by the devil's spirit. Even though the manifestation of his spirit being is through mankind perception. It is still mankind manifesting the devil's spirit that deceive the world.

World, remember wherever mankind dwell the devil, demons, or both dwelled. Wherever they dwell deception is there as well in the flesh of man or in the atmosphere or both. Whatever the case might be they are present. The deception is in whom?

The spirit realm like to destroy you by any means of deceptiveness. Brethren, demonic forces are out to deceive the entire world but people appear to ignore such manifestations because they are participants of the evil and wickedness in the world.

Spiritual deceptiveness is rampant and most prevalent throughout the world than ever before. People of all races and ages are deceiving one another to get that which they are seeking. People will lie, steal, and even kill to get what they are seeking for. There is no respecter of person whom Satan will not use to deceive the other. As I've stated the flesh in always susceptible of spiritual deception because Satan spirit acknowledge how, when, and where to bring about the manifestation of deceptiveness.

Church, therefore, do not be deceived by Satan's false deception that you cannot be deceive. All flesh is vulnerable of spiritual deceptiveness. The truth is not in the flesh but in the spirit. It is the flesh that Satan and demonic forces use in attempt to bring condemnation upon soul and spirit of mankind.

If Satan can get the flesh to deceive man's natural spirt that which his spirit is doing at an alarming rate all over the world, souls will be lost is well. It is the spirit and soul of a person that Satan and demons like to destroy for eternity.

The spiritual realm of Satan has nothing to lose, it acknowledges its destiny. Satan and demons acknowledge they are spirit beings without bodies. They realize the soul and spirits of a person will either live after the first death for eternity in heaven or hell.

Hell, which is called "the Lake of Fire" was created for the devil and demon spirits in the Earth and universe and those who choose to follow them during this lifetime because of spiritual deceptiveness.

Spiritual deceptiveness lives among us; it has been and it always will as long as there's a devil and demons in the Earth.

Spiritism and Demonologies Hidden Dangers

It is scriptural we live in a Spirit world, a world that is more spiritual than physical. Therefore, affirming this truth individuals believe that the dead communicate with the living as through a medium. A person thought to have the power to communicate with the spirits of the dead or with agents of the spirit world of another dimension, demons.

More people today than ever before (the world) are attempting to get in touch with the spirit world either directly or through a human medium not acknowledging spiritism open avenues to bring persons under the influence of many kinds of wicked spirit demons.

Daily multitudes of people get involve with mediums, astrologers, and psychics "dial a demon" activities of various kinds. They like to experience the spirit world out there; however, they tend to forget or perhaps never realize that man who give themselves over to powers they do not understand have not come out the same again.

Spiritism or demonology also bring a person not only under the influence of demons but also demon possession. Which mean a person is captive, controlled and influenced by an invisible wicked spirit or demonic forces.

When Jesus walked the Earth and as well as the present time demonized and demon-possessed person were afflicted in various ways, some were unable to speak, some were blind, some acted insane, some possessed superhuman strength, or other predicted.

A case of prediction is pointed out in the Bible of a certain servant girl in the City of Philippi. She used to furnish her master with such gain by practicing the art of prediction, one of the things related to spiritism. The account plainly says that the source of her prediction was not God but a demon of divination, a wicked spirit. Hence, when the Apostle Paul expelled the wicked spirit, the girl lost her powers of prediction.

Yet demons or wicked spirits still exercise dangerous power over men, women, and children as well and with the help of demons. Satan is misleading the entire inhabited Earth about communicating with spirits of the dead.

Any person who claim communications with dead persons, if not a deliberate lie on the part of the claimant must be from an evil spirit that stands in opposition to God. The Bible clearly indicate that wicked spirits, demons are the evil source that pretend to be spirits of the dead.

Even though God has legislated against spiritism and divination. It is still being practice of trying to find out about the future or about something unknown with the help of unseen spirits, demons. That mean Satan spirit mediums still appear throughout the world.

But God's law says, "Do not turn yourselves to the spirit mediums and do not consult professional foretellers of events so as to become unclean by them (Lev. 19:31). There is an example in the Bible of a wicked spirit or demon who pretended to be a dead prophet of God, Samuel.

A powerful army of Philistines had come up against Saul's Israelite army and he was afraid. However, Saul knew God's law. But Saul was so eager to learn about what was going to happen that he went to a spirit medium in En-dor. She was able to bring forth the "form" of a person that she could see. By her description of the "form," Saul identifies him as Samuel "a spirit of deception." At this, the spirit person pretending to be Samuel spoke, "Why have you disturbed me by having me brought up?" Saul answered, "I am in very sore straits, as the Philistines are fighting against me." The spirit person replied, "Why then do you inquire of me when God himself has departed from you and proved to be your adversary" (Sam. 28:3–19).

Obviously, it was not really Samuel that the spirit medium had contacted. Samuel was dead and at death a person goes back to his ground, in that day his thoughts do perish (Ps. 146:4).

Remember, Samuel was God's prophet. So he had opposed spirit mediums. And as we have seen while he was alive, he had refused to speak any more with disobedient Saul. Think, too, God's law was against spirit mediums and God refused to give Saul any information. Could a spirit medium who God was against force God to give Saul a message through dead Samuel? This gives an idea of methods that demons use to mislead people.

Also, divination embraces generally the whole scope of gaining secret knowledge about future events through the aid of spiritistic occult powers. Spiritistic and divination are in the same spiritual realm. They both operate together to be effective against God's law.

Divination is gaining secrets knowledge about future events through the aid of spiritualistic occult powers. Those that teach and believe such doctrine also believe in spiritism that claim communication with the dead.

Since the dead are conscious of nothing at all, communication with such dead persons are actually impossible. Which explain the claimant communication is not with the dead but demon spirits pretending to be spirits of the dead communicating with the living. Spiritism or divination can communicate only with the flesh or carnality of mankind but not the spirituality of man.

Church we live in a spirit world that which all spirit beings angelic and demon spirits see and is aware of everything mankind says or does. But God is above all invisible and visible overseers of the physical and spiritual realm. If He weren't mankind would be in trouble big time with the devil and wicked spirits.

As I've stated, spiritism and divination bring people under the influence of demonic forces as well as it's methods that demons use to mislead people. The fact is that wicked spirits are out to harm humans and church. The time is now to find out the characteristics of demons by way of demonology.

It is imperative that the human race beware and acknowledge we live in a spirit world and cohabitate with millions of demon spirits in the Earth's atmosphere and in human bodies of the demon-possessed.

Men, women, and children of all ages become victims of demon possession or demonized in their lifetime. When many demons gain possession of a person simultaneously their possession is compound which cause persons to be disobedient toward God.

So don't be misled about wicked spirits, demons they possess great power over the lost and even some Christians are being misled by demonic leadership in congregations throughout the world. The spirit realm is not to be compromise with. Satan and demons are God's enemies and an enemy of God whether man or spirit is an enemy of man.

Church, even though the devil and wicked spirits, demons are defeated foes they are still powerful and more prevalent performing through the lost and possessed. Their spirit and spiritual perceptions must be in mind and body of a person to be effective in the physical world. Their spirits are also effective in the physical world pretending to be persons or spirits of the dead, that which have led many to believe.

However, there are many kinds of wicked spirits, demons pretending to be someone through another person that rule under the rulership of God's adversary Satan the Devil. But before we learn about them let us acknowledge when and how wicked spirits originated.

Demons as such were not created by God. The first to make himself one was Satan the Devil, who became the ruler of other angelic sons of God who also made themselves demons. Hence, scriptures indicate that the creature known as Satan did not always have that name. Rather, this descriptive name was to him because of his taking a course of opposition and resistance to God.

Therefore, the one becoming Satan was when created a perfect righteous angelic creature of God. He is a spirit person which Jesus said of him, "That one was a manslayer when he began. And he did not stand fast in the truth because truth is not in him" (John 8:44).

Satan was once in the truth but forsook it beginning with his first overt act in turning Adam and Eve away from God. Thereby, he was a manslayer for he brought about the death of Adam and Eve which in turn brought sin and death to their offspring (Rom. 5:12).

It is clear that Satan exist as a person as is his demons are persons without bodies who speak in their own language and possess great power and influences over the minds and lives of men, women, and children of all ages. Even having the ability to enter into and possess humans and animals and the truth show the purpose of all such demonic activity is to turn people from God and the pure worship of God.

However, demons cannot enter nor possess the mind and body of a person under their own demonic or supernatural power. Unfortunately, Satan the Devil, God's adversary possess such power, which he uses insidiously the power of influence that create habits for human beings through his spirit. His spirit creates false perceptions that opens up avenue or accessibilities that which allow his spirit to enter all kinds of and as many demons he like to enter into a person's mind and body that which control them.

Such false perceptions create habits and false habits and false personalities and identities in individuals. Drug and alcohol abuse are created habits, tobacco chewing or smoking are created habits just to name a few. False personalities and identities that create alternate lifestyles and the belief of being the opposite sex or be in denial of one biological sex are all created by Satan spirit being and are all demonically controlled. A person without Jesus Christ as Lord and Savior has no power over a spirit or spirits greater than their own natural spirit.

In Bible times, demonized person was afflicted in various ways, some were unable to speak, some were blind, some acted insane and some possessed superhuman strength. All were woefully mistreated by the invisible enemies of God and mankind.

I became a victim of demon possession at the age of six and a habitual alcohol drinker. Many demons gain possession over my mind and body for which they possessed and controlled for over forty years which force me to become an alcoholic of over thirty years.

When God cured me of demon possession many demons was expelled out of my body. It was at that time, I returned to a sound and sane state of mind. Which confirm the spirit realm is real as well as demon spirits are real and alive in the Earth atmosphere and human bodies.

Its imperative mankind acknowledges the spirit realm is a supernatural realm where the manifestation of the unseen reveals its presences in physical form is well as in spiritual form through humans, in human bodies and human characteristics.

What I'm saying is that the devil and demons has penetrated human hearts contending with Christ to condemn mankind as persons without bodies by way of possessing human bodies for their purpose to destroy human lives and to turn mankind away from God Almighty.

Forming an Opinion Satan's Access to the Human Mind Sermon and Message

Congregation, we have all at some point or time formed an opinion of someone or something and above all, even ourselves. No one has control of themselves of forming opinions which happen more than we ever know.

Note: Congregation, consciously or subconsciously we form opinions that is part of life without self-opinions, the mind would become weak which is the opportune time for Satan the Devil to gain access to the mind of persons to use as giving his own demonic perception while his spirit acts and perform in and through individuals, "who assume he or she is performing their own agenda."

Children of Jehovah God, an opinion is a belief or conclusion held with confidence but not substantiated which is to support with proof or evidence.

Note: Ninety percent of times, it is Satan who form's mankind's opinions which cause individuals to act accordingly as though they were acting out their own perception of an opinion.

Forming one's own opinion is an act of unbelief. Some people have their own opinion of the Bible, being God's "Word" even have their opinion of Jehovah God existence and the Lord Jesus Christ being the Son of the Living God, Jehovah.

Note: And for many, their opinion going to cause their eternal separation from Jehovah God.

Note: Congregation of all denominations, people in general that form their opinion or belief of God and Jesus Christ nonexistence have already been judged.

Read John 3:16–18.

> For God so loved the world that he gave his only begotten Son, that whosoever believeth in Him should not perish but have everlasting life.
>
> For God did not send his Son into the world to be its judge, but to be its savior.
>
> Those who believe in the Son are not judged, but those who do not believe have already been judged because they have not believed in God's only Son.

Note: Forming opinions for others can be misleading and often dangerous because they aren't their support.

Church, there is a "world of opinions" of Jesus Christ not being the Son of God, the Father, which is sin, an eternal sin.

Scripture says of such belief, "They have already been Condemned!" The world's sin is unbelief in Jesus Christ. Scripture says, "Fools say to themselves, 'There is no God!'" (Ps. 14:1).

Children of God, forming one's own opinion is not always his or her; or your own. Satan the Devil has his right of forming or giving one's opinion as their own.

Remember him, Satan, a deceiver, who has deceived the whole world and at this very hour in the process of deception of forming multitudes opinions by deception. Satan is deceiving the whole world by deception, "as a transitional human person in human form as a human being. A person of any nationality he chooses to appear as to deceive the entire world!"

Note: Congregation of Jehovah God, it's not being preached nor taught in the pulpits of all denominations nor in homes that Satan has his hands and plans in everything, I mean everything mankind does. His spirit is always at work by way of a thought, by perception or opinion. His spirit can appear in an instant or as quick as a person think.

Church, Scripture says Satan the Devil is a deceiver, which means he must appear as a demonic perception or thought or as a spirit person to become that which Scripture describe him to be the deceiver of the world as a human being, a real spirit person!

Whether mankind (you) admit it. We have all been deceived at some point in one's life. We have all formed deceptive opinions of ourselves as well as other people.

As long as there is a devil on the Earth, mankind will never be exempt from forming deceptive opinions.

Remember Satan is at his best, when deceiving the "world," as a person at no other time, he is at his best when deceiving the "whole world," as a real human being. Walking and talking while roaming the Earth among us appearing as a person. A real human being!

The world (people) never speaks of Satan or devil as being a deceiver nor speak of him openly in the world or publicly; nor roaming the Earth, nor the world system of things, which he controls drug traffic, money laundering, sex, pornography, and other illegal activities. That's because his spirit has demonic opinions and perceptions in the world's mind, which people in general has accepted as normal and a way of life; which is a deceptive lie of Satan.

Child of Jehovah God, the devil, Satan won't never give a good opinion of one's self nor others. However, his spirit will always form an opinion negatively of one's self and on any occasion, he will appear as an angel of light always ready to deceive at any place and time. Scripture says,

Read 1 Peter 5:8. "Be alert, be on watch! Your enemy, the devil roams around like a roaring lion, looking for someone to devour."

Child of Jehovah God, there are others being deceived with demonic opinions not of their own but of that of the devil, Satan. No good deeds are ever rewarded in different opinions because they can go either way, both can be deceiving.

The world, the people, does not realize it has already been deceived in spirit and deception is coming to pass through them, the population of the world.

Children of God, have you heard of public opinion? That's when the public or the world, people in general give their opinion on or about any or everything.

A worldly or secular opinion is part of Satan, world system of things. You recall Satan has his hand in everything mankind does for himself and others.

Never think nor believe you are alone; Satan spirit is there when you least expect he'll show up appearing in and through you. Mankind performing that which he does best "deception."

Note: Congregation of Jehovah God, an angel of light is one of the devil, Satan most successful disguises. He appears to mankind as of a perception of thought in or from another person or persons as the right thing to do even yourself to agree on that which others agree is the right thing to do but in reality is against all principles of righteousness and the end result is failure.

Scripture tells us, "Well, no wonder! Even Satan can disguise himself to look like an angel of light!" (2 Cor. 11:14).

Therefore, children of Jehovah God, stay alert. We must not be ignorant of the devil's disguises and machination. The act of Satan plotting for the accomplishment of a sinister end.

Read Proverb 28:26. "It is foolish to follow your own opinions. Be safe and follow the teachings of wiser people."

Amen.

"Thus," Says the Lord, "Teach and Preach!" How Demon Spirit Enters "You" Humans

Note: It's imperative the world, people, believers, and nonbelievers acknowledge who demon spirits are where they come from and their purpose on the Earth.

Answer: Who are demon spirits? They are fallen angels cast out of heaven down to Earth because of their conspiracy with Lucifer, which mean light-bearer another angel who attempted to "dethrone" Jehovah God; and he, Lucifer, were cast out of heaven and became the devil, Satan who deceived the whole world.

Read Revelation 12:7–9. "The huge dragon was thrown out- that ancient serpent named the devil or Satan, that deceived the whole world. He was thrown down to Earth, and all his angels with him."

Note: The cherub, Lucifer was going to be God, in his deception way. No longer Light-bearer but now an adversary (enemy) of God and humankind.

The name *Satan* means "adversary." His angels who conspired with him, now became demons or evil spirits on the Earth. A third of the angels united with Satan in the conspiracy and rebellion.

Read 1 Peter 5:8. "Be alert, be on watch! Your (our) enemy, the devil roams around like a roaring lion looking for someone to devour."

He's not only looking to eat up greedily, but to steal, kill, destroy, and consume mankind permanently by way of habits and deception.

Note: I want the entire population of the world *acknowledge* the spirit realm is "real and alive," and exist throughout the Earth. The world is living in deception even though it affects all livelihoods and how mankind live; age nor gender is no exception.

We aren't never alone. Wherever we travel, we are in their presence. Evil spirits, *demons* in the atmosphere of our homes, company, public places, and yes, even in church sanctuaries.

Note: The spiritual world is not of the deceased which a vast number of people, Christians and non-Christians, choose to believe.

The spirits without bodies are demons or evil spirits disguised in search of persons to enter.

Note: Children of God, a demon or evil spirit cannot enter a human body under their own power. It takes power greater than its own which is the spirit and power of the devil, Satan.

Even as powerful as the devil he cannot enter a demon or evil spirit into the mind and body of a person. Therefore, Satan must create avenues or accesses which he does by creating habits in individuals to enter controlling spirits into the mind and body of a person.

Note: Therefore, the creating of habits of all kind open avenues and accesses which allow Satan to enter all types of demonic spirits into a person's mind and body which literally translate into a demon or evil spirit now has demonically control of that person's body and mind, not as a word or perception but as a spirit entity, a spirit being with its own perception and characteristics.

After the demon or demons have enter the person body and mind that person become influenced and controlled under its power. Which at this time such power control's that person or humankind by ways of habits that the devil's spirit created in that person or humankind.

We are all vulnerable of possessing some kind of habit or habits, manmade habits or demonic created habits, both are avenues or accesses to demonic control habits.

Brethren, the devil nor demons do not discriminate against race, age nor gender. All human beings that has a bad or detrimental habit of any kind is being control internally with power other than their own ability to control. Including children of any age. Anyone under the power of influence of a demonic spirit has the potential of inflicting great harm to him or herself and humankind. Read Matthew 17:14–18. "Jesus heals a boy with a demon." Also read Matthew 15:22. "Vast number of children of all ages are living under demonic influence and control but does not realize their condition and neither does the parents."

Note: "Satan created habits for the purpose of entering demon spirits into the minds and bodies of mankind to cause and create death and destruction."

Demons are also evil spirits are here to steal, kill, or destroy mankind and perform Satan's assignments and purpose through mankind. Which is to steal, kill, or destroy by manifestation of demon spirits throughout the human race. Which age is no exception.

Children of God, it is the devil purpose to kill us, remember, habits are detrimental to one's "health" and life. Habits will either kill or get you kill and as I've stated, it is their purpose to kill or destroy mankind.

Note: Take notice at the vast number of people control with habits beyond their natural ability to control. Young and elderly people dying as the results of such habits. Alcoholism, lung cancer, the result of smoking tobacco, sex, the results, many types of sexual related (venereal) diseases transmitted by abnormal sexual (anal or sodomy) copulation, some types aren't listed in the medical manual and all types of drug abuse which led to drug addiction, just to name a few habits beyond humankind control which are all detrimental.

Note: Does people know this generation of people are confined living with habits which control their lives and destiny, even though they think they are in control which they aren't? Yet you ask, why won't you quit such detrimental and harmful habits? Their response is, "I can, but still killing or harming themselves and others without remorse."

If a person were in control, he or she would not be dying habits related deaths. This should tell or reveal to them something is seriously wrong with them. If he or she is control by a habit beyond his or her natural spirit's ability to control, the habit is demonically control.

Note: "Child of God, you aren't never in control of habits. If a person was in control, there would not be any habits."

Regardless how small or how large habits may appear to you to be in control. You aren't never in control of bad degrading or detrimental habits. If you were in control, there would be no habits!"

I know, I've been where you are today. I was under Satan power and power of influence for over forty years, control with many habits beyond my ability to control.

Children, there will come a time the devil want you to believe you are in control, which is a false perception and deception and not one's own perception.

Conceal and Camouflage Spirits

Note: Yes, there are hidden demons that possessed the minds and bodies of mankind. These evil spirits remain conceal and go undetected. Hidden demons or evil spirits, demonically control people without one's knowledge, they even control some habits which people isn't aware of.

"These wicked spirits cause a person to lose their temper or lose one's mind. There are multitudes of people not in their right mind, even though they appear and act normal in every aspect of life, yet they aren't in their right mind!"

Note: It's saddened me to see children of all ages demonized, wandering why can't they control their behavior. Even parents do not know what's wrong with their child.

Are children born into the world demonized? Some certainly are. A vast number of infants are born into the world of possessed or demonized parents, conceived and develop in the womb of addictive mothers. Which both mother and father victims of demonically control habits such as alcoholism or drug abuse.

These demon control habits just to name a few are detrimental to one's health.

Note: Fetus, the unborn is in the womb of addictive mothers receiving everything in their blood as that of the mother. Whether orally or intravenously which a vast number of women get pregnant under such conditions.

It's time for people to wake up and realize there's a devil in the world along with millions of unseen evil spirits, demons roaming the Earth and in the Earth's atmosphere waiting for the opportunity to enter human bodies of any age and bring the unborn under their control.

Note: The human race should also realize these evil spirits are real, alive, and active and bring destruction on the human race. They aren't made of flesh and blood but possess all human characteristics that cause mankind to reject God and Jesus Christ.

Thereby, without Jesus in one's life, they are free to do whatever they choose to do, to and through humans that is weak in faith and beliefs and all nonbelievers. Brethren, the spirit realm recognize believers and nonbelievers.

Note: Demon spirits can articulate, which means the spirit realm of Satan and demons has the power of speech. The spirit realm can imitate or mimic any nationality in their own language and in and through the ones of those they possess or control!

Several times I've heard my name called out of the atmosphere. When no one was near nor in the vicinity. I've heard a voice called me whom I thought was my Mother's voice, which it wasn't.

Believe me they know when and where to get mankind attention. I can't stress strong enough how Real and Alive demon spirits are and their ability to cause mankind to perform under such power.

Once evil spirits enter a person, nothing but the Name of Jesus can cast or expel it out. Man does need to be a believer nor have Jesus in his life as Lord and Savior to be cured of demon possession.

However, you must be a believer in God and have faith in Jesus Christ to expel demons out of human beings. My friend, the spirit realm is aware of one's faith and beliefs. They know who possess such power to cast them out of humankind and make them obey in the atmosphere of the spirit realm.

Therefore, don't attempt to expel demons out if you lack faith and belief in Christ Jesus. Friend, it's demon spirits that prevent persons from accepting Jesus as Lord and Savior. The spirit realm knows any man, woman, or child without Jesus Christ in their lives as Lord and Savior is subject to be influence of the devil and come under the power of demons.

"Demon Spirits know us individually and by name. They know who's in the Body of Christ and who's not. Therefore, all mankind must accept Jesus in their lives as Lord and Savior.

Read "The Sons of Sceva."

> Some Jews who traveled around and drove out evil spirits also tried to use the name of the Lord Jesus to do this. They said to the evil spirits, "I command you in the Name of Jesus, whom Paul preaches."
>
> Seven brothers, who were the sons of a Jewish High Priest named Sceva were doing this.
>
> But the evil spirit said to them, "I know Jesus, and I know about Paul, but you who are you?"
>
> The man who had the evil spirit in him attacked them with such violence that he overpowered them all. They ran away from his house, wounded and with their clothes torn off. (Acts 19:13–16)

Note: DON'T ATTEMPT TO EXPEL DEMONS (EVIL SPIRITS) OUT, IF YOU ARE LACKING FAITH AND BELIEF IN JESUS CHRIST!"

Children of God, you must be a believer to be effective against and in the spirit realm of the devil. All mankind must possess spiritual power of Jesus to protect him or herself as well as others against spiritual beings, demon forces in the air or atmosphere and in bodies of humankind!

Note: I reiterate, I cannot stress strong enough the realization how real and alive demon forces are in the Earth's air or atmosphere and in humans.

These evil spirits cannot be seen by way human vision nor touch by human flesh; however, their touch can be felt by human flesh. Which amaze me because demon spirits aren't tangible, they cannot be touch, nor felt by way of human flesh but yet can be felt by the spirit's touch.

Note: "All my past and current life, demon spirit has physically through the Earth's air and atmosphere persistently harass me from out of the spirit realm and unto this day and time. I'm still being harass!"

Note: Jehovah God is my witness in this short testimony.

This date, February 20, 2018, approximately 10:00 a.m. While shopping at a major food market, I approach the eggs and milk refrigerator to get a carton of eggs. Suddenly the full-size cabinet door of the refrigerator opened and closed as I approached the door. I posed to think maybe, it's something new when a shopper approaches the refrigerator, the cabinet doors automatically open.

To my surprise, that was not the case, because when I approach the same door that had open and closed when no one was near it, nothing happened.

Then it dawned on me: this act I just witnessed was performed by an invisible spirit demon in the spirit realm! True testimony: Jehovah God is my witness!

CREATIVE HABITS

Note: Children of God, it isn't difficult for demon spirits to enter a person body. The devil, Satan, has many avenues and use many tactics to enter demon spirits of all "kinds" into a person to control that person's mind and body, by way creative habits.

There are many believers, claim the titles as Christians but weak in faith and still possesses uncontrollable habits. Am I saying some Christians are living with demonically control habits? Yes, I certainly am.

Note: Many Christian believers are under demonic power of influences but does recognize it. And as stated earlier, any person that have a habit beyond or not beyond their control regardless how small or any person does something against their will power, mean he or she does not possess the power to resist something performing spiritually through them, other than their own natural spirit.

Oh, yes, many who claim to be Christians are performing under some kind of spiritual force other than their own and some Christians are demonized but don't recognize nor acknowledge their demonic condition nor the invisible enemies.

Note: Man, mankind can take upon himself to allow the enemies enter his or her body to gain or possess supernatural power over their counterparts in the world.

Therefore, it's imperative all humankind, believers and nonbelievers be strong in the faith and believe in God and not give in to the devil's plan and tactics.

Brethren, the devil and demons are defeated foes, it is through Jesus Christ our Lord and Savior who protects us from the invisible works of Satan and demon forces and demons' dominance and power to control our lives throughout the world!

Note: Demon spirits aren't effective against the human race without their spirit in a human body. "The Return of the evil spirit."

Read Luke 11:24–26.

> When an evil spirit goes out of a person, it travels over dry country looking for a place to rest. If it can't find one, it says to itself, I will go back to my house.
>
> So it goes back and finds the house clean and all fixed up.
>
> Then it goes out and brings seven other spirits even worse than itself and they come and live there. So when it is all over, that person is in worse shape than at the beginning.

Note: Therefore it's imperative all mankind believers and nonbelievers be strong in faith and belief and not give in to the devil's plan and tactics.

Note: A minister and I and another gentleman was discussing the spirit world of our experiences in it. We live in a spirit world, which people in general have very little or no knowledge at all, some not even know there is a spirit world we live in.

As we discuss our spiritual experiences and events, the gentleman injected, he had seen or had visitations of his deceased mother, father, and sister.

I could not let him continue to believe that "lie" of the devil, which multitudes believe to this day, they have seen spirits of "loved ones."

I corrected him, there is no spirits of the deceased on the Earth. What he had thought to have seen weren't his "loved ones," but spirits or demons, "the fallen angels who joined Satan in rebellion against God, masquerading in disguise pretending to be spirits of loved ones, family members whom has died.

Oh! They will frighten you by pretending to be ghosts of the deceased! "Why do they pretend to be persons who have died? It is to deceived the world that the dead are still living, when the Bible is very clear when it says, "As for the dead, they are conscious of nothing at all" (Eccles. 9:5).

Children of God, Read These Writings with a Clear Mind!

The spiritual realm of Satan aren't physically effective against the physical world, of humankind, us, unless evil spirits, demons enter human bodies, fathers, mothers, sisters, or brothers all mankind are vulnerable.

They cannot accomplish Satan assignments unless their spirits enter human bodies, they cannot perform mentally nor physically until manifestation of the spirit by way of the flesh of a person body and mind.

Believe me the spirit realm are aware of human weakness of every area of life. Once the spirit or spirits enter, the spirit take's control of the person's body and mind as its own.

Therefore, the person's body takes on the manifestation of the spirit as it performs, becoming demonically control.

Note: The revelation is some individuals or persons are representatives of the devil or demon spirits. There aren't any exceptions, all mankind are vulnerable of representing him or demon spirits in one's lifetime.

I've discovered the devil and demons can speak to and through worldly people. Believe me the forty years, plus I was serving Satan and the "world system of things," I didn't realize there were so many ungodly and demonize people in the world whom Satan use to open up avenues in each other to allow kinds of evil spirits, demons to enter each other, age, gender is no exception.

Note: When I was in the world, I also discovered the devil's spirit was always present 24-7, which his representatives was also presence at all times attempting to open up avenues or accesses in an attempt to remind godly people to be like; talk like; and act like; and become like the world.

Again, I discovered the world (the world is the people) like to remind godly people about their past and things which they used to like and do, and show them what they (we) are now missing in the world!

Note: Children of God, when I was in the world, I knew where to go whenever to dialogue with the spirit world of demon spirits disguised like myself in the flesh.

Wherever the world congregated to speak of world and worldly events, demons in disguise openly spoke to discuss their Heinous works and assignments in the world among and against its people (the world is the people) through mankind, which man or humans are used to perform under demonic influences and power.

Note: "Remember, I once was under demon possession!"

Demon spirits dialogue among people speaking to and through individuals, like "myself," without the person nor the world knowledge. However, a person's tongue and speech reveal their presence as well as the manifestation of the invisible enemies' presence. Therefore, do not be deceived by people's words and speech.

It's important to know demon spirits are territorial, which mean belonging to or limited to a specific territory, districts, and jurisdictions. Therefore, I speak out daily at demon spirits in the midst of my home to obey me in the Name and authority of Jesus Christ.

It is the supernatural power in Jesus's Name that as a believer, the devil and demons "obey" and be expel out of human bodies. All power over the spirit realm is the Name of Jesus Christ. This is in the Name, now imagine how powerful Jesus is in one's life as Lord and Savior!

Amen.

Satan's Master Plan

The devil's master plan is to counter and defeat the works of God through the human race throughout the world. His plan is to manifest demon spirits and himself as persons in the flesh of mankind to assist his efforts in accomplishing his plan.

He wants to stop and prevent humankind from proclaiming victory over him, demon spirits and the spirit realm. In all reality, the devil and demons has declared spiritual warfare against the human population of the world.

Spiritual warfare is now at its highest form in human lives which mankind does not recognize. Therefore, it is spiritually imperative for the human race acknowledge Jesus Christ as Lord and Savior in their lives.

The spirit realm knows without Jesus Christ in man's heart as Lord and Savior man has no power over himself nor the spirit realm. Virtually, he is helpless in defending him or herself from the attack of the spirit realm.

As a Christian and soldier of God's army, I know we are engaged in war with the devil, demons in the body of humankind in the atmosphere and the entire spirit realm. Satan and demons are attacking all mankind and all denominations. They are attacking the Body of Christ, the Church and everyone in the church. There aren't any exceptions.

The spirit realm does not want the human race to claim victory over it. Therefore, its strategy is to keep reminding people of their past to turn back as many to their past lives to live the lives they once lived for the devil and demons.

Which put mankind in spiritual warfare with himself and the world without his or her knowledge. Friend, you must realize the human race cannot recognize spiritual warfare without acknowledging Jesus Christ as Lord and Savior in their lives, because the devil and demon spirits that reside in human bodies won't let them. Because the spirit realm know Jesus is greater than human's natural spirit.

And yet man believe he's in his right mind when in fact he's in the grasp of the devil and demons using him to perform their work against mankind. I reiterate, spiritual warfare is at its highest level which appear it still escalating.

I've spoken to people in war with themselves, and you may be among them. Yet they believe they are at peace with themselves when in fact they are being irritated by their mind. Many cannot make just decisions of what and what not to do for themselves nor loved ones. Yet they appear normal in every humanly aspect.

But, friend, you are far off from being normal. Satan's spirit gives you the perception to appear normal that fools you and those around you. Friend, it would not be spiritual warfare if you knew those things about yourself and other as well.

Spiritual warfare is spiritually fought. However, the battle has been won but mankind must seek spiritual helps to combat the spiritual attacks of the invisible enemies internally as well externally. Thereby accepting Jesus Christ as Lord and Savior, Jesus becomes man's protector as well.

Jesus will supernaturally give you victory over the spirit realm. As I stated, the battle has been won, but you, mankind must claim victory over the spirit realm through Jesus Christ.

People, no one can claim this victory for you, you must claim it yourself by way of our Lord and Savior by accepting Jesus into your heart as Lord and Savior. Even though the devil and demons know they are defeated foes they will try to stop to prevent the human race from accepting Jesus Christ as Lord and Savior.

Brothers and sisters, I've been in spiritual warfare all my life which I'm still is in spiritual warfare, but the Lord is fighting my battles. Yet I've claimed victory over sin, the devil, demons, and the spirit realm; and yet Jesus is still protecting me while showing me the way, the truth, and the life.

Now you may wonder what spirit warfare is and how can a person recognize or acknowledge he or she; or even yourself is at war with the spirit realm. First of all, you nor mankind has to wonder whether or not you are in spiritual warfare. Because all mankind is in some kind of spiritual battle with themselves and the world included.

As I've stated, it is Satan's master plan to stop or prevent the work of God by way of the human race and you are no exception. I was in the world for over forty years fighting against demon forces I didn't know exist because no one never told me the devil and demons was real persons without bodies, not made of flesh and blood.

They are the culprits that are fighting in and through mankind and against us in the world and through the world atmosphere. In essence, mankind is fighting themselves by way of demon forces in the flesh of the human race which is demon possession of human bodies.

Man is in spiritual warfare but does not recognize it. Entire families are in spiritual warfare among themselves and do not realize it. Youth gangs are in spiritual warfare but does not know it.

Gang members think it's cool to fight against and kill each other or drive by and shoot indiscriminately into homes not caring whom they shoot. People that's spiritual warfare. The enemy, the devil is here to steal, kill, and destroy human lives and the works of God by way of humankind which he's doing throughout the four corners of the world.

Children killing children of all ages, infants included because they became bored in which the devil and demons tells or give them the perception to do something, so they destroy innocent lives, some even get bored and take their own life.

When people commit such hideous acts, they aren't in their right mind. They are at war with the invisible enemies within their body controlling the mind and body spiritually performing.

People, no human being in their right mind regardless of age would engage in sexual intercourse with an infant or toddler. It's true that any person who does it or commit incest are control by a spirit or spirits other than their natural spirit! "A person's natural spirit won't allow it."

That's why people do things beyond man's comprehension. Because it isn't humanly possible for a person to commit such hideous and perverted acts against other human beings, we are all God's temples and are holy.

But Satan the Devil is trying to destroy God's temples by way of mankind, which is spiritual warfare. Which mean any human being that commit such acts against another aren't in their right mind but under the power and control of the devil, demons, and spirit realm.

Believe me, we are under a demonic attack, those persons without bodies, not made of flesh and blood. They are possessing bodies of human beings of all ages committing acts never before committed, which tells us there are people even though they appear normal in every aspect but aren't in their right mind.

All humankind is supposed to have the mind of Jesus; however, by way of their works and acts tell us some people has the mind and spirit of the devil and demons. Only Satan and demons commit such works and acts utilizing the human race mind and body for their tools and weapons against each other.

People, spiritual warfare is real. It is a real war which people are getting kill and lives are being destroy. Mankind does not need to be demon-possessed to be in spiritual warfare. It exists all around us and is effective in world peace and living.

People kill without remorse. They kill infants as they would kill an animal. Some people will tell you they can and will kill and think nothing of it.

Friend, believe me, any person who says that isn't in their right mind, therefore, it isn't their natural spirit speaking. It is the devil or a demon spirit perception manifesting by way of such person speaking the devil's spirit or demon perception that he or she perceive to speak.

Yes, the devil and demon spirit possess power to speak intellectually by way of the mind and mouth of humankind.

That's part of spiritual warfare manifesting through the body of humankind. People, spiritual warfare would not exist had not Satan and demons inhabited the Earth. Therefore, humankind isn't safe without Jesus Christ in his or her life.

Lucifer, the angel known as Satan the Devil, God's adversary, was dispelled out of heaven and a third of God's spiritual Son's angels followed. They came to Earth seeking vengeance. That is to avenge against the works and Word of Almighty God through the human race.

Unfortunately, the spirit realm's power lies in the body and mind, the flesh of humankind. So don't be fooled nor misled of their existence. Satan and demons can and will possess your body to operate through to obtain their objective. Matter of fact, they may currently be operating in you which is to steal, kill, and destroy mankind, and the works and Word of God.

We are all vulnerable to spiritual warfare during one's lifetime. Which mean spiritual warfare is here to the end of time. Therefore, mankind must forever wear the whole armor of God, which is His Word.

People, it is Satan's plan to cause us to destroy ourselves through spiritual warfare. And in some areas of mankind's life he has accomplished that, and yet he's still working on that which he has yet to accomplished.

Brethren, we are in spiritual warfare whether you believe or not. Mothers against daughters; fathers against sons; brothers against sisters and brothers, daughters against fathers and sons against mothers. This family matters are displayed throughout the world, but no one appeared to recognize what is happening.

Why? Because Satan and demon spirits have blinded the minds of the world and its worldly inhabitants. And those that recognize spiritual warfare has taken it for granted or ignore it as though it doesn't exist.

Which is a mistake, we are in the midst of something that is trying to kill and destroy us. Take off the veil Satan has place over your mind and eyes. Wake up, use the whole armor of God, which is His Word against spiritual warfare and assist other in their warfare against the invisible enemies of the world.

People do not ignore anything that the spirit realm is involve or concerning the spirit realm. Spiritual warfare isn't a game. The devil is here to steal, kill, and destroy us by any means possible.

Spiritual warfare isn't a game, it is the devils master plan which is to destroy mankind, the works and Word of God by way of this evil world. Spiritual warfare has moved into the Body of Christ, the Church, the place of worship.

We have brothers and sisters claim to be who they aren't. But yet they say God called them to teach, preach and prophesy. Some called themselves prophets, prophetess, bishops, and apostles—all disciples of God, yet they live immoral and unrighteous lives.

Friend, you are in spiritual warfare with yourself. The spirit realm is using you and others to defile the Body of Christ, the Church while bringing condemnation upon this nation and throughout the world. This is part of the spirit realm master plan against humanity throughout the four corners of the world.

I believe if people in general know demon spirits are responsible for their behavior against themselves and the world, they would accept Jesus Christ into their hearts as Lord and Savior throughout the world.

But people in general take the spirit realm as though it doesn't exist, and they are the people in spiritual conflicts with themselves. The devil's spirit has blinded their eyes and dull their minds and given them his spirit false perception to perceive they know everything. Which mean mankind can't tell them anything of morally living nor the Word of God.

Anytime mankind perceives a false perception about of the Word of God, he's not in his or her right mind. Remember, we all have the mind of Jesus and must think as Jesus think that is to believe and act on the Word of God.

But Satan's plan is to victimize mankind with his spirit false perceptions into believing that their perception of the Word of God is of their own mind when in fact their perception is that of his spirit being.

Thereby, it is imperative all humankind accept Jesus Christ into their heart as Lord and Savior, which make "He that is in them is greater than he that is in the world and the world's atmosphere."

People, the devil and demons see everything we are in the process of doing in which they are involve internally as well as externally.

There isn't anything man does that the spirit realm does not see and a part of. You know if they are in the Body of Christ (the Church), they are in the body of the living. That should tell you we are in spiritual warfare throughout the four corners of the world.

Children of God, there aren't no other way but through Jesus Christ to defeat the spirit realm and its master plan. Jesus Christ has already defeated the devil and demons, our spirit foes. But it is up to man and you to claim victories over the spirit realm and spiritual warfare through Jesus Christ.

Without Jesus Christ as Lord and Savior, you nor mankind will never have victory over the devil nor demons in your life. You and mankind will forever be in spiritual warfare with—yourself, the world, and in the devil's master plan.

What Mankind Should Know Satan the Devil and Mankind's Perception Sermon and Message

Note: Scriptures indicate that the angelic being (creature) known as Satan the Devil did not always have that name. It was given to him because of his taking a course of opposition and resistance toward Jehovah God.

His challenge of God and his charging God's servants with lack of integrity. Satan lived up to his title devil which mean accuser, slanderer which titles he deserved for having slandered Jehovah God in the Garden of Eden.

Note: The Apostle Paul associates Satan with the wicked spirit forces in the heavenly places and speak of them as the world rulers of darkness; therefore, we must,

> put on all the armor that God gives you so that you will be able to stand up against the devil's evil tricks.
>
> For we are not fighting against human beings but against the wicked spiritual forces in

the heavenly world, the rulers, authorities, and cosmic powers of this dark age. (Eph. 6:11–12)

Satan is the "supreme adversary" or enemy of Jehovah God and the world and so are demons. He is the prince of "darkness" and god of the world system of things.

Read 2 Corinthians 4:4. "They do not believe because their minds have been kept in the dark by the evil god of this world."

Note: Congregation, Jehovah God did not place the devil over mankind, man allowed his "intellectual perception" (mind) place the enemy or enemies over him or herself to rule and be control by demonic influences.

Note: Servants of Jehovah God, there is a great need for you, this nation and the world (people) to stressfully preach or teach the realization of spiritual warfare we the world are in against demonic forces that are real and alive on the Earth and in our lives which are at work in work influentially performing even as you (I) speak.

The spiritual realm and warfare is a part of the message of the Gospel, which Jesus stressed throughout his ministry. It is responsible for the teaching of the Gospel message, not mankind. Spiritual warfare begin with Job, in the Old Testament time.

Note: Spiritual warfare begin with a challenge. When Satan challenged Jehovah God that he could turn humankind in general away from Him.

It began with Job and is still in effect or still stand to the day and will continue until the end of the Age.

Congregation, people with demonic influences are responsible in this time and age that cause them to bring upon themselves condemnation by allowing Satan control of the mind or their intellectual perceptions to achieve his goal, or plan.

Mankind wonder how is it, Satan so powerful in their lives being a defeated "Foe" or why did God give him such power and authority?

Brothers and sisters, Jehovah God did not give Satan or demon forces authority over His Creation. People, man give the devil and demons power to control over oneself because lack of spiritual knowledge.

Had God given them authority and power over people or mankind, Jehovah God would've given demonic forces authority and power over Himself, His holy temples.

God's spirit resides in "believers," which believers body is the temple of the Holy Spirit.

Read 1 Corinthians 6:19. "Don't you know that your body is the temple of the Holy Spirit, who live in you and who was given to you by God? You do not belong to yourselves, but to God."

Note: Congregation, Satan took upon himself to possess and control human minds when he chose mankind to represent him in spirit by grasping control of man's perception for his own.

Definition of *perception*: The process of perceiving to become aware of directly through any of the senses, specially sight or hearing. Which Satan adversely use against humans.

Note: *Are you ready for this?* Satan's power to control mankind is in mankind inability to distinguish the two, his own perception or that of Satan's perception. Which he uses to deceive mankind and the whole world.

Note: Satan's perceptions which he put in man's mind to perceive of his own is his ability to know one's thoughts. He knows the perceptions or thoughts he put in a person's mind to act on as or perform as their own.

Note: Satan can only perceive a person's natural thoughts which he placed in man but not of the Holy Spirit. His ability to control is relied solely on those that his spirit gives to perceive as one own intellectual belief.

Servants, clergies, ministers of Jehovah God, human perceptions allow Satan to know when, where and how to perform throughout the entire world against anyone, anywhere.

A person or human perception produces his spirit just with a thought to appear simultaneously when and wherever the perception lead which gives his spirit ability to appear throughout the Earth simultaneously.

Note: It is human beings' own perception that gives the evil one, Satan the Devil's spirit power to manifest to control people with a thought all over the world.

His power of influence is in the mind and how we perceive that's his ability to know when, where and how to appear in people (human beings) across the Globe. Satan know whom he can control to manifest through and so does demon spirits.

Note: But Jesus Christ has given Christians and believers power and authority in his name over Satan and the spiritual realm he exists in and over demons of the Earth and universe.

Just with a thought or perception man can place Satan spirit perception wherever he wishes. Therefore, we must guard our minds at all times. Scripture says,

Read 1 Peter 5:8. "Be alert, be on watch! Your enemy, the devil roams around like a roaring lion, looking for someone to devour."

However, Jesus defeated the devil, Satan at the Cross at Calvary. When he died but three days later was raised to life by the power of God and is now alive at the Father's right hand, which he had been given authority over hell and death.

Note: Congregation, I reiterate, Christian believers have authority over the devil and demon forces in the air of the atmosphere and in the flesh of the world, only in the Name of Jesus.

Although Satan is a defeated "foe," He does not accept defeat in multitudes of individuals lives (people) because his presence in mankind is essential for his purpose of being who he is in the world. Which is to steal, kill, or destroy people livelihood.

Read John 10:10. "The thief comes only in order to steal, kill, and destroy, but Jesus says, "I have come in order that you might have life—life in all its fullness."

Recognizing Who Satan the Devil Is

Note: Congregation, never forget, Satan is a representative of two spirits, a spirit in the spiritual realm and a spirit person of a human being supernaturally in the physical realm a transitional change from spirit to a spirit person just as you and I are spirit persons.

Jesus rebuked Satan spirit in Peter. "You recall when Jesus spoke of His death, Peter rebuked him but Jesus rebuked Satan spirit which had entered Peter.

Read Mark 8:33. "Jesus turned around, looked at his disciples, and rebuked Peter, 'Get away from me Satan,' he said, 'Your thoughts don't come from God, but from human nature.'"

Note: In Jesus's reply, he spoke of Peter's "thoughts."

Jesus said, "Get away from me Satan, your "thoughts" don't come from God but from human nature.

Children of Jehovah God, Jesus knew Satan is a spirit person for he appeared in heaven in the presence of God. Jesus Christ said of him, "That one was a manslayer when he began and he did not stand just in the truth because the truth is not in him."

Jesus Christ knew this time and age without Him in our lives we are vulnerable of his attacks and Machinations also Jesus know that it is a person's mind and body Satan spirit use to vocalize to express (*speak*) to and work through humankind.

Therefore, it is essential that you (humankind) recognize Satan or demons approach, which is to listen for the manifestation of his (their) spirit which is in the articulation of the tongue while guarding the mind.

Which was Jesus's purpose, commanding Satan the Devil to get away from him.

Satan verbally manifest himself in spirit through Peter's mouth and tongue to oppose Jesus.

Note: Human eyes cannot visually see the devil as a natural being, spirit; however, mankind can visually see him as a person. A materialized or transformed human being but yet spirit. Which makes it imperative to listen for his approach through vocalization (articulation) of man's words, action and tongue which reveal the manifestation of his presence and spirit being.

Note: Church, Satan operation is effective in both spiritual and physical realms because the power of influence to control is through the flesh and in spirit.

Remember Peter, a Christian and Disciple of Jesus, he was caught in the flesh for a short period. When he denied and rebuked Jesus but Jesus recognized Peter fleshly condition.

On one occasion, Peter three times denied knowing Jesus and giving way to cursing of his denial on the other occasion Jesus recognize Peter fleshly condition and said, "Get away from me Satan, your 'thoughts' don't come from God, but from man, human nature, which confirms Satan the Devil is a spirit and a person (man)."

Note: Thereby Christians and believers, stand firm and stay alert against the attacks of the devil and demonic forces, wear the whole armor of God at all time.

Don't give into demonic influences nor perceptions that cause deception and remember Satan power to control is in "realm" of the "mind" and "how" we mankind perceive things.

Note: Without a human perception, Satan is powerless, thereby he has nothing to operate nor manipulate. No perception, no power. No power, no influences to control.

Note: Congregation, you must know when and how to recognize Satan spirit in yourselves which is stay vigilant and alert of what you speak and what you think because the power to control is in mankind perception where the tongue and mouth create action along with manifestation of Satan spirit which mean you must listen at all time for Satan spirit or demons approach in yourselves or others which is in a person's tongue and vocal and verbal expression.

Brothers and sisters, it's imperative to listen to yourself and your own words, articulations, and dialogues of that which you speak to know whether it's your own perception you speak or someone else's ("the devil or demonic") perception.

That's why it's imperative to guard the mind, listen to that which you speak and what others speak. Think before you speak. "Think."

Read James 1:19. "Remember this, my dear friends! Everyone must be quick to listen, but slow to speak and slow to become angry."

Note: Congregation, since you can't see neither, the devil or demons approach. You man must listen for their approach to see the manifestation of the spirit, the devil or demon or both, which is in a verbal or vocal expression in the tongue and mouth of people, humankind! Never forget that!

Amen.

The Holy Spirit Satan Waging War against the Holy Spirit Sermon and Message

Note: "Our Father which are in heaven, hallowed be thy name. Thy Kingdom come, thy will be done on Earth, as it is in heaven."

Children of God, God's will shall be done in us, through us, as it is done in heaven. God's will for all mankind bring to pass that which has been done in the spiritual heaven.

God's will for mankind is made known by the Spirit, but not the flesh, which I know without a doubt, "When I was part of the world, disobedience was constantly at work through the flesh of my heart."

Note: Being born again of the Spirit and not of the flesh. I truly say without any doubt, "Greater is He in me, than He that is within the world."

Read 1 John 4:4. "Ye are of God, little children and have overcome them, because greater is he that is in you, than he that is in the world."

Note: How do I know, "Greater is He in me, For the Bible, God's Word told me so, plus Jehovah God have shown me. "I'm Greater than he, the devil, Satan, he that is in the world and greater of those of the world, by the Power of God's Spirit, the Holy Spirit which dwell in my body which is the Temple of the Holy Spirit.

Read 1 Corinthians 6:19–20.

> Don't you know that your body is the temple of the Holy Spirit who lives in you and who was given to you by God? You do not belong to yourselves but to God.
>
> He bought you for a price. So, use your bodies for God's glory.

Note: Congregation of God, Satan at this very moment attacking the Holy Spirit. Satan only avenue of attacking God's Spirit is not in a physical manner but in a spiritual manner Internally and Externally against God's will for humankind of born-again believers.

Note: The devil is waging war against the Holy Spirit through the flesh of man, who hasn't any clue the devil's spirit is at work in himself, not only in the flesh, he has no control over but He that is in him, the Greater One, God's Spirit.

Note: The Holy Spirit in born-again believers is under attack Internally without the assist of man's knowledge.

The Holy Spirit is also God's free gift which he grants to those who sincerely seek and request it. A right Heart is the key factor of God's requirement of His free gift.

But Water and Spirit is the requirement of born-again believers, which all mankind must be born again of water and of the Spirit.

Flesh

Note: Children of Jehovah God, you should know flesh can't war against flesh which God created perfect from dust of the ground; however, Satan chose to war against the flesh while using simultaneously the flesh to war through against the Spirit of God in man.

Read Galatians 5:16–17. "For what our human nature wants is opposed to what the Spirit wants and what the Spirit wants is opposed to what our human nature wants. These two are enemies and this means that you cannot do what you want to do."

Note: It's an internal spiritual war being individually fought, Spirit against the flesh which the Holy Spirit serve as Helper which helps mankind to understand God will and purpose in their lives, that which the devil is against.

Satan told Jehovah God that he could cause mankind to curse him to His face which he fails to do.

Satan appeared to me as a transparent spirit whom I saw at the age of six; I didn't know it was the devil, who telepathically communicated with me—to tell me to curse God; however, I knew not to.

Note: I revealed my age because age is no exception in the devil's attacks against the "will and purpose" of God in human lives.

Read Job 2:4-5. "Satan replied, 'A person will give up everything in order to stay alive.' But now suppose you hurt his body; he will curse you to your face."

Note: The devil has a will and purpose of his own, to steal, kill, or destroy human lives by any means. He counteracts and oppose all God's wills and purposes against the human race by deception of deceiving the whole world.

Read Revelation 12:9. "The huge dragon was thrown out—that ancient serpent named the devil or Satan that deceived the whole world. He was thrown down to Earth and all his angels with him."

Note: He's a counterfeiter, a duplicator, and a deceiver; he appears at times as an angel of light, even after he told God he could cause man to curse Him to his face.

Satan has openly changed his once conceal strategy attacks against the flesh, he's now attacking the "works" of the Holy Spirit internally of man, using man and himself as spirit against God's will and purpose in human beings' lives.

This message of truth isn't preached in pulpits nor taught in seminaries by theologians because Satan possess power and ability which he uses to blind the physical eyes and mind of man to hinder or prevent mankind from performing the will and purpose of God in our lives.

Note: I was in the process of praying, when I received this Revelation internally the "works and strategy," which he has changed to prevent the will and purpose to not take place or come to pass, not only in our lives but throughout the entire Earth.

Note: Children of God, Jesus Christ tells us how to pray, the Lord's prayer of "God's will be done on Earth as is in heaven." Confirmation of God's will for all human beings has already been done or taken place in heaven," which shall now come to pass individually through us human beings of the Earth.

Note: Congregation, laymen, clergies, servants, pastors, ministers, theologians of all denominational seminaries, I, a servant of God, writes, "God's will and purpose" of this message of truth, did not come from any Earthly source but from above, if it had come from an Earthly source, Satan or demons would've prevent, stop, or hinder me of receiving and revealing this message of truth.

Note: The spirit realm of Satan and demon spirits are attacking and waging war internally against the Word of God throughout nations all around the world, which is global.

However, humankind can rely on the Holy Spirit as helper to bring to pass God's will, plan, and purpose prevent disobedient or rebellious living.

"However, sadly to say, the message of truth isn't being taught in seminaries nor told or preached in pulpits across the Earth."

Note: Believers and nonbelievers, there are Bible Scriptures throughout God's Word where Satan spirit is counteracting against the Word of God internally through the five-fold ministry of some apostles, prophets, evangelists, pastors, and teachers which are for edification of the Body of Christ, the Church.

"Satan is counteracting through the flesh, without one's knowledge!" As proof, read Matthew 16:21–23; Jesus speaks of his suffering and death.

> From that time on Jesus began to say plainly to his disciples, "I must go to Jerusalem and suffer much from the elders, the chief priests, and

the teachers of the Law. I will be put to death but three days later I will be raised to life."

Peter took him aside and began to rebuke him, "God forbid it, Lord!" he said, "That must never happen to you!"

Jesus turned around and said to Peter, "Get away from me, Satan! You are an obstacle in my way, because these thoughts of yours don't come from God, but from human nature."

Question: Was Satan present? Jesus spoke of him being present there among them. Where? In the spirit of a thought or perception of Peter which he spoke out of the flesh, which is evidence of Satan's control of the flesh or nature of human beings without their knowledge. Waging war internally against the Spirit of God through believers and against the Name, Jesus Christ of nonbelievers.

Note: Children of Jehovah God, believers and nonbelievers, we (you) can't see the devil's approach. You must listen for his approach through a person's spoken Words which his spirit manifest himself in and through the person's tongue!

Therefore, pay attention to the Spirit but also discern who is speaking to you and through whom.

"Discernment is one of the nine gifts of the spirits. He that is in you, a believer is greater than he that is within the world, and those of the world."

Note: Satan and demons sometimes addressed or called evil or wicked spirits of the Earth. They are real and alive without a body. We, humans are real and alive on the Earth with bodies.

However, some have set up residency in human bodies, performing internally. While expressing their action externally through whom they reside in or possess.

Note: We believers and churchgoers, often quote the Scripture.

Read 1 John 4:4. "But you belong to God, my children and have defeated the false prophets, because the Spirit who is in you is more powerful than the Spirit in those who belong to the world."

Note: Which is true, however Satan has now placed this Scripture on display of the hearts of believers while he challenges believers, quoting this Scripture verse, actually believe, "Greater is He in them, than he that is within the world. "The devil speaking of himself."

Congregation of God, the devil will test every person on the face of the Earth, beyond one's imagination and self-endurance quoting that Scripture. You shall be tested, whether a believer or nonbeliever, just quoting scripture.

Note: One must remember, he that is within the world, the physical and spiritual world can very well enter the mind in spirit to work or challenge or attack believers or nonbelievers in and through themselves.

Quoting the Bible verse 1 John 4:4, "Ye are of God, little children and have overcome them, because greater is he that is in you, than he that is in the world."

Note: "He that is in the world" is responsible for many who has "backslid" back into the world, even some "servants," males and females who was called into ministry.

Quoting this scripture verse is evidence, the entire world is being attack or being challenged in the spiritual realm, internally and externally of mankind.

I reiterate, all mankind shall be tested, whether a believer or nonbeliever, just quoting scripture.

Note: All children of God are under attack, age is not an exception. Man need not be provoked in a war he can't see because we aren't fighting against "flesh nor blood," which take place Internally of man as well as Externally which is a battle aren't physically seen; however, can be seen and heard spiritually with the ears, "Yes, the ears."

Note: Yes, children of God, we all possess the ability to see and hear the devil's spiritual works and actions right before you through your hearing.

"Satan, demons acknowledge their waging war against us can be seen and heard only through human ears and vision of the Holy Spirit."

All spiritual and physical action of the devil or demons can be seen and audibly heard in spirit, by way of human ears.

Humans can't literally see with the Ears, but can see spiritually with the ears, spiritual things, you cannot imagine of ever seeing visually with the eyes.

Note: Children and congregation of Jehovah God, He that is in us believers, the Holy Spirit, hasn't lost a battle nor spiritual war nor never will internally nor externally.

Every spiritual war that has been waged against the human race, internally and externally in the past, present or in the future has already been defeated but because of man lack of knowledge, some failed the test.

The devil and his household, demons of the Earth acknowledge they are defeated foes. I am a living witness and testimony of their defeat!"

Amen.

Satanic Dictator, Dictatorial, and Dictatorship

I

Note: These three dictator, dictatorial, and dictatorship are satanically control in the physical and spiritual world, which is beyond human comprehension which mean to have knowledge or the capacity to understand.

Dictator, an absolute ruler over people's lives. I was once a recipient and victim of the devil, Satan dictatorship and direction of how to live and follow his instructions and way of performing his will and purpose, which were to steal, kill, or destroy by any means.

The devil, Satan is a dictator in all human lives, he is the chief leader of all dictatorial and dictatorships throughout the Earth. Who speaks and govern by his Words through the flesh of the human race in the physical realm.

A person would be shocked to know of themselves in the percentage of the world's population living by the influence and dictatorship of the devil at work in and through them, "The One who deceives the whole world."

Satan's dictatorship lies in the minds of persons, even loved one's perceptions and the world also perceives in the mind as its own perception, which become persons will and purpose to perform as their own, which is the opposite and contrary of that of God's will and purpose in one's life.

Note: Children of Jehovah God, if only a person would take time to think, "Who is it in control of their thoughts, perception, mind, and actions and acknowledge?" What lies ahead in the future, the world and persons would not be in the condition it's in today.

Note: Satan's dictatorship is contrary to human beings eternal salvation. The physical world or realm is satanically influenced and controlled more than ever before in both area of human lives. Externally in the physical realm and internally in spirit of human bodies in the spiritual realm, which mean Satan is the Earth's greatest dictator of the world.

Note: We, human beings are up against two entities, that exist as a discrete united spirit, which operate and dictate through person's minds and bodies without their knowledge to perform it's will and purpose among the living.

Jesus tells us to pick up the Cross (life) and follow Him. Jesus is speaking to us through His Word today to all mankind.

Following Jesus, man can see that which the human heart and eyes can't see because a person sees that which is natural not that which is supernatural.

Congregation of God, yes, the spiritual world which we live is a world where spiritual events and phenomena occur. Where Satan's dictatorial over rule the lives of multitudes internally and externally.

Therefore, you (mankind) must listen to a person "words" which are spoken to recognize Satan's spirit presences. You (we) can't see his approach, you must listen for his spirit approach which is in the person "Words," "the manifestation of his spirit is in and through that person (mankind) tongue. Satan dictation is heard in that person mouth and tongue.

Note: Satan's dictatorial is throughout the entire world (land), which the world, the whole world is under dictatorship power of the devil but does not recognize nor realize being driven and control by an invisible satanical and demonic entities by a force beyond human ability to control or even comprehend.

Note: The thoughts of perceptions which the world (people) perceives are often that of the devil, Satan, the one who deceives the whole world.

Satan is the dictator of the whole world. Jesus spoke of and addressed the devil as a liar and the father of lies.

Read John 8:44. "From the very beginning he was a murderer and has never been on the side of truth because there is no truth in him. When he tells a lie, he is only doing what is natural to him because he is a liar and the father of all lies."

Satan's dictations are control and perceived as human perceptions of the mind to act and perform as their own.

Note: Jesus and the disciples were at supper. The devil had already put into the heart of Judas, the son of Simon Iscariot, the thought of betraying Jesus. Read John 13:2.

Congregation of Jehovah God, a dictator is an absolute ruler. Here mankind has an invisible Ruler, that Rule internally and externally over multitudes of human lives, without being seen nor acknowledge.

Some churches' congregations are under satanical dictatorial leadership without any knowledge, deceiving themselves and the world.

Note: Jesus spoke of the spirit world more than anything else while in the world. He spoke of the spirit adversaries who live among us, which we, mankind, face daily and will continue to face daily until Jesus's return.

Note: While on the Earth, Jesus and the Jews knew Satan was a spirit person that possess transitional power to transition unto a spirit person that could be seen and transition back to an invisible spirit person. That which he does today for any occasion.

Note: "I honestly say, Jehovah God is my witness. I have witnessed the devil's transitional change as a visible spirit person or human being and transition back to an invisible spirit being!"

Congregation, Satan walk's the Earth today as a Person, a human being. I believe others than myself have encounter him, exchanged word's without knowing who he was, nor whom he or she were in the company of.

Note: Whenever Satan appear as a person, a human being, not a person in all the Earth can identify him as the devil, nor Satan. It is totally impossible only God can open one's mind and eyes to identify this spirit adversary that walks daily among us as another person and dictator, deceiving the entire world in and through mankind.

Note: Congregation of God, it's imperative that this "truth" be heard, preached, and taught!"

Our government, local and world is being satanically attack like never before. The head of our government, the president of the United States is in spiritual warfare from both sides of the democracy. Men and women, Democrat and Republic, internally and externally is being used by the devil, Satan to dictate how to govern his invisible or unseen government, he has established inside the true government of the United States.

This satanic and demonic invisible force is attacking all the righteous leaders dictatorially to bring or cause destruction upon the human race. Jehovah God's people throughout the land, through all of whom his spirit is in control of, race, age, nor gender are no exception!

Note: Sisters and brothers, I praise and commend those who stand for true democracy and for not allowing the works of the devil to dictate his plans for the human race, God's people!

Note: Satan, satanic dictatorship starts at the highest level of any government. Note: If he can control the highest level or echelon of any government, he can and will control a nation of people, including Christians, which is his will and purpose to steal, kill, or destroy deceiving the entire world spiritually just by his spirit.

II

The Dictator

The World's Worst Enemy or Adversary

Note: Who are the Enemies of the entire world? Satan and his counterparts, Demon spirits. They are responsible of turning human beings against God and against one another. However, Jesus says, "Love Your Neighbor" as you love yourself!"

The Great Commandment

Read Matthew 22:39: "The second most important commandment is like it. Love your neighbor as you love yourself."

Jesus also says in retrospect

Read Matthew 10:34–36.

> Do not think I have come to bring peace to the world. No, I did not come to bring peace, but a sword.
> I came to set sons against their fathers, daughters against their mothers, daughters-in-law against their mothers-in-laws.

Note: Because, to quote, "Your worst enemies will be the members of your own family."

Note: "Including oneself, you, man or woman or herself a worst enemy as well!"

Note: God's people are up against two enmities, one in mankind and the other in the spiritual realm of Satan.

Jesus Christ says of him, Satan.

Read John 8:44. "From the very beginning he was a murderer and has never been on the side of truth because there is no truth in him. When he tells a lie, he is only doing what is natural to him because he is a liar and the father of all lies!"

The devil's first overt act was turning man away from God. He was a manslayer, he brought about the death of Adam and Eve which in turn brought sin and death to ("us") their off springs.

Read Romans 5:12. "Sin came into the world through one man, and his sin brought death with it. As a result, death has spread to the whole human race because everyone has sinned."

The question is, how can that be, everyone has sinned?

Note: Answer. As help in your understanding, think of what happens when a baker bakes bread in a pan that has a "dent" in it. A mark will show on all the bread that is baked in that pan.

Adam became like that pan and we are like the bread. He became imperfect when he broke God's law. It was as if he received a "dent" or a bad mark. So when he had children all of them ("us") received this same mark of sin or imperfection.

Note: The one becoming Satan, the dictator is a spirit person that no human being knows the identity of the one misleading the whole world. Only the name Satan can be identified by his actions which he brings men, women, and children without their knowledge under his dictatorial leadership and control.

Satan does this by way of the mind, a thought of perception perceived by individuals as their own human thoughts allowing the devil to dictate that which the person perceives as his or her own perception which manifest as his will and purpose through the person tongue and action.

Note: It is biblically confirmed Satan is a spirit person that has access spiritually to an individual mind and perception and his spirit ability to enter a human being.

Read Matthew 16:21–23.

> From that time on Jesus began to say plainly to his disciples, "I must go to Jerusalem and suffer much from the elders, the chief priests and the teachers of the Law. I will be put to death, but three days later I will be raised to life.
>
> Peter took him aside and began to rebuke him, "God forbid it Lord! He said, that must never happen to you!"
>
> Jesus turned around and said to Peter, "Get away from me Satan! You are an obstacle in my way, because these thoughts of yours don't come from God, but from human nature."

Also read Luke 22:3, Judas betrays Jesus: "Then Satan entered into Judas, called Iscariot, who was one of the twelve disciples."

Note III: Entering Human Bodies "Dictation"

Demon spirits, Satan's counterparts also enter person's bodies and possess as their own body and mind and dictate while living internally in a person life dictating how to live and think. All of which contrary to God's will and purpose for mankind. Demon spirits has the ability to speak, "articulate" through a person's body as their own!

Note: They also take control of a person's biological perception of being a different gender which cause a person to believe he or she is the opposite sex. While causing others to believe he or she is of both biological sex's which create in them to believe they are of both male and female gender, therefore, they can perform as either sex! No human being can make them believe anything different, man nor medication!"

Note: Children of God, it takes the Spirit of Jehovah God and the works of Jesus Christ's name to change or cure any and all persons under demonic bondage that believe He or She is the opposite sex or believe he or she is of both biological genders. They all are demoniacally control of the body and mind, other than their own natural spirit and mind!

Note: Children of God, I reiterate, it is biblically confirmed, Satan is a spirit person that possess spiritual access of an individual's mind of thoughts and his spirit the ability to enter a human body as it did Judas in the presences of Jesus.

Note: The devil, Satan spiritual capabilities on the Earth is beyond human comprehension. The Bible tells us,

Read Matthew 26:41. "Keep watch and pray that you will not fall into temptation, 'The spirit is willing, but the flesh is weak.'"

Note: Dictatorial dictatorship through Satan human representatives is how the evil one govern his government on the Earth, which no human has come to the "knowledge" of nor spoke out against, which I believe is in fear of the evil one retaliation!

Satan's Spiritual Manifesto of Order and Rank

There is invisible realm at work among this nation government and government throughout the four corners of the Earth. There is a chain of command in spiritual order and rank which Satan is in control.

Satan employ thousands and thousands of demon spirits that administer to him throughout the world. They are demon agents, evil spirits that are alive in spiritual force. Their assignments and levels of responsibilities is to control this nation and governments the world over though humankind.

Satan spiritual government and foremost power and authorities exist in all levels of governments. It is his manifesto of order and rank which mean both government of all levels are in similar echelons according to their governmental assignments.

Unfortunate mankind governments throughout the Earth does not recognize nor acknowledge an invisible demonic spirit force at his side performing in opposition against his government.

Which mean the Earth governments are in spiritual warfare, a conspiracy spiritual warfare which the devil strategically controls throughout the Earth in spiritual order and rank of position.

The devil's ranks of demons are positioned in the highest levels of governments strategically place to oppose all government personnel. The Bible reveals that there are invisible governments that are good as established by God as well as those that are wicked established by Satan, control by demons.

Which mean we aren't fighting against people in high principalities but evil and wicked spirits persons not made of flesh and blood. Demons sometimes called fallen angels possessing superhuman power in and out of the body because they possess the ability to enter into human to instill great power and influence over the mind and lives of people.

They are responsible for wrong human conduct in our nation's government. There isn't any government affairs Satan or demons does not intervene in. His government is set up to oppose and destroy the integrity of humanity.

Hence, his government and headquarters are strategically located and housed inside our nation government. The purpose of his insidious governmental demonic activities is to turn people or a nation away from God morally way of life and to steal, kill, and destroy human values by any means possible.

Demonic influences in human affairs are more prevalent in this nation than ever before and is escalating at an alarming pace. The writing is on the wall. All nations are in spiritual warfare.

There are two echelons of demons, a high and lower echelon. The responsibilities of the higher echelon are governmental issues and lower echelon dwell in societies of the secular movement and worldly affairs of human issues and morals.

Also, the lower echelon is responsible for human conflicts with the world gender and adverse societies. Thus, demons have their own jurisdictions and are territorial among people of adverse societies which they respond to higher echelon demons of higher principalities that are established throughout the Earth.

People, there isn't a house nor home demons does not occupy. The lower echelon of the demons are in public schools and places and in homes in the atmosphere or in the body of the residency or both. They are there as an observant of everything and to exhibit evil and wicked advice.

That's why it is imperative that this nation focus on the devil and spirit realm existence, it's power, influence, spiritual designs, and method of operation so it can fight spiritual foes with spiritual weapons that God provide "The Word of God" and not with monetary weapons.

People in general should focus on the spirit realm instead of things that are visible. I've been in spiritual warfare my entire life; however, I did not realize because my eyes and mind was fixed on things which are seen and not on the unseen where spiritual development exist. It is the unseen that bring condemnation into the nation and world.

I've been victimized and demon-possessed, but now my mind and eyes are fix on the invisible things. I recognize demonic influences and demonic activity in people. I recognize demonic activity in government and system of things. I recognize demonic influences in all ages of the general population and societies that has formed their own demonize demonically control societies and municipalities.

I've witnessed demonic activity in the atmosphere of homes, public schools and places, sanctuaries, and throughout the streets of this nation. I reiterate, spiritual warfare does not discriminate against age or gender. We are all in some kind of spirit war.

Why can't the government recognize we are in spiritual warfare? Why can't they realize we are under a spiritual attack and that it is our own self-government that Satan's spiritual government is using through mankind against ourselves as an opposing spiritual force.

The spirit realm is real and alive; however, only a small percentage of mankind recognize it and those that do are fearful of exposing Satan because of political reasons. That's why mankind must focus on the unseen things rather than the seen.

Believe me, we are in spiritual war with ourselves and with the government. Demon spirits are opposing us, in us, through us, and against us through the spirit realm. Even though man is appointed to govern world affairs the devil's government and spiritual forces are disguised masquerading as politicians in the carnality of mankind performing as both governments spiritually and physically.

The manifestation of the devil's spiritual order and rank are in both governments in which many politicians are demon-possessed, demonize or under demonic influences. All of which are partakers of the spirit realm and spiritual warfare.

Satan's insidious plan is to take us out collectively or individually by any means possible. Their objective is to steal, kill, and destroy human morals through our government. He disguises himself, his real nature and purpose by performing through mankind. All demonic nature is manifest by proxy through the carnality of humankind.

However, man has the mind to see the visible effects of the spirit realm before it's manifestation. If he focuses on things aren't seen rather on things that are seen. The mind is the spiritual realm headquarters; therefore, man must focus on both physical and spiritual things.

Because there are evil and wicked spirits disguised as humans masquerading in the flesh as humans. Demon spirits are in the Earth's atmosphere as well observing their own wickedness being perform by humankind.

They know backsliders as well as hypocrites, evil doers whom the spirit realm is in control of. People, it isn't anything the spiritual realm does not see or know about (us) you. It is man whom the spirit realm uses the continuation of oppositions toward God and governments.

Spiritual government has advantage over the world's physical governments because the world's inability to see into the spirit realm. The world does not realize mankind cannot see into the spirit realm nor it's government with the eyes, it takes the mind, a mind that is spiritual train and motivated by the "Word" of God that no weapon will not form against.

The only time the world sees the spiritual effects of the devil's governmental operations are after the manifestation becomes a reality in human lives and livelihood. That's why it is imperative for mankind to focus on things not seen rather on things are seen. What I'm saying the devil and demons, wicked spirits have a role in everything our government says or does.

I would like to know what percentage of this nation government officials know Satan's power is in political arena. Satan know wherever his power exists, his government exist as well. That mean demonically control individuals are serving in all levels of world's government. Which mean the devil along with the fallen angels, demons are everywhere and every place. Now what percentage of government officials will acknowledge the truth and conform to it?

People, it isn't a game. We are at war with the spirit world. Mankind of all levels of life are in spiritual combat with the devil and wicked spirits. And if man does not believe he's in spiritual warfare; therefore, he does not realize the devil control the world system of things and not mankind nor this political position.

Man thinks he's in control but in spiritual reality the spirit realm is controlling the world system of things through man. However, God Almighty is still in control of the Earth but man must let God be God over world affairs though himself and not the devil.

I would like to know what percentage of the world population acknowledge we are in spiritual warfare? A small percentage because a vast multitude does not believe there's a devil roaming the Earth along with millions of demon spirits in the Earth atmosphere and dwelling in human bodies of the demon-possessed and those in the atmosphere are waiting for the right moment and opportunity to enter human bodies which thousands have already entered the bodies of the human race. Age nor gender is no exception. We're all vulnerable to demon possession.

Therefore, the Bible says we are to wear the "whole armor of God," which is the "Word" of God. The devil is out to destroy our Christian nation and heritage in which he is utilizing government resources as strongholds in an effort to bring condemnation upon the Earth, which he is doing.

People we have invisible enemies out seeking whom to destroy. We must wear the "whole armor of God" everywhere, so we can stand against the devil's strongholds. The Lord know where he isn't welcome or his name not allowed, Satan and demonic activity exist.

Satan and demons know where God Almighty aren't recognized and the Name Jesus Christ is abolished. He is in power and control, and wherever his power exists, his spiritual government is in control.

Now how many governments and judicial courts of law acknowledge Satan's power in their office.

I wrote a letter to the highest court of authority of our government, "The United States Supreme Court."

I stated, "The Lord says let my people pray!" in public schools and places throughout the nation and the Earth. Prayer is a spiritual language to communicate with God and a spiritual weapon that essential in all lives to combat the spiritual realm insidious plan against the human race throughout the Earth.

SHAKE HANDS WITH THE DEVIL

All humankind must know who Lucifer and demons are but unfortunately, we don't. Friend, Lucifer is the devil's original name in and now on the Earth as well. However, his Earthly name became Satan the Devil.

The Bible reveals that Satan was once a powerful cherub angelic of high rank called Lucifer, the light-bearer. He became perverted, wrapped up in his own power and beauty. In an outburst of envy and jealousy, he led one third of the angels (God's spiritual sons) in a rebellion against the authority of God. The rebellion was repulsed, and Lucifer became Satan the Devil ("the adversary of God") and his angelic cohorts became demons.

They all became persons without bodies and not made of flesh and blood. Yet they are spirits beings that manifest their spirit in and through the body of humankind by demon possession, age is no exception, all humans are vulnerable of demon possession.

Their power and strength are in the influence and manifestation of their spirit in whom they use to represent their spirit being. Lucifer isn't a common name in today society because such name represents God's adversary. However, multitudes possess his credentials which is to steal, kill, and destroy everything God stands for.

And it's imperative that it be known, an adversary of God is an adversary of humankind. However, man does represent his spirit but not all mankind approves of being named or called Lucifer because it acknowledges the presence of the devil or the manifestation of his spirit in society.

But it isn't man who choose to represent or manifest his spirit being but the devil himself that does these things. I should know, I was a representative for over forty years and during those years, I was demon-possessed and under the power and influence of his spirit.

However, I did not discover until after God cured me of demon possession that I had served as representative of Satan spirit and the spirit realm without acknowledging who I was. In reality, people over the years shook hands literally with Satan's spirit through me, and I've shook hands with him in the flesh of mankind.

I also discovered people indulge in dialogues daily with the spirit Satan and demons as well but does not recognize their human attribute. People, the devil and demons make themselves present in our everyday lives. There isn't anything you nor mankind does without their presence.

Which mean Satan can and does manifest through anyone as an angel of light that dwells in the dark to accomplish evil and wickedness. All mankind is vulnerable to become representatives of his manifestation, which there aren't no exceptions.

However, it's imperative to know the devil's spirit is powerless without the aid of humankind. He knows as well as his agents, demons without the aid of human bodies they are powerless against humankind. Human beings are their source of power.

Thereby, they display their spirit being by manifesting through the flesh of mankind to perform. Which mean on any given day you can shake hands with the devil or a demon spirit manifest as a person, any person.

In family members, friends, relatives and associates, church members and in some clergies, people ordained for religious service and those claims to be men of God. I've shook hands with the devil and demons in sheep clothing, people pretending to be Christians which they weren't.

When I was in the world, I served the devil and demons, I did not attempt to serve both God and Satan while serving the spirit realm.

The devil and demons have many Earthly disguises which wolves in sheep clothing are some of them and they are all in the body of mankind. They are here to deceive the world which they are doing in the form of persons.

You never have to look nor search for them because they aren't never far from you. Matter of fact, their spirit dwells in you disguise as a person, you and the fact are they are persons without bodies that use human beings' bodies to manifest through.

The devil and demons are two and operate as two. First, they are evil spirits beings and secondly, they are persons without bodies that use bodies of mankind to materialize as persons to manifest their spirit to operate in and throughout the world.

In reality, the devil and demons are persons and are disguise as persons which they perform as persons. Thereby, the next time you shake someone's hand you could very well be shaking hands with the devil or a demon spirit in disguise.

There isn't no respectful person that represent the spirit realm as the devil or demons. Everyone is vulnerable sometime in their life to be use as flesh for their spirit being without acknowledging his or her involvement.

Thereby, as I've stated earlier Lucifer, the devil and demons are spirit being's persons without bodies which all their attributes are in the flesh of humankind whom they use so successfully to perform through.

As I've said, Man never has to look nor search for Satan nor demons. They are in the midst of us disguise in the flesh of mankind and in the Earth's atmosphere waiting precariously on the will of mankind.

The spirit realm depends on the will and favor of the human race. That's why and how the devil and demons are so successful in the physical realm. Their success is contributed to their human attributes which are difficult to detect.

But if you, mankind would listen you can hear the devil or demons' approach in man's words spoken in the mouth and see the manifestation of their spirit by way of man's tongue. People, it's imperative that you listen for their approach. You can always hear their approach in man's words and speech.

He nor demons can't deceive you if you listen for their approach. You can always hear the devil's approach in man's mouth. Their presences are heard in Man's mouth. Therefore, don't let man's physical appearance mislead or fool you because of his or her articulation.

Satan and demons are great articulators. Their deception is in the mouth of humankind throughout the four corners of the world, age is no exception. They will use the body of a toddler as well as an adult to speak and operate through. I reiterate, there aren't no exceptions.

People, we live in the midst of a spirit world, surround by evil spirits. Therefore, the awareness of their presence needs to be more vocal and made known their existence throughout the world.

It is imperative that mankind know that Satan spirit exist as a spirit in the atmosphere and in human bodies as a person as well as demon spirits exist as persons without bodies, but all possess human characteristics.

Demons are agents of Satan and Satan is the chief adversary of God. Scripture indicate that the creature known as Satan did not always have that name. It was given to him because of his taking a course of opposition and resistance to God.

Satan has many different names and descriptions; however, they do not confuse his character but serve to identify him as the source of all aspects of evil. He was a murderer from the beginning and does not stand in the truth because there is no truth in him. When he lies, he speaks according to his own nature for he is a liar and the father of lies.

By way of his spirit, he does all these things through the flesh of mankind and the world. Friend, there aren't no respectful person the devil's spirit use to manifest his presence. All mankind is vulnerable to represent him or a demon in spirit as a person in one's lifetime.

I confirm this truth and their presence in my body and mind. I heard demonic voices in my head. I've actually heard dialogues or conversations in my head for over thirty years. Now after God cured me of demon possession (alcohol demons) the voices left which I've not heard voices since.

However, occasionally, I hear my name called out in the atmosphere. Oh yes, Satan and demons know us by name that which they speak in their own language. Therefore, do not be surprise when the devil or demons manifest their spirit being to you in the spirit or in the flesh or body mankind.

To shake hands with the devil and demons are not mystery. Demon spirits has been in spiritual and physical contact with mankind ever since demons inhabited the Earth. Demons does not need to be in the body of humankind for man to have physical or spiritual contact or communication with.

Let no one fool you to shake hand with the devil and demons is common throughout the Earth. In homes, sanctuaries, schools, offices and wherever you travel; you will spiritual and physical contact persons that are representatives of his spirit being. Wherever mankind exists, the devil or demons or both are in the midst of them in the atmosphere, in spirit; or in the flesh or body. There isn't any place on Earth that the devil's spirit or the spirit of his agent's, demons does not exist, no place.

And yes, the spirit of the devil or a demon can shake hands through you, there aren't no exception in the spirit realm. We are all vulnerable at all times. I was a servant of the spirit realm well over forty years. the devil's spirit leads me into places I would not have gone into had I been in my right mind. This occurred daily for over forty years without any knowledge, I was living in the midst of a spirit realm.

There are multitudes living as servants of this spirit being, control by demons, evil spirits and does not realize it. Thereby, when you shake hands with the spirit of the devil or a demon spirit you don't know whether you are shaking hands with him or through him or whether he's shaking your hand or both.

I'm a living witness of a hand shake with the devil and demon spirits as well as family members. I've encountered Satan and demons in members of my family. I've drunk and indulged in dialogues with the devil and demons in family members. However, at the time I did not recognize nor realize I was in the midst of a spirit realm in disguise and neither did they.

My friend, alcohol demons possessed several members of my family, myself, and many relatives without their knowledge. In which several family members and relatives died as the result of alcohol abuse.

But by the grace and mercy of God, I was cured of alcohol demons as well as demon possession of over forty years. Which means, I and some family members were representatives of the spirit realm. Therefore, I truly say a vast number of people have shaken hands with the devil's spirit but did not realize it.

Oh yes, even in children (age no exception) in which they display hand signals or signs as do members of gangs does to each other. This is the devil and demon spiritual signs of identifying their territorial ground.

Demons are territorial; they like to be identified with their territorial ground or jurisdiction by hand signals and signs. Which they will kill to protect their territory. You hear more people are killed in some areas than others, that's because demon spirit by way mankind protect their territorial ground by hand signals or hand signs.

It's imperative to know any person in agreement with the spirit realm whether it be a family member, or a gang member can spiritually and physically communicate with Satan and demon spirits in the atmosphere and in the body humankind.

I have physical contact with the spirit realm or I can say is that the spirit realm made physical contact with me. It was a period in my life that physical contact was so frequent I thought demons were literally trying to drive me out of my home. Once, I thought they wanted to communicate with me to be in agreement with the spirit world to prevent me from exposing these revelations.

People, I've witnessed and still witnessing, things in the spirit realm beyond humankind imagination. Some of these things man would only see in the movies, some of the things I've seen in the spirit realm had it not been for the Holy Spirit "He that dwells in me and is greater than he that is in the world." I could not have faced the spirit realm and remain sane in my right mind.

I've stood face-to-face with demon spirits in the midst of my home. I've been physically abused. I've been slapped several times, physically punched on, and struck by demon spirts in midst of the atmosphere. What I've reveal to you, the Holy Spirit is my witness.

I've witnessed some awesome sights and supernatural happenings in the spirit world. I saw Satan the Devil whom I witness through the vision of the Holy Spirit at the age of six which at that time he telepathically communicated with me and command me to curse God. I did not know any better, but the Holy Spirit led me not to.

Even though I once was the devil advocate and representative, whom I represented well but he was trying to kill or eliminate me since the age of six and he is trying to eliminate you. Although most people have some form of belief in God, many find it much harder to believe that there is a devil.

That is exactly what the devil wants. If he can be thought of as a figment of our imagination. A bygone fantasy of medieval superstition, he has the perfect disguise to perform his role of adversary of God and enemy of mankind.

Do you think I am overstating Satan or demons? The devil has penetrated human hearts everywhere. In your heart, and in mine, the devil is contending with Christ. The devil is at work in the midst of everything we do. The devil is at work and has not yet been completely conquered nor defeated in all lives.

Satan is wily, cunning, and deceitful. He works deceitfully, quietly, and insidiously. He knows how to arouse man's curiosity and he can play on mankind insecurities and fears. Satan's devises are people which I myself was use as a devise.

Now you know to shake hands with the devil is no mystery. We've been in spiritual and physical contact with the devil and demons all our lives. Even as I write these revelations, I'm in the presence of demon spirits in the midst of my home; however, the Holy Spirit have told me "not to be afraid."

However, there were times I was frighten until I discovered "greater is He in me than he that is in the world and in the midst of the Earth's atmosphere." Thereby, Jesus Christ conquered all fear for me in the spirit realm.

It was by way of Jesus Christ that I defeated sin in my life, the devil, demons in the flesh of the living and in the Earth's atmosphere. I have authority over the spirit realm in the Name of Jesus and I've displayed it over Satan and demon spirits in the atmosphere and in the body of mankind. And yes, I still shake hands with the devil's spirit and demons.

It is imperative that the world realize humankind are the spirit realm representatives. The only way to shake the hand of the devil is through humankind. Humankind are Satan and demons power source throughout the world and universe.

So do not expect to see horns on a person's head nor a folktale on a person's body. Mankind must listen for their approach in man's words with the manifestation of their spirit being is in man's tongue.

Jesus said of him, "That one was a manslayer and did not stand fast in the truth, because truth is not in him." Jesus also said, "The ruler of the world is coming, and he has no hold on me." Therefore, all mankind need Jesus Christ as Lord and Savior over our lives.

I'm so thankful through God's Word, we Christians and believers are enlightened to realize Satan and demons' existence, their power in mankind their design devices disguises and purpose of their operations so that we can fight these spiritual foes with the spiritual weapons God provides that is to wear the "whole armor of God" His Word.

Amen.

What the World Is up Against Sermon and Message

I

I, a servant of God know who Satan the Devil is of both worlds the physical world and the spirit world. My knowledge didn't come from any human source it was reveal to me. Jehovah God gave me revelation of who and what Satan look like upon the Earth in spirit and as a spirit person appearing as a human being, a person just as you and I.

Note: Since I know who Satan is and what he looks like or appear as, I honestly believe I'll have more encounters with him in person and more personal conflicts with him in public since the public know not what to look for; however, I do.

God is my witness and the revealer; therefore, I know him as he walks the Earth among us deceiving the entire whole world as a real person but not a human on the Earth can recognize Satan or devil without Jehovah God revelation unto you to witness his presence among the human race.

Satan has showed and demonstrated his power of influence over the human race of how his unseen spirit perform while dictating that which he wants an individual to perform or speak his spirit inspired perception with only a thought.

His unseen or invisible spirit can prompt anyone at anytime, anywhere throughout the land with only a thought to act and perform evilness and wickedness against persons and their neighbors. Therefore, the devil is classified as being wicked.

Satan acknowledge multitudes does not take his existence seriously nor believe of his presences on the Earth. He walks and talks among us, mankind daily acknowledging he is not recognized as "the huge dragon that was thrown out of heaven, that ancient serpent, named the devil or Satan that deceives the whole world. Children of God, the Bible tells us he was thrown down to Earth and all his angels with him.

Which he is at this very moment performing that which his name represents, he and the other one-third angelic beings or sons of God, who has now become demon spirits of the Earth along with their chief Satan the Devil.

Note: Since I'm no longer of the world any longer, I know from experience what the world think of the devil and demon spirits. The world (people) doesn't take the world seriously. The world doesn't have time to think of the devil nor demon spirits, the very ones here to steal, kill, and destroy them by any means, they are here to harm, using the human race as their shields while they perform their evil, wicked and murderous acts in and through the very ones that says or does not believe in the existence of Satan the Devil or demons.

Questions have been and are still being asked, "Why God allow Satan to perform and do the things he does without mankind knowledge.

Note: Children of Jehovah God, Jesus Christ has showed the world. Jesus has told us the world who Satan is, Satan himself has given us, the world his location as being on the Earth and in the world among us.

When asked by God, "What have you been doing?" Satan told God, because he could not lie to the Creator, Satan answered, "I have been walking here and there roaming around the Earth."

Read Job 1:7. "Satan himself told us, mankind from his mouth who he is amongst us and his inspired intentions are whom he can devour. Scripture warns us or make aware in advance of actual; of potential harm, danger or evil."

Read 1 Peter 5:8. "Be alert, be on watch! Your enemy, the devil, roams around like a roaring lion looking for someone to devour."

Note: Why are man (you) complaining? Read the Bible, the Holy Bible. God's Word and the Gospels of Jesus Christ tells us Satan is a person just as you who ask the question. "Why does God allow the devil perform to do the things he does without mankind knowledge?

Ask yourself, Why aren't I in the Word reading the Word of God? Any question pertaining to the devil, Satan are there written and spelled out for the human race to read for themselves. Any question concerning the devil or demons, the answers are there in the Holy Bible, "any questions."

II

Note: The children of Jehovah God and the children of the devil, it's imperative to know there is an eternal place which has been prepared for the devil and the fallen angels who has become demons of the Earth and those, persons of the Earth that follow them.

Read Matthew 25:41. "Then he will say to those on his left. Away from me, you that are under God's curse! Away to the eternal fire which has been prepared for the devil and his angels!"

Revelations: Questions and answers for nonbelievers

Question 1: What are demon spirits and Satan purpose and function in the Earth?

Answer: Demon spirits are one-third fallen angelic sons of Jehovah who conspired with the cherub, another angelic son of God of high rank who was cast out of heaven down to Earth. The fallen angels became demons or evil spirit in the Earth along with once light-bearer, who became Satan the Devil their purpose is to follow and obey orders of their chief, the devil and to bring humankind, people under their power of influence and control by entering them (human bodies) to perform evil and wicked works through their own spirit to bring condemnation upon all human beings. Scriptures says in Luke 8:1–2.

> Jesus travel through towns and villages preaching the Good News about the Kingdom of God. The twelve disciples went with him.
> And so did some women who had been healed of evil spirits and diseases. "Mary, who was called Magdalene from whom seven demons had been driven out.

Note: Children of God, demons cannot enter human bodies under their own power; however, individuals have invited demon spirits to enter to possess and control them at their commands and inspired actions.

But to enter human beings, Satan, their chief must create desires, accesses, or avenues, which he does by spirit creating habits which control the mind and body which was placed there by Satan for various reasons.

Read Luke 4:33–35.

> In the synagogue (place of worship) was a man who had the spirit of an evil demon in him, he screamed out in a loud voice.
> "Oh" What do you want with us Jesus of Nazareth? Are you here to destroy us? (There was more of them.) I know who you are. You are God's Holy Messenger!
> Jesus order the spirit, be quiet and come out of the man. The demon threw the man down in front of them and went out of him without doing him any harm.

Question 2: What are demon spirits purpose of entering people?

Answer: To bring human beings under their power and demonic influence to do evil and wicked works against Jehovah God and the Word of God and deny Jesus Christ and the Gospel of Christ.

Question 3: How does demon spirit enter people?

Answer: Basically, through Satan's techniques and creatorship of habits. Habits of a person is basically avenues of entering all kinds of evil and wicked controlling spirits.

Note: Children, congregation, believers and nonbelievers of God. Satan and demonic spirits are real and alive! Don't ever forget there is a live demonic force we are contending against (fighting) against us.

Note: I reiterate, children of God, a demon spirit cannot enter a person or human body under its own power. It takes the spirit of Satan, even though Satan is a defeated foe, it is his craftiness which he uses to create accesses such as habits as avenues in people which allows these controlling evil spirits to enter a person.

However, there are people who has given demonic spirits permission to enter through the power of Satan to control their life and commit evil and wicked acts in and through them.

Note: Satan, creates avenues to access habits of all kinds, that allow demonic spirits of all kind to enter into persons minds and bodies which is termed demon possession or oppression. Which literally translate an evil spirit or spirits has totally control of mind and body of a human being.

Once an evil spirit or demon enter a person, it takes a believer to cast it out in the Name of Jesus Christ. The person that's being deliver or set free of demon possession or oppression, need not be a believer nor Christian. Believe me, congregation, the spirit world knows whether you are neither.

After a spirit or spirits enter a person, he or she become influenced and controlled of the mind perception, a thought of the spirit's power at which time the demonized person(s) is controlled with false personalities and habits beyond their control which Satan has created and crafted in person(s) (people) as their own.

Satan nor demons does not discriminate against age, race nor gender. Observe, you'll see their performance all around you and throughout the land among same-sex marriages, homosexuals, lesbianism, bisexuals, those that prefer both men and women as sex partners. There are many other abominations and vile destructive alternate lifestyle living.

Question 4: Where does demon spirits habituate?

Answer: They dwell throughout the land and the Earth atmosphere and human bodies all around us and constantly in search of human bodies to enter by the power of Satan.

Evil spirits, demons are more effective internally of human bodies, than they are throughout the Earth atmosphere; however, they do masquerade in the atmosphere as spirits of deceased loved ones but they need to be in a physical human body to be effective on the Earth against God's people and the Word of God.

Scripture says you have eyes, can't see? You have ears—can't not you hear? Congregation, you must possess the Spirit of God, the Holy Spirit to see that which the Scripture says, "You can't see nor hear. You must abide in the Word and the Word abides in you, in Spirit. In the Spirit, you can see and hear all things."

Note: The Return of Evil Spirits

Read Luke 11:24–26.

> When an evil spirit goes out of a person, it travel's over dry country looking for a place to rest. If it can't find one it says to itself, I will go back to my house (the human body).
>
> So it goes back and find the house clean and all fixed up.
>
> Then it goes out and bring seven other spirits even worse than itself and they come and live there "IN THE PERSON," so when it is all over, that person is in worse shape than at the beginning.

Congregation, this is currently happening to people of this day and age! There is more "evil" in the world today as never before!

Children of God, Scripture clearly state and confirm where demon spirits dwell and habituate; however, mankind must possess spiritual insight and knowledge to comprehend their invisible presence even in one's self.

Scripture also inform us, mankind,

Read 1 John 4:4. "He that is in us is greater than he that is in the world."

Which is true but not all children of God is in the Word and neither the "Word" is in all mankind. Which mean man (you) must possess the Spirit of God in him or herself to be greater than he (the devil) that is in the world.

Question 5: How does a person know or whether he or she or a loved one or anyone is demonized or living under demonic oppression or demonic influences?

Answer: A demonized person can't or won't distinguish right and wrong or normal (good) or abnormal (evil), thy both perceived intellectually the same perception.

While some demonized persons appear to be emotionally disturbed. Which they are yet believe as though he or she is normal in all respect even after performing acts out of the norm or the natural realm.

Note: In today's world, the natural or physical realm, the acts of possession performing "good deeds" and "evil" are accepted as the same in individuals lives as being good is accepted of being evil, yet still good, and being evil is accepted as being good but yet still evil.

This is today's world, people performing out of the norm while acting under demonic possession or oppression or demonic influences.

Yet the world (people) does not recognize we live in a demonic realm. Where demonic activity is prevalent throughout the Earth.

Therefore, any person without Jesus Christ as Lord and Savior over their lives becomes vulnerable of becoming a victim of Satan demonic guest.

Congregation, I can't stress strong enough the realization of evil spirits, demons in our midst and in persons whom we interact daily with and those whom we transact business with.

Scriptures warns us we aren't fighting against flesh and blood which explain demons are persons without bodies, evil spirit that are superhuman intelligent and intellectually adapted to the world system of things. "Demons are wicked and powerful."

Note: Children of God, at all times, wear the whole armor of God.

Read Ephesians 6:10–18.

> For we are not fighting against human beings (flesh and blood) but against the wicked spiritual forces in the heavenly world, the rulers, authorities and cosmic powers of this dark age.
>
> At all times carry faith as a shield for with it you will be able to put out all the burning arrows shot by the Evil One.
>
> Do all this in prayer always asking for God's help. Pray on every occasion, as the Spirit leads.

Note: Here are some of their physical and camouflaged appearances, which we mankind represent.

Read Luke 6:18: "They, 'People' had come to hear him [Jesus] and to be healed of their diseases. Those who were trouble by evil spirits also came and were healed."

Also, read Luke 9:37–42:

> A man shouted from the crowd, "Teacher, I beg you look at my son, my only son.
>
> A spirit attacks him with a sudden shout and throws him into a fit, so that he foams at the mouth. It keeps on hurting him and will hardly let him go.
>
> "Jesus said to the man, bring your son here."

> As the boy was coming, the demon knocked him to the ground and threw him into a fit. Jesus gave a command to the evil spirit, healed the boy and gave him back to his father.

Note: Congregation and children of God, today there's multitudes of people in condition as that child, young and elderly alike but unaware of their condition.

Question 6: Does Satan possess control over demon spirits?

Answer: "Yes. The devil is the Chief and Leader of fallen angels who became demons or evil spirits on the Earth. Which you'll find in a number of scriptures.

Read John 12:31. "Now is the time for the world to be judge. Now the ruler of this world will be overthrown."

Also, read Revelation 12:9. "The huge dragon was thrown out, that ancient serpent named the devil or Satan that deceived the whole world. He was thrown down to Earth and all his angels with him."

Note: "He is the king or the prince of the evil world in which we live in this day."

Question 7: Do demons or evil spirits speak audibly?

Answer: "Yes." Demons speak and communicate in their own language in their natural habituate which is in spirit and also through the articulation of human beings.

I've personally heard demonic voices of several occasions called out of the midst my name in the spiritual realm or out of the atmosphere.

Demon Spirits also speak in their physical habituate through the articulation of the human race throughout the Earth!

Here are some examples of evil spirits speaking through their physical habituate articulating through the body of a person.

Read Acts 19:13–16. "Seven brothers who were the sons of a Jewish High Priest named Sceva, were doing this, casing out spirits. But the evil spirit said to them, I know Jesus and I know about Paul, but you, who are you?"

Note: The evil, a demon spoke audibly through a human body, a person whom it had entered.

Question 8: How demons or evil spirits communicate in the world?

Answer: When a spirit speaks out or communicate in spirit or in public places; facilities or sanctuaries, the spirit speaks similar to us as we speak in a human voice.

Note: Jesus heals a man with evil spirits. Read Mark 5:1–20.

> As soon as Jesus got out of the boat, he was met by a man who came out of the burial caves there. This man had an evil spirit in him
>
> He was some distance away when he saw Jesus, so he run, fell on his knees before him.
>
> And screamed in a loud voice, "Jesus Son of the Most High God. What do you want with me? For God's sake, I beg you don't punish me!
>
> He said this because Jesus was saying, "Evil spirit come out of this man.
>
> So the spirits begged Jesus, "Send us to the pigs, and let us go into them."
>
> He let them go, and the evil spirits went out of the man and entered the pigs.
>
> As Jesus was getting into the boat, the man who had the demons begged him, "let me go with you."

Also read Luke 4:34.

Note: A man with an evil spirit speaks out in the sanctuary.

Read Luke 4:34. "Oh, what do you want with us Jesus of Nazareth? Are you here to destroy us? There's more than one evil spirit in the sanctuary! I know who you are, you are God's Holy Messenger!"

"Jesus ordered the spirit, 'Be quiet and came out of the man! The demon threw the man down in front of them and went out of him without doing him any harm'" (v. 35).

"Congregation, the demonic realm know and acknowledge Jesus!"

Question 9: Can a Christian become or act under demonic influences?

Answer: "Yes." A negative thought or perception is subject of being demonic. The Apostle Peter confirms a Christian or a Follower of Jesus Christ are subject to speak under demonic influences.

Note: Jesus speaks of his suffering and death.
Read Mark 8:31–33.

> Then Jesus began to teach his disciples, "The Son of Man must suffer much and be rejected by the elders, the chief priest and the teachers of the Law. He will be put to death but three days later he will rise to life."
>
> He [Jesus] made this very clear to them. So Peter took him aside and began to rebuked him.
>
> But Jesus turned around, looked at his disciples and rebuked Peter, "Get away from Me, Satan," he said, "your thoughts don't come from God, but from human nature."

Note II: Questions, answers and messages. Habits = habits are created. Avenues and accesses for Satan to use to enter demoniacally control demon spirits. Which are real and alive into human bodies to inhabit and reside in and control.

Question 1: What and Why does people possess especially detrimental habits?

Initially, first and foremost, a habit is an established disposition of the mind and character of a person, which acquired through frequent repetition. Which Satan use to become habitual.

However, there are good habits person have which leads to better and healthful living and there are "demoniacally" control habits which lead to death which are detrimental such as substance abuse (drugs) alcoholism, eating disorder, and there are others which Satan use to enter internally to use in spiritual warfare.

Observe around you at the vast number of people control by detrimental habits of all kinds beyond human ability to control or quite the habits.

Spiritual Warfare

Scripture warns us, "The thief, the devil is here to steal, kill, or destroy humankind!" *Us*.

Children of God, congregation, spiritual warfare is different from any other wars ever fought in the past, present or in future wars on the face of the Earth.

Spiritual warfare is an invisible war against invisible enemies whom can't be seen in the flesh fighting against us, mankind. These invisible enemies (demon spirits) are also Jehovah God enemies which occupy both physical and spiritual realm.

Mankind war take place in both realms in the physical realm which is in spirit and physically in the flesh which is in spirit and flesh. Scripture tells us (the people) we aren't fighting against flesh and blood but against wicked spiritual demonic forces, real demon spirits in the bodies of the living, humans.

Read Ephesians 6:12: "For we are not fighting against human beings, but against the wicked spiritual forces in the heavenly world, the rulers, authorities and cosmic powers of this dark age."

Note: Brothers and sisters in Christ, we all are in spirit warfare, the entire population (world) to some degree. Whether Christian or pagan, believer or nonbeliever are in spirit warfare.

Scripture warns us, "All mankind put on the whole armor of God."

Read Ephesians 6:10–18. "We do all this in prayer, asking for God's help. Pray on every occasion, as the Spirit leads. For this reason, keep alert and never give up, pray always for, all God's people."

Note: Congregation of Jehovah God, God also warns us of whom we are up against which is in spirit. Which mean our weapons aren't carnal but every Word of God, which is the whole Armor of God! "His Word."

Question 2: Who and what is a ghost?

Answer: Children of God, a ghost is nothing more than a demonic spirit's image of a demon spirit which appears in a faint or false image pretending while masquerading as a deceased person or a loved one. The Bible is very clear when it says, as far the dead, they are conscious of nothing at all.

Read Ecclesiastes 9:5. "Yes, the living know they are going to die, but the dead know nothing."

Also read 2 Corinthians 5:8. "We are confident, I say, and willing rather to be absent from the body and to be present with the Lord."

Note: Wicked spirits, "demons," are powerful. These spirits or demons are the angels who joined (Satan) Lucifer, the cherub angelic creature of high rank in rebellion against Jehovah God.

Why do they pretend to be persons who have died but never the living? It is to advance the belief that the dead or deceased spirit is alive on the Earth.

Many have been falsely led to believe such a lie which is of the devil. The Bible, Jehovah God "Word," says the dead is conscious of nothing.

There's a description in the Bible of a wicked spirit (*demon*) who pretend to be Samuel, a dead prophet of Jehovah God.

Samuel knew God's law and also King Saul, which said, "Do not turn yourselves to the spirit Mediums and not consult professional fortune tellers, so as to become unclean by them.

Read Leviticus 19:31. "Do not go for advice to people who consult the spirits of the dead. If you do, you will be ritually unclean. I am the Lord your God."

Note: In time, King Saul turned away from Jehovah God. Therefore, Samuel, who at the time was alive refused any longer to see King Saul. Samuel died and all the Israelites came together and mourned for him. Then they buried him at his home in Ramah.

Now in time of trouble, King Saul was desperate because Jehovah God would not listen to his calls for help. King Saul was so eager to learn about what was going to happen that he went to a spirit Medium in En-dor.

The medium brought forth the "form" of a person that she could see, and King Saul identified him as "Samuel." The spirit person pretending to be Samuel, spoke, saying, "Why have you disturbed me by having me brought up?"

Note: "Demon spirits can and does speak in their own language."

Note: Remember, Samuel was dead and at death a person goes back to the ground and his thoughts do perish.

Read Psalm 146:4. "When they die, they return to the dust, on that day all their plans come to an end."

Congregation, the voice was not really that of dead Samuel. Samuel was God's prophet. He opposed spirit Mediums and while he was alive Samuel had refused to speak anymore with disobedient Saul and God refused to give King Saul any information.

Now, could a spirit Medium force Jehovah God to give Kings Saul a message through dead Samuel and if the living could actually talk with dead loved ones surely a God of love would not say that they had become "unclean" because of turning to spirit Mediums.

Note: So it is not the spirits of the dead that pretending while masquerading as spirits of loved ones. Those spirits which claim to be the (ghost) spirit is demonic. They are demons, the fallen angels who joined Satan in rebellion against God.

Children of God, demons are the culprits pretending to be the ghost or spirit of the deceased "their purpose is to advance the 'lie' that the spirits of the dead are alive on the Earth."

Note: (3) Demonized children or adolescents

Question: Can infants be born into the world demonized, possess by or as if by a demon?

Answer: "Yes." The fetus of an unborn young in the womb of an addictive mother receive everything through the blood as that of the mother. Whether orally or intravenously which a vast number of women conceive and become pregnant under substance abuse habits.

Note: Children of God, it is sad and it hurt to have an infant born demonized (medical term, addictive) into the world and in later years wonder why he or she can't control their behavior nor emotions. Even parents and some doctors wonder why they can't.

Are these children born into the world demonized or drug or alcohol dependency? "Yes." I believe some certainly are, which need to be address in pulpits throughout the land.

Note: Children of God, a vast number of infants are born every day into the world of demonized or demonic oppression; or demonic influences; or possessed parents when was conceived in the womb of addictive mother, which at the time of conception both mother and father were victims of demonically control habits such as drug and substance abuse and alcoholism just to name a few.

Note: Jesus heals many people of demonic possession and demonically influences.

"Jesus heals a child with an evil spirit."

Read Mark 9:17–29.

> A man in the crowd answer, "Teacher, I brought my son to you because he has an evil spirit in him and cannot talk."
> Jesus ask, "How long has he been like this?" Jesus ask the father. "Ever since he was a child," the father replied.

Note: Does this Scripture answer your question, "Can a child be born under demonized conditions?"

Questions 4: Do evil spirits, demons like human beings?

Answer: "No." Demons are evils spirits, their name warns us who they are, evils spirits here on assignments. Which is to possess human bodies to use as to steal, kill, or destroy human lives and livelihoods by way of any means. Demons are adversaries of Jehovah God and humankind.

Read Luke 4:38–46.

> Scripture says after sunset all who had friends who were sick with various diseases brought them to Jesus, he placed his hands on every one of them and healed them all.
>
> Demons also went out from many people, screaming, You are the Son of God!

Also read Luke 6:17–26.

Jesus Teaches and Heals

Read Luke 7:17–26. "People came to him [Jesus] to be healed of their diseases. Those who were trouble by evil spirits also came and were healed."

Note: Demons are evil and wicked spirits.

Question 5: Does wicked spirits (*demons*) possess power to hurt or harm?"

Answer: Yes. They are vicious having superhuman powers in persons whom the evil spirit or spirits has entered.

Read Matthew 8:28–29.

> When Jesus came to the territory of Gadara on the other side of the lake, he was met by two men who came out of the burial caves there. These men had demons in them and were so fierce that no one dared travel on that road.
>
> At once they screamed, "What do you want with us, you Son of God? Have you come to punish us before the right time?

Note: Also read the "Sons of Sceva"

Read Acts 19:13–16.

> Some Jews who travel around and drove out evil spirits also tried to use the Name of the Lord

Jesus to do this. They said to the evil spirits, "I command you in the Name of Jesus whom Paul preaches."

Seven brothers, who were the sons of a Jewish High Priest named Sceva, were doing this.

But the evil spirit said to them, "I know Jesus and I know about Paul, but you, who are you?

The man who had the evil spirit in him attack them with such violence, that he over powered them all. They ran away from his house, wounded and their clothes torn off.

Children of God, evil spirits, demons aren't physically effective against us unless enter into human bodies, thereby taking on the appearance of a person, a camouflage appearance of whom the spirit enter.

They cannot perform their assignments mentally nor physically unless manifest their action in and through human bodies!

Question 6: Are we under attack of Satan and his cohorts, demons?

Answer: "Yes." We all are under attack; the entire land is under attack, a demonic attack. We are in spiritual warfare in a demonic realm, in a physical world, the Earth.

Read Revelation 12:9. "The huge dragon was thrown out—that ancient serpent named the devil or Satan that deceived the whole world. He was thrown down to Earth and all his angels with him."

Also read Revelation 12:12. "And be glad you heavens and all you that live there! But how terrible for the Earth and the sea! For the devil has come down to you and he fill with rage, because he knows that he has only a little time left."

Question 7: Are there friendly demons or evil spirits?

Answer: "No." In our time, which is currently, demonized persons are afflicted in various ways; some are dumb, some blind, some acted like lunatics and some possessed superhuman strength. Men, women, and children are victims of these invisible enemies.

Jesus Christ Says of the Devil

Read John 8:44. "From the very beginning he was a murderer and has never been on the side of truth because there is no truth in him. When he tells a lie, he is only doing what is natural to him because he is a liar and the father of all lies."

Satan's cohorts, demons, are so evil and wicked they are classified as evil spirits and their chief, Satan, is called the evil one.

Read Matthew 6:13. "Do not bring us to hard testing, but keep us safe from the Evil One."

Note: Also read John 10:10. "The thief [Satan] comes only in order to steal, kill, or destroy!"

Note: Human beings and livelihoods

Children of God the demonic realm is a threat to the whole human race but only through the flesh or body of those whom Satan influence or brought under demonic control. It very well could be a mother, father, sister, brother, or any family member, relative, friend, neighbor, or an associate.

Note: This isn't a Fairy-tale, it is known for toddlers and young children to have imaginary friends whom they talk to and play with in the demonic realm, which is in the air or atmosphere of their room or house.

Because of humans' lack of knowledge of the spiritual realm, the so-called imaginary friends that exist in the air or atmosphere of the house are wicked spirits, demons pretending to be playmates in the air while waiting for opportune time to enter the child or an adult body.

Note: Therefore, it is vitally important that it be preached or taught the Earth, air and atmosphere is demonically populated with invisible wicked spirits, demons which has set up residency among us, the human race throughout Earth in observance while waiting to enter human bodies to use as their own which became subjective to Satan rules.

Note: Brothers and sisters, Satan the chief of the demonic realm, is called the ruler or prince of the air who boast of having all the Kingdoms of the Earth at his disposal, now worketh in children of disobedience.

The devil, Satan is in charge or ruler of the Earth's demonic world, and its atmosphere, who broadcast wrong motives, attitudes, and moods.

He influenced people and nations, stir's them up and blinds them; however, Jesus Christ is the true and faithful ruler of the world.

Read Revelation 1:5. "And from Jesus Christ, the Faithful Witness, the first to be raised from death and who is also the ruler of the Kings of the world."

Jesus revealed to us Satan is a murderer and liar. Which tells the world Satan is a person. He hates and want to destroy any who pose a threat to him or his demonic spirit kingdom.

He hates the preaching and teachings of the full true Gospel of Jesus Christ because it spells his defeat and demon spirits' doom. And the "END" of his invisible control over the world's population and nations. Read John 5:19. Scripture, says, "We know that we belong to God, even though the whole world is under the rule of the Evil One."

Note: Scripture also says, "Now is the time for the world to be judge. Now the ruler of this world will be over thrown" (Jn. 12:31).

Question 8: Does evil spirits, demons or Satan know human thoughts or human mind?

Answer: "No." Only the perceptions or thoughts perceived by the demonized. Which is demonic and that's because the perception of the demonized is a demonic perception of the evil spirit(s) residing in demonized or demon-possessed persons which are the thoughts or perceptions of demons which the person perceives as their own natural thoughts or perceptions. But not, *I reiterate*, but not the person natural spirit mind nor born-again spirit perceptions.

Question 9: How does we, human recognize Satan or any other demonic spirit that may speak or articulate through people?

Answer: We, humans (you) must possess the "gift of inspired utterance." Which is one of the nine fifths of the Spirit, thereby having the ability to discern whether an inspired expression is of human origin or a spirit other than one's natural spirit.

Secondly, Satan or demons appearance and approach among people is deceptive in the flesh of humans. Humans must remember Satan and demons represent two realms, one is the spiritual, the invisible realm as spirit and the other as a spirit person in the physical realm.

They can appear through both as a human; however, only Satan can materialize or transition to become and appear as human, a human being, speak or articulate as a person, appear as a person yet spirit and dematerialize or transition back to spirit, invisible to human eyes and not be seen.

Note: Children of Jehovah God, God is my witness. This I've witnessed and experienced, Satan's transitional powers.

Ordinarily, humans can't see neither Satan nor demon spirits nor their approach with natural vision. However, humans (you) can hear the spirit or spirits invisible approach in the person mouth and words spoken or speech.

It's imperative to listen for the spirit or spirits approach, Satan or any other evil spirit approach is in the person words. LISTEN TO WORDS BEING SPOKEN." The manifestation of demonic spirits in the person is in the person's tongue, even yourself!

Question 9: "Demon spirits in Christian sanctuaries?"

Answer: "Yes." In the midst of the atmosphere, the pews, in pulpits preaching or teaching doctrine of demons.

There are demon spirits in observation of all sanctuaries, synagogues, mosques and all institutions of worship and public facilities.

Read Luke 4:33–34.

> In the synagogue was a man who had the spirit of an evil demon in him, he screamed in a loud voice.
>
> "Oh!" What do you want with us, Jesus of Nazareth? Are you here to destroy us? I know who you are, you are God Holy Messenger.

Note: "Yes," there are demon spirits, demonic or demonized oppress individuals setting in pews and in the atmosphere of institution. Also read 2 Timothy 4:3–4.

> The time will come when people will not listen to sound doctrines but will follow their own desires and will collect for themselves more and more teachers who will tell them what they are itching to hear.
> They will turn away from listening to the truth and give their attention to legends.

Note: "Doctrine of Demons"

Congregation of Jehovah God. A doctrine of demons is a system of principles that Scriptures that are taught or preached that are non-scriptural that some clergies and ministers who were called to preach the Gospel of Jesus Christ and teach Jehovah God's message turn biblical scriptures around, alter or change the true biblical meaning to comply with their carnal mind (flesh) to preach that which their congregation is itching to hear.

Read 1 Timothy 4:1–2.

> [False teaching] The Spirit says clearly that people will abandon the faith in later times, they will obey lying spirits and follow the teaching of demons.
> Such teachings are spread by deceitful liars whom consciences are dead as if burnt with a hot iron.

Question 10: How does evil spirits appear to humankind?
Answer: The same as we appear to one another, some of us appear as an angel of light, yet wicked and evil.

They appear to us in the flesh of human bodies yet is spirit.

Demons speak (articulate) in and through humans of whom its spirit has enter the body of. They speak with personalities, biological personalities of those which the spirit(s) use to appear through. "As the man in the synagogue spoke!" In the synagogue, there were more evil spirits in the pews of worship.

Note: Children of God, a person appearance can be deceptive, but hearing can't because that which you hear come out of a person's mouth, reveal the spirit's approach and that which he or she speak reveal the manifestation of such spirit through the tongue.

Remember evil spirits (demons) can and do appear as angels of light with all characteristics of human beings, a person must possess the "spirit of discernment," which is one of the nine-fifths of the Spirit, the Holy Spirit which gives the ability to discern whether an inspired expression of message is of human origin or a spirit other than one's own natural spirit.

Note: Children of God, the potential and vulnerabilities are great among the human population of becoming a victim of demonic influences, oppression or even demon-possessed, age nor gender is no exception!

"Jesus Christ, our Lord and Savior forever protects the believer and nonbeliever from the works of the evil one, Satan and the fallen angels, that has become demons, evil spirit on the Earth.

Amen.

The Congregation of God Has a Target on Its Back! Sermon and Message

Congregation of Jehovah God, all God's people have a target on their back which the devil, Satan is shooting invisible arrows, some of the burning arrows are hitting the mark without being felt or seen in many cases while others are being hit without one's knowledge.

"Many invisible arrows are being shot daily at individuals whom Satan is attempting to stop or prevent from speaking out or performing against him or his cohorts, demons."

Note: It may sound irony, but the devil can shoot arrows from all direction, still yet hit the target on mankind back, "you."

People in general are the arrows and targets, which come in many shapes and forms. Drug abuse of all kinds, diseases, lies, alcohol abuse, use of tobacco of any form, sex, eating disorder, every kind of self-induced habit, which allows controlling demon spirits to enter the human body that control habits from within. Perversion or a perverted or demonic thought are all burning arrows being shot externally as well as internally.

The arrows being shot are invisible, but all are sin nature and becomes detrimental to human beings' lives; however, the tongue is the most frequent and commonly use burning arrow, which can be shot anywhere at any time in and under any circumstances.

Note: Children of God, it may sound strange; however, it is the "full Gospel truth." Satan the Devil does the aiming of the burning arrows, but mankind is the shooter and the recipient of his works.

Note: Children of Jehovah God, all mankind are vulnerable of the works of Satan; therefore, at all time, wear the full armor of God, so that you will be able to stand up against the devil's evil tricks.

Some arrows shot at us and mankind, appear to be good in nature while some appear to be angels of light as sheep but are really wolves in sheep clothing.

We, Christians, must think of ourselves as warriors in the army of Jehovah God always alert and vigilant because targets on our backs are everlasting until Jesus Christ return.

Note: "I said everlasting because when we, mankind was born into the world, just as Jesus were born. We were just as Jesus were born with a target on His back which remain on His back until he went to the Cross for you, me, and the world.

To this day, every nation and person, age nor gender is no exception, in the past, present and future have and will have a target place on the back which there isn't no exception whom burning arrows are shot at.

Congregation, since I've been in the world, no one told me, I have an invisible target on my back. "Why? Because Satan has shut the mouth of some clergies, servants, and pastors, as well as the congregation of God."

Note: Every burning arrow shot by the devil's representatives, bring detrimental consequences in all kinds of shapes, forms, and fashions. The devil holds nothing back of trying to get you and I," and the world to steal, kill, or destroy one another. Satan use methods as burning arrows to steal one's health, kill, or destroy persons.

Note: He like for the nation to sin against God, by denying the "Word" of God and the Gospel of Jesus Christ.

Therefore, it is imperative to study the Word of God, act on the Word and perform the works of the Word, when and Where action is called for. Never allowing the devil to catch you off guard.

Therefore, stay alert and vigilant because Satan is looking for whom he can destroy. His plan is to kill, steal, or destroy mankind and his works against him and his cohorts by any means which I'm at the head of the "hit list."

Note: Children of God, Jehovah God is my witness of this truth, which I've revealed." Everywhere I traveled, I experience unbelievable encounters in the spiritual realm of Satan with mankind. Satan representatives or in the spirit realm against real demon spirits in persons, in the atmosphere of my dwelling, in the Earth atmosphere and in public places.

Everywhere I go, I'm in physical contact and physical conflict with demon spirits (everywhere).

Note: Servants, clergies, and ministers "pastors" of Jehovah God, it is imperative that you, your neighbors and throughout the nations be made known and acknowledge there is an invisible target on the backs of all humankind, which Satan is aiming and shooting burning arrows at all directions from directions you didn't know exist.

"Age is no exception nor gender." Adolescents are doing and performing the works of the devil while themselves are being demonically motivated and control.

Note: Children of Jehovah, every arrow shot at you or a person is for a cause and purpose, none are wasted.

When a person says to you, "Watch your back," even though it may sound proverbial or an old saying but, brothers and sisters, it has unbelievable meaning in spirit but true. Never take for granted, when told to "watch your back." Which literally mean, be alert at all time and watch out for Satan representatives.

The world is in a spiritual battle, anytime a person has a target on their body, believe me, the enemy or enemies are shooting to kill or destroy. Satan is on the "Earth" to accomplish just that.

Mankind can't hide nor can he (you) conceal oneself because it's the devil's spirit or demons working in and through the flesh of people.

Note: Jehovah God tells us through His Word the battle is not ours, but the Lord. Why is it the Lord? Because we can't see, even though we know who's responsible, which the invisible arrows that are being shot only God and Jesus Christ see the spirit realm that which is in spirit being shot continually at the children of God.

However, Jehovah God's Word says, "Put on the whole armor of God," which is our defensive weapon and protection wherever we travel. Yet the Battle is still the Lords that which we must acknowledge at all times.

Note: Believe me, children of God, the devil know unbelievers and he know the believers of Jehovah God's Word, believe me He knows, and He will try those that are in the Word and wear the whole armor of God.

Satan will put you through the test 24-7 continually. "Don't ever forget that." A target of any kind placed on a person's back is to be destroyed.

Note: Whether Christians acknowledge, "there is a diversion between Christian nations and the world. Which all have different targets placed on the back, one is faith.

Every nation is under the attack of the devil of their faith in Jesus Christ. Nations are continuously shooting burning arrows at other nation of people and at themselves which Satan is in control of their faith and unbelief.

Note: The world sin is unbelief in Jesus Christ. Because of their faith and unbelief many have already perished.

Beliefs of the Christian faith in the Lord Jesus Christ and the Father Almighty God and because of their unbelief, many will perish which many have already been judged and have already perished because of their beliefs.

Note: Scripturally speaking to shooting a burning arrow, there must be a target, which the target the evil one, Satan is shooting at is "mankind faith."

In all areas of a person's life, Satan is attempting to destroy "faith." Faith will quench or put out all burning arrows the evil one, Satan is shooting against mankind's life.

Note: Children of God, faith can cure all diseases and all kind of human induce habits which allow demon spirits into entering human bodies as controlling spirits. Faith will even defeat unbelief's in one's life of demonic thoughts of the Lord and God, Jehovah also it takes faith to control the tongue.

Brothers and sisters, faith will quench every arrow the evil one shoot at you, his targets are the world's population. Have been in the past, present, and will continue into the future.

"Satan's aiming is at the world's faith. He knows faith without action is dead."

Note: Therefore, a person must acknowledge there is an invisible target on his or her back, which it takes faith from which every direction arrows are being shot or come from.

Faith in Christ, our Lord and Savior and believe in God the Father and His Word. Faith will quench all burning arrows shot by the evil one, Satan or his demons!

Amen.

DOCTRINE OF DEMONS IN THE CHURCH: THE BODY OF CHRIST

Note: I addressed to congregations of all denominations of Jehovah God.

Question: Why is there still being preached and taught doctrine of demons in the Body of Christ, the Church, and Jehovah God's congregation across the land?

DOCTRINE OF DEMONS

Answer: Church, a doctrine of demons is a system or principle that are scripturally preached or taught, which are nonscripture, that some clergies and ministers who were called to preach the gull Gospel of Jesus Christ, also teach or preach the Good News, God's message. Jesus brought of His Father but have turned biblical Scriptures around, alter or changed the true biblical meaning to comply with their carnal mind (flesh) to preach that which their congregation is itching to hear.

Jehovah God gave the "Body of Christ, the Church" a ministry through His Son Jesus Christ, and His message through the gifts of the five-fold ministry, apostles, prophets, evangelists, pastors and teachers.

Note: Also, there are gifts of Jehovah God, Spirit, the Holy Spirit.

The Apostle Paul named nine different manifestations or operations of the Spirit. Paul describes those gifts in born-again believers.

(5) Speech of wisdom, (2) speck of knowledge, (3) faith, (4) gifts of healing, (5) powerful works, (6) prophesying, (7) discernment of inspired utterance, (8) different tongues, and (9) interpretations of tongues.

Note: Neither of them comes from human beings or any human source, the gifts of the Spirit is from God, it is Jehovah God that's responsible for the performing of the gifts of the Spirit.

Note II: The Confession of Apostle Paul

The Apostle Paul's confession of the Jewish law of its Jewish rules and commandments.

(1) Tell the truth.
(2) The day of the Lord.
(3) The Jewish law and its rules and commandments, "abolished at the Cross."
(4) The true righteousness of which Paul had to say of his rules and commandments in the Body of Christ, the Church.

Note: Prophetess, a woman who prophesies or of the work of a prophet. Miriam is the first woman designated or called a prophetess in the Bible.

Note: Anna served as a prophetess. She spoke of Baby Jesus in the temple and spoke about the child to all who were waiting for God to set Jerusalem free. She conveyed the "Good News" of Jesus birth which was the beginning of Jehovah God's message as well as the Gospel of Jesus Christ.

Note III: Excommunication and Persecution in the Church

(1) I choose to obey Jehovah God, not humankind.
(2) Humankind can and will persecute or excommunicate but not whom Jehovah God has called.
   Question: Whom do you dear? Jehovah God or humankind and their rules?

(3) Whom to fear is God.
(4) There are signs, wonders, and miracles today in the Body of Christ, the Church.

Amen.

Doctrine of Demons in the Church Sermon and Message

I

To all congregations of all denominations of Jehovah God. My question is, "Why is there still being preached and taught, doctrine of demons in the Body of Christ, the Church of Jehovah God's congregation across the country and throughout the world?"

Note: To all servants, clergies, ministers including the five-fold ministry, apostles, prophets, evangelists, teachers, and preachers after acknowledging the "truth." Doctrine of demons is more "prevalent" today than ever before.

Doctrine of Demons

Denominations of God, a doctrine of demons is a system or principle that are scripturally preached or taught that are nonscripture that some clergies and ministers who were called to preach the full Gospel of Jesus Christ, also teach or preach the Good News, God's message. Jesus brought of His Father but have turned biblical Scriptures around, alter or changed the true biblical meaning to comply with their carnal mind (flesh) to preach that which their congregation is itching to hear.

Jehovah God gave the "Body of Christ, the Church" a ministry through His Son Jesus Christ, a five levels of ministry which are the five-fold ministry of Christ for edification of the Church which Christ is head of, which Christ-appointed five spiritual positions. He appointed and gave gifts to those whom He called.

(5)Apostle. One sent forth to represent the sender Christ Himself.

(2) Prophet. One through whom divine will and purpose are made are known. True prophets are no ordinary person in the Spirit they are spokesmen for God who speak in behalf of Jehovah with

Inspired messages. They stand in God's intimate group and He reveals His confidential matter to them which they the prophets reveals Jehovah God-inspired message by divine revelation to nations (people) and the world.

Jehovah God transmit divine revelation to true prophets by means of His Holy Spirit and occasionally by spirit directed by angelic messengers.

Note: That which I experienced in the year of 1984, two angelic messenger (angels) presented me God's Word, the Holy Bible.

Read Revelation 22:6. "Then the angel said to me, 'These words are true and can be trusted. And the Lord God, who gives his Spirit to the prophets, has sent the angels to show his servants what must happen very soon.'"

(3) Evangelist. A preacher of the Gospel or Good News for the building up of the body of the Church. The work of such evangelizers was missionary work. Evangelist would open new fields where the Good News had not been previously preached.

(4) Pastor. A Christian minister or priest having spiritual charge over a congregation or other groups, "a shepherd."

(5) Teacher. To advocate or preach to impart knowledge and to provide knowledge of the Gospel or Good News or cause one to learn.

Note: "Servants of Jehovah God after you were called and given gifts of the Spirit to preach or teach the full Bible of the Gospel of Jesus Christ and the Good News. He brought of His Father some clergies, pastors, and teachers after being in the pulpits fifty or sixty years still preaching or teaching in disobedience of Jehovah God's Word. Compromising Scriptures for the sake of their counterpart and the congregation of what they are itching to hear. While acknowledging he or she aren't addressing nor in compliance of God's message, His Word nor preaching the full Bible.

Congregation, children of God and servants regardless of your stay in pulpits, one year or sixty years, you will suffer consequences in due time of disobedience of not preaching or teaching the full Bible.

II

Spiritual Gifts in Men or Mankind

Note: Apostle Paul describes those gifts in men that Christ gave the congregation, before His ascension into heaven. Paul named nine different manifestations or operations of the Spirit.

(1) "Speech of wisdom," a miraculous ability to apply knowledge in a successful way to solve problems arising in the congregation.
(2) "Speech of knowledge," speech of knowledge was something above and beyond the knowledge shared by Christians in general, it was miraculous knowledge, concerning God's will and his requirement for life.
(3) "Faith," a gift of the Spirit that aided the individual to overcome mountain like obstacles that would otherwise hinder service to God.
(4) "Healing," the gift of healing was manifest in the ability to cure diseases completely, regardless of the nature of the affliction.
(5) "Powerful works." Powerful works included raising dead persons, expelling demons, and even striking opposers with blindness. The manifestation of such powerful works resulted in adding believers to the congregation.
(6) "Prophesying." Prophesying was a greater gift than speaking in tongues as it built up the congregation, moreover,

unbelievers were aided thereby to recognize that God was among the Christians.

(7) "Discernment of inspired utterance," involved the ability to discern whether an inspired expression originated with God or not. This gift would prevent its possessor from being deceived and turned away from the truth and protect the congregation.

(8) "Tongues." Gifts of tongues, the miraculous gift of tongues was the out pouring of God's omnipotent, omnipresent, and omniscient Spirit on the Day of Pentecost where the 120 disciples and followers assembled in an upper room were thereby enable to speak about the magnificent things of God in the native tongues (Earthly languages) of the Jews and those that came to Jerusalem and faraway places.

Note: Congregation, these gifts all come from Jehovah God and it is Jehovah God that perform the gifts by signs, wonders, and miracles. God is omnipotent having unlimited or universal power, authority, or forces.

God is omnipresent, present everywhere simultaneously. God is omniscient having total knowledge, knowing everything, everywhere.

Thereby, wherever God's Spirit dwell or habituate so does the gifts of the Spirit.

Note: Congregation, Jesus Christ spoke in "tongues" on the Cross but in an Earthly language spoken by Jews in Palestine and by other people in the Middle East at the time of his death.

Read Matthew 27:46. "At about three o'clock Jesus cried out with a loud shout, ELI, ELI, LEMA SABACHTHAI? Which means, 'My God, My God, Why did you abandon Me?'"

However, servants, clergies, and ministers of all denominations of Jehovah God, "There is a heavenly language that is spoken in another tongue, which is evidence of being born again, from above with the Spirit or the full nature of Jehovah God, a heavenly language. No one understand except Jehovah God Spirit and the "born-again spirit" in man.

This heavenly language is evidence of the "new birth," which is a requirement of Jehovah God through Christ of being "born again" of above of the Spirit and of water below, that which Jesus spoke to Nicodemus of being "born again" of water baptism below and by the Spirit of God of above.

Note: "Denominations of God, Man baptize with water below; however, it is Jesus Christ that baptize with the Spirit from above."

Note: Children of God, it is imperative that you understand, there is a heavenly language which is spoken in tongues which is evidence of being "born again" from above of the Spirit or the Full Nature of God, a heavenly language no one understand but Jehovah God and the born-again spirit of Christian believers.

> Those who speak in strange tongues do not speak to others but to God, because no one understands them. They are speaking secret truths by the power of the Spirit. (1 Cor. 14:2–4)

> Whoever does not have the Spirit cannot receive the Gifts that come from God's Spirit. Such a person really does not understand them, and they seem to be nonsense, because their value can be judged only on a spiritual basis. (1 Cor. 2:14) ("Ye must be born again of the spirit.")

Note: More about gifts of the Spirit

> But those who proclaim God's Message speak to people and give them help, encouragement and comfort.
> Those who speak in strange tongues help only themselves, but those who proclaim God's Message help the Whole Church. (1 Cor. 14:3–14)

> The person who speak in strange tongues, then, must pray for the gift to explain what is said.
> For if I pray in this way, my spirit prays indeed, but my mind has no part in it.
>
> So then, my friends, set your heart on proclaiming God's Message, but do not forbid the speaking in strange tongues. (1 Cor. 14:13–14, 39)

"Thus, says the Lord!"
(9) "Interpretation of tongues," the ninth gift of the Spirit was manifest to translate a language unknown to the one having the gift. Read 1 Corinthians 14:5

> The Apostle Paul says, "I would like for all of you to speak in strange tongues, but I would rather that you had the gift of proclaiming God's message. For the person who proclaim God's message is of greater value than the one speaks in strange tongues, unless there is someone present who can explain what is said, so that the whole church may be helped.

Note: If the one speaking in a tongue other than their own was unable to translate, then he did not understand what he or herself is saying. Paul encourage those having the gift of tongues to pray that they might also translate and thereby edify all listeners.

Because neither of them come from human beings or any human source, the gifts of the Spirit is from God. It is Jehovah God that is responsible for the performing of these gifts.

Note: Scripture say man is called by the Gospel to minister which is true. All Jehovah's children is called to minister; however, not all is called into the five-fold ministry as apostle, prophet, evangelist, teacher or preacher. Scripture tells us in 1 Corinthians 12:27–30.

> All of you [us Christians] are Christ's body, and each one is a part of it.
> In the church God has put all in place, in the first-place apostles, in the second-place prophets, and in the third-place teachers, then those who perform miracles, followed by those who are given the power to heal or to help others or to direct them or to speak in strange tongues.
> They are not all apostles, or prophets or teachers. Not everyone has the power to work miracles.
> or to heal diseases or to speak in strange tongues or to explain what is said.

I'm a living witness and testament of what Jehovah God Spirit performs in and through me. The very things, miracles, supernatural healing. I can testify to as Jehovah God; the Lord Jesus Christ and the Holy Spirit are witnesses of this truth.

Note: In this True Testament, written in Scripture and a servant of Jehovah God. Some clergies, servants and ministers of God still preaching and teaching in pulpits, a doctrine of demons against this truth across this land and the world, which is an abomination and sin against God, his Word and works.

Note: "Thus, Says the Lord," this truth which is reveal by My Spirit through man My

Servant, whom I've called to write and speak in behalf of Me this truth in My Name, Jehovah, the

God of all mankind, must be preached and teach not by mankind carnal perception but by the power of My Spirit which reveal's "all truth."

Note: I, Jehovah, does not send out My Word nor My works to return "void." Clergies, ministers and servants of all congregation receive and acknowledge this "notice." "My Word nor My works shall not be compromised nor neglected, nor ignored, neither My servants." "Thus," says the Lord.

Clergies and ministers of all Jehovah God, congregations, you have heard or read the written "truth." Now this written truth must be "carried out" and put into practice in all churches of the Body of Christ, there aren't any exceptions in proclaiming the truth.

Note: Churches of the Body of Christ and all denominations of God, I'm not writing under normal conditions nor my own authority, even though I possess authority to speak or write in behalf of Almighty God.

This writing and message are being divinely, under the inspiration of the Holy Spirit. Not by my power nor my might but by direction of the Spirit.

Therefore, don't hold me accountable for any consequences you may encounter for not preaching the "full Bible" or revealing the truth, which is in the full Gospel and in Jehovah's message, the Good News.

II

Apostle Paul's Confession of the Jewish Law

Note: Which is a revelation of women preachers and teachers are servants of Jehovah God in the "Body of Christ," the church of all denominations that preach Jesus Christ as Lord and Savior.

Don't take my word. Digest that which Apostle Paul has written and that which the Lord Jesus Christ did while His flesh was nailed to the Cross at Calvary.

Tell the truth

Note: Churches of all denominations have compromised My Word and My works for decades, if not centuries, time have caught up with My plan to stop the existence of preaching and teaching, "doctrine of demons," the demise, "death" of Satan, My and mankind's adversary's deception has come to an "end."

"Thus," says the Lord God. "It is written, My Word nor My works shall not return void!"

The Day of the Lord

Read Joel 2:28–29.

> Afterward, I will pour out my Spirit on everyone. Your sons and daughters will proclaim my message, your old people will have dreams and your young people will see visions.
> At that time I will pour out my Spirit even on servants both "Men and Women."

Note: "That were My message. Then and is my message today!"

Peter's Message of Jehovah God

Read Acts 2:17–18.

> This is what I will do in the last days. God says, I will pour out my Spirit on everyone. Your sons and daughters will proclaim my message. Your young men will see visions and your old men will have dreams.
> Yes, even on my servants, both Men and Women. I will pour out my Spirit in those days and they will proclaim my message.

Note: "I, Jehovah, God spoke to My servant, prophet in an audible voice, "To tell the truth if he loves me." Which mean my written truth is being compromised throughout the Body of Christ and across the Earth.

But now servants, clergies, ministers of all denominations has no excuse performing my works in obedience to My Word, preaching the full Gospel truth. However, you must repent, confess the truth or suffer consequences, "Says the Lord."

Lay hands on the sick they shall recover by the supernatural power of My Spirit. Speak in Tongues which My Spirit leads too, which is a heavenly language a believer receive after baptism of the Holy Spirit which show evidence one has been "born again" from above of the full nature of My Spirit. "Man baptizes with water. My Son baptize with the Holy Spirit from above!"

Congregation, it is "sin" to come under the conviction of Almighty God, "Stop." I ask you, stop your traditional preaching and teaching the Jewish law and its commandments and rules, which Jesus Christ abolished on the Cross and that which Apostle Paul confesses himself Jesus abolished the Jewish law with its rules and commandments which the Jewish people live by.

Read 1 Corinthians 14:26–40.

> Because God does not want us to be in disorder, but in harmony and peace as in all the churches of God's people.
>
> The women should keep quiet in the meetings. They are not allowed to speak, as the "Jewish Law says," they must not be in charge.
>
> If they want to find out about something they should ask their husbands at home. It is a disgraceful thing for a woman to speak in a church meeting.

One in Christ

Note: "The Jewish laws and its rules and commandments"

Gentiles and Jews became "one" in the Body of Christ by way of the Cross. Therefore, Jewish laws and its rules and commandments was abolished at the Cross.

Read Ephesians 2:11–19.

> For Christ himself has brought us peace by making Jews and Gentiles "One People." With his own body he broke down the wall that separated them and kept them enemies.
>
> He Abolished the Jewish Law with its Commandments and Rules, in order to create out of the two races "One" new people in union with himself, in this way making peace.
>
> By his death on the Cross Christ destroyed their enemies by means of the Cross he united both races into One body and brought them back to God.
>
> It is through Christ that all of us, Jews and Gentiles are able to come in the one Spirit into the presence of the Father.

Note: "The true righteousness" of what Apostle Paul had to say of his "rules and commandments" in the Body of Christ, the Church.

> I was circumcised when I was a week old. I am an Israelite by birth of the tribe of Benjamin, a pure-blooded Hebrew. As far as keeping the Jewish Law is concerned, I was a Pharisee.
>
> and I was so zealous that I persecuted the church, as far as a person can be righteous by obeying the Commands of the Law, I was without fault.
>
> But all those things that I might count as profit I now reckon as loss for Christ's sake.
>
> Nor only those things, I reckon everything as complete loss for the sake of what is so much more valuable the knowledge of Christ Jesus my Lord. For his sake I have thrown everything away, I consider it all as mere garbage, so that I may gain Christ.

> And be completely united with him, "I NO LONGER HAVE A RIGHTEOUSNESS OF MY OWN," the kind that is gained by obeying the "Law." (Phil. 3:1–11)

Note: Congregation of God, "Who has the right or authority to overrule or control God's Spirit? Man or God, himself. God who says, I'll pour out my Spirit on both servants, men and women to proclaim my message.

Therefore, it's imperative. All churches of Christ in the Body of Christ acknowledge the whole Bible or suffer consequences. The Bible is a Book of Jehovah God's Word, which may divide the Word of truth but not added to nor subtracted from.

Note: Servants, clergies, and ministers of all denominations, Jehovah God cannot and does not contradict Himself nor His Word which is stated twice in Scripture of "Old and New Testament." God himself in Joel 2:28–29 and Acts 2:17–18 (old and new covenants).

Read Joel 2:28–29.

> Afterward I will pour out my Spirit on everyone. Your sons and daughters will proclaim my message, your old people will have dreams, and your young people will see visions.
>
> At that time I will pour out my Spirit even on servants both men and women.

Note: Therefore, Apostle Paul complied in obedience to Jehovah God's "Word," which is written in verse 7: "But all those things that I might count as profit, I now reckon as loss for Christ sake" (Phil. 3:7).

Note: "Therefore, thus," says the Lord, "women has the right to proclaim, preach, and teach the Gospel and deliver My messages of whom I pour out My Spirit upon. My Word nor My works, will not return void! I, Jehovah, have spoken!"

III

Note: Women In Jehovah God, Earthly Congregation

Prophetess, a woman who prophecies or carries on the work of a prophet.

Miriam is the first woman designated a prophetess in the Bible. God conveyed some messages through her, perhaps inspired her to sing.

Read Exodus 15:20–21.

> The Prophetess Miriam, Aaron's sister, took her tambourine and all the women follow her playing tambourines and dancing.
>
> Miriam sang for them, "Sing to the Lord, because he has won a glorious victory, he has thrown the horses and their riders into the sea.

Note: Thus, she and Aaron are recorded as saying to Moses, "Is it not by us also that Jehovah has spoken?"

This was in fulfillment of Joel 2:28–29, which foretold Jehovah God, declaration, "I will pour out My Spirit on your sons and daughters and they will proclaim My message" ("Old Covenant").

Note: Anna served as a prophetess, "Baby Jesus is presented in the temple" ("New Covenant").

Read Luke 2:23, 36–38.

> As it is written in the law of the Lord. Every first-born male is to be dedicated to the Lord.
>
> There was a very old prophet, a widow named Anna, daughter of Phanuel of the tribe of Asher. She had been married for only seven years and was now eighty-four years old. She never left the Temple, day and night she worshiped, fasting and praying.

> That very same hour she arrived and gave thanks to God and spoke about the child to all who were waiting for God to set Jerusalem free.

Note: As a result Anna, the prophetess was privileged to see the young child Jesus and bear the Good News about him.

Which was a fulfillment of Joel 2:28–29. Where Jehovah God poured out His Spirit on sons and daughters to Proclaim His message, read Acts 2:17–18 (New Covenant).

Note: The prophetess Anna delivered the Good News of Jesus's birth. Churches of all Jehovah God congregations and denominations, women shall and is preaching and teaching the full Bible, in some pulpits of Jesus Christ and delivering God's messages through Christ by faith.

Thereby I must say, I've heard and witnessed several full-Gospel sermons and messages of women servants of Jehovah God congregation whom God poured out His Spirit on.

Philip, the evangelist four virgin daughters, prophesied under the power of God's Holy Spirit. Philip was one of the seven men who had been chosen as helpers in Jerusalem.

Read Acts. 21:9. "He had four unmarried daughters who proclaimed God's Message."

This was in fulfillment of Joel 2:28–29.

Note: Also foretold, Scripture, "I will pour out My Spirit on everyone, your sons and daughters will proclaim my message."

Note: Clergies, ministers, and servants of all denominations, women who God has call, prophetess, whom God poured out His Spirit into is being denied, neglected, and ignored or unrecognized in some Churches, where Christ Jesus is the head.

Whether you know or not, it is an abomination toward Jehovah God. Also, the Church is believing and teaching a "doctrine of demons," which is "sin" in Jehovah's sight.

Woe unto you, who are under Conviction of God at this very hour, there will be consequences suffered if Repentance is not in your heart and mouth.

Believe Me, you would be better off for not knowing the Gospel or teaching the Full-Bible of Christ than to know but yet teach or preach a different Gospel with Christ as Head. Apostle Paul says, "May a Curse be upon you."

Note: Children of God, Satan the Devil has a demonically control gospel being preached and teach as a doctrine of demons," right before our eyes. He has ministers who claim to be ministers of Jehovah God deceiving themselves while deceiving the world.

Note: Satan has his own agenda in ministry, lesbians and homosexuals, in pulpits across the land as preachers and teachers sworn in over the Bible by once truthful religious men and women of God but has now abandon the "truth" for a "lie." A lie of the devil while still under oath, a solemn formal declaration of promise to Jehovah God but thy allowed Satan turn their oath into an irreverent, blasphemous, vile act against that which is sacred.

IV

Excommunication and Persecution in the Church

Definition of excommunication: to deprive of the right of Church Members or to exclude by or as if by decree from membership or participation in a group.

Definition of *persecution*: to oppress or harass with ill treatment as on the basis of "In my case" prayer.

Note: Servants, clergies, ministers, if you are facing opposition in your church or group or dogma or a doctrine or system relating to matters such as principles, beliefs, or teachings, or statements of ideals or opinions considered to be absolutely true but biblically speaking is not but misleading in the Body of Christ, the Church.

Servants, clergies, and ministers, if there is misleading in Scripture reading. Wake up, make an effort to correct it, Jehovah God will do the rest through you. Correcting his Word and works, which you must allow Him to.

Note: However, you will face opposition and persecution, for your righteousness and will come under the attack of the devil through family members, church members or congregation, in and outside of the Church.

Are you servants of God afraid of "persecution" in the Body of Christ, the Church for preaching, teaching the "whole Bible," or obeying the Holy Spirit for performing that which "He" guides you to "perform," and that which God's Word says to do, "lay" hands on the sick, and they shall recover? Which I've experienced or speak in Tongues that which I also do, speak in tongues. Which is One of the gifts of the Holy Spirits, "He that is in me and believers."

"Church don't "Quench," the Holy Spirit allow Him to work in and through you, in and outside of the Church. Obey, God's Word and Spirit!

Note: Never again will I allow man stop me from performing that which I am called and showed to performed, by Jesus Christ Himself, which was confirmed by Jehovah God. Never again! No man nor devil or devil in man or spirit regardless who or whom shall never again stop nor prevent me from which I'm called and showed to do!

Note: Congregation of God, Jehovah God, Jesus Christ, and the Holy Spirit are my Witnesses of that which I've professed openly to.

Man persecutes and excommunicates, Jehovah God does not. "Who do you fear, man or God?"

I'm a servant, called by Jehovah who placed and position me in the spiritual realm to speak and perform in behalf of His Word and works. I was persecuted for performing such prayer by divine guidance of a member who refuse to stand in the presence of Jesus Christ Who says, "For where two or three are gathered in my name, there am I in the midst of them" (Matt. 18:20).

Note: The member had "cancer," which I didn't know. I request her to stand, she refused. I'll forever believe had she stood in Jesus's presence, He would have supernatural healed her.

I requested permission to pray for her yet persecuted by a minister and member of that congregation for performing that which I was called to do.

Yes, I was directly persecuted in the Body of Christ in the sanctuary. A pastor openly condemned me in the sanctuary, "Go home and pray!" Yet over years of ministry, he now sat in the pew, blind of the disease diabetes.

Note: Brethren and sisters, if Jesus called you into the five-fold ministry of Jehovah God, as an apostle, prophet, evangelist, pastor, or teacher, do not compromise, alter, nor change God's Word nor His works as in a "clique," teach or preach the "whole Bible truth." Therefore, you won't suffer or face Consequences in the future, whether you preach one day or seventy years. Preach or teach the whole Bible truth and in your latter years, you'll enjoy the "fruit of your labor."

Question: Do I fear man? "No." Nor man's clique, nor organization. God is whom to "fear." So brothers and sisters, you may be persecuted for your righteous acts. Regardless, be obedient in your call. If you are called to heal the sick, in the home or sanctuary, heal the sick. If you speak in tongues while in the sanctuary, speak in tongues in an orderly manner. If you are called to lay hands on the blind, the lame, the deaf, the dumb, do so and pray in the Name of Jesus. Again, do not fear man, fear Jehovah God.

Read Acts 4:19–20.

> But Peter and John answered them, "You yourselves judge which is right in God's sight, to obey you [man] or to obey God.
> For we cannot stop speaking of what we [I] ourselves have seen and heard. "And Neither Can I."

Note: I chose to obey God

Read John 14:12–14.

> I am telling you the truth, those who believe in me will do what I do. Yes, they will do even greater things, because I am going to the Father.

And I will do whatever you ask for in my name, so that the Father's glory will be shown through the Son.

If you ask me for anything in my name, I will do it.

Note: "It was not until late I learn that the woman whom I had prayed for had "Cancer," which I didn't know, until several weeks later."

Healing

Don't have time, take time. "Thus," says the Lord, thy God Jehovah.

Church, you'll be amazed to see the supernatural power of God at work right before your eyes in the sanctuary, which also edifies the Church.

(1) Healing = To heal is restoring of health to the sick.
(2) The making sound or whole that which is broken or injured.
(3) The curing of various diseases and defects.
(4) The returning of a person to the general state of well-being, with a sound mind.

Spiritual healing comes from Jehovah to repentant ones.

Note: The congregation, clergies, and ministers should know that faith without action prevents healing."

(1) Faith = failing to act upon or lack or have no faith in God, prevent healing.
(2) Unbelief = lack of belief or faith, prevent healing, especially in religious matters. Church, the "world sin" is "unbelief in Jesus Christ."

Read Mark 16:16. "Whoever believes and is baptized will be saved. Whoever does not believe will be condemned."

(3) Sin = a transgression of a religious or moral law. Deliberate disobedience to the will of God, prevent healing.
(4) Trust = failing to trust or place reliance in God prevent one's healing.
(5) Unforgiving = reluctant or refusing to forgive, prevent healing.

Note: Spiritual healing come from Jehovah God to repentant ones in the Name of Jesus.

Note: Spiritual healing can take place anywhere at any time. Don't have time; take time. "Thus," says the Lord thy God, "My Word nor My works shall not return void."

Tongues

Note: Tongues, servants, clergies, and ministers (teachers and pastors). One must be "born again," of above to receive the gift to speak in tongues which is true evidence a believer had been born again of above.

"Born again" takes place supernaturally internally and is spiritual tangible to the spiritual discern. This is the "new birth." Therefore, any man be in Christ, he is a new creature. Old things are passed away, behold, all things are become new.

"Thereby speaking in tongues are "new" it's one of the gifts of the Spirit which is a heavenly language spoken that the "born again" spirit communicate with the Spirit of Almighty God.

Note: After being "born again" of the Spirit, I began speaking in a language I heard spoken in the Body of Christ which I had no knowledge of; however, I heard other believers speak which was evidence of being born again of above with the full nature of God's Spirit.

Note: Apostle Paul says, read verse 14 and then read verse 13.

Read 1 Corinthians 14:13–14. "For if I pray in this way my spirit prays indeed but my mind has no part in it. The person who speaks in strange tongues, then must pray for the gifts, to explain what is said."

Note: Which mean the ninth gift of the Spirit which is "interpretation of tongues must be implied.

Note: "Whoever does not have the Spirit cannot receive the gifts that come from God's Spirit. Such a person really does not understand them and they seem to be nonsense because their value can be judge only on a spiritual basis."

Whoever has the Spirit, however, is able to judge the value of everything but no one is able to judge him.

Note: As the Scripture says, "Who knows the mind of the Lord? "Who is able to give Me advice? "Thus, Says the Lord, Thy God."

Read 1 Corinthians 14:2. "Those who speak in strange tongues do not speak to others but to God because no one understand them. They are speaking secret truths by the power of the Spirit."

Note: Servants both men and women whom I've poured out my spirit. My Word nor my works shall not return, "void." As of now, the present nor in the future. You teach and preach My Word; however, You, whom I've called does not act nor carry nor perform, laying of hands on the sick or curing diseases in My Son's name. You are in disobedience of My Word and My works.

You preach on "faith," but where is action? I Jehovah God does not perform on "faith" alone, it takes action alone with "faith" for Me, Almighty God to supernaturally perform in or out of the presence of mankind.

Note: The sickly need no faith to be healed, just believe. Neither does a nonbeliever but you the believer must have faith; however, if it's alone and include no action, then it is dead.

Read James 2:24. "You see then, that is by our action that we are put right with God, and not by our faith alone."

Note: Now, my servant, speak in behalf of me, Jehovah God! Church, put your faith into action, in the sanctuary, where Jehovah God can manifest His presences, where signs, wonders, and miracles can be seen throughout the "Body of Christ" in the Name of My

Son. Where two or more come together in Jesus's name, there He is in their midst. "Thus," says the Lord thy God.

Read Hebrews 11:6. "No one can please God, without faith, for whoever comes to God must have 'faith' that God exist and rewards those who seek Him.

(5) (1) "Signs." Jehovah gave Signs as an assurance of truthfulness and dependability of His Words they gave evidence of God backing His servants.

Read 2 Corinthians 12:12. "The many Miracles and Wonders that prove that I am an apostle were performed among you with much patience."

(2) "Wonders," gave strong assurance that God cares for mankind and that he can and will protect those who serve Him. Jehovah God Wonders break the "law of nature."

Congregations of all denominations, Jehovah God is the same, yesterday, today, and forever.

(3) "Miracles," served a number of important purposes, they helped to establish or confirm the fact that a man was receiving power and support from Jehovah God.

Some denominations does not see God performing such miracles by the hands of Christians servants nor believers because of preaching or teaching "doctrine of demons" of unbelief's and denying the existence of miracles or either does not believe in an invisible "miracle performing" God and Creator that still exercise His supernatural power.

Read Matthew 13:57–58.

> And so they rejected him, Jesus said to them, "A Prophet is respected everywhere except in his hometown and by his own family.
> Because they did not have "Faith," he did not perform many Miracles there.

Note: But unbelief does not make the Word of God of no effect.

Read Romans 3:3–4. "But what if some of them were not faithful? Does this mean that God will not be faithful? Certainly not, God must be true even though all human beings are liars."

Note: Church, the biblical account of God's miracles and the good purpose that they accomplished, always in harmony with the truth and principle found in Jehovah's Word.

Miracles builds faith that Jehovah God still intervene in a miraculous healing and blessing faithful humankind.

Excommunication Plus Persecution

Note: For My sake, "Thus," says the Lord, thy God. Do not fear excommunication nor persecution. "Fear Me, Jehovah." Do not fear man regardless of man theology background. "Fear Me, Jehovah!"

Do not allow the devil, Satan, my adversary and the adversary of mankind stop My works nor hinder you from performing nor speaking the truth. "Fear Me, Jehovah!"

Do My work and perform in faith, I Jehovah God, Almighty will do the rest. I have spoken in behalf of My servant. "My servant, who is My prophet, whom I called by name!"

I called in my own voice to place him in my five-fold ministry. He did not make himself a proclaim prophet. I, Jehovah God, placed him in the position before he was born into the world and where he is now, "I, Jehovah, placed him where he is today!"

Note: Excommunication, the state of being excommunicated, relating to a church as an organized institution of being "outed" by a church congregation or deprived of your church or denomination membership for not traditionally preaching or teaching a "doctrine of demons" but teaching and preaching and proclaiming the "full Bible truth."

What Is Truth?

Note: The truth is contained in God's Word. Not a portion or division or piece or segment but the full Bible truth. Jehovah's Word, which is the source of the "ultimate truth" that can only come from the Almighty Creator Himself.

Question: Why is there some Churches of the body of Christ of all denominations does not preach nor teach nor proclaim the full-Bible truth?

It's because Minsters today of all denominational churches in the Body of Christ have drifted far away from the uncompromised biblical teaching of Jesus Christ even though many honest ministers and clergies won't admit that they know better and that they are simply teaching what they believe people, the world, not the congregation need to hear but people the world. Which is a "doctrine of demons." Yet the vast majority of Christians go along with man traditional preaching or teaching while they sit in pews like a bump on a log, afraid to speak out.

Note: Children of God, I reiterate, a doctrine of demons is a system or principle that are scripturally preached or taught that are nonscriptural that some clergies and ministers who were called to preach the full Gospel truth of Jesus Christ, also teach or preach the Good News, God's message, Jesus brought of his Father but have turned biblical scriptures around, alter, or changed the true biblical meaning to comply with their carnal mind (flesh) to preach or teach that which their congregation is itching to hear.

"But woe unto them that does such."

Note: If servant of Jehovah God whom God have poured His Spirit out to preach or proclaim the full Bible truth but instead proclaim a doctrine of demons, should not be allowed in pulpits in the Body of Christ. "And woe unto you!"

Multitudes of churchgoers and Christians are living in total darkness (sad to say) in hearing the truth, the full Bible truth and real purposes of God "genuine" message and understanding His inspired "Word" of healing the sick, laying on of hand, curing diseases, all in the Name of Jesus Christ and all of which performed supernaturally throughout the Body of Christ, in sanctuaries, homes, hospitals, supermarkets, and public places. Jesus says in Matthew 18:20. "For where two or three come together in my name, I am there with them."

Note: "Servants of God, healing the sick is not only for the believer but for nonbelievers as well."

Jehovah God says, "Do not place me in a box," which some clergies and men of God has already done, deceiving themselves while deceiving others with demonic deceptions.

The Bible make exceedingly clear over and over Satan the Devil deceives the whole world including the Body of Christ, the churches of all denominations.

Note: Clergies, ministers, and priests, I've expressed before, I do not wish to hurt anyone feelings nor frighten you. However, I must tell the truth as a servant called by the Living God in an audible voice and told, "If you love Me, tell the truth."

Some of you must "wake" up; you have been absolutely neglectful proclaiming that which you were called or told to do.

Reiterate: You will be held accountable and suffer consequences in this life for not teaching nor preaching the "whole and true" counsel of God as the Apostle Paul taught, for he said in Acts 20:27, "For I have not held back from announcing to you the whole purpose of God. And neither have I."

Amen.

A Doctrine of Demons

A doctrine is a teaching of humankind or a rule of principles of law or a principle or system presented for acceptance or belief as by a religious or philosophic group. Man acknowledge the manifestation of all doctrines are available through mankind. However, we have a doctrine of doctrine manifesting to and through the Body of Christ that which scripture speak of.

Demon spirits does teach as articulators, its spirit manifesting in the organs of speech such as the lips or tongue or both through the carnality or flesh of mankind. They have the ability to think abstractly or profoundly and the ability to learn and reason in and outside of the Body of Christ, the Church.

And because of their articulation through man, the Spirit clearly says that some people will abandon the faith in later times, they will obey lying spirits and follow the teachings of demons.

Scripture tells us the time will come which it is here now when people will not listen to sound doctrine but will follow their own desires and will collect for themselves more and more teachers who will tell them what they are itching to hear. They will and have already turned away from listening to the truth and gave their attention to doctrines of demons. Such doctrines are spread by deceitful liars whose consciences are dead.

Many false doctrines are being demonically teach which bring about denominational division into the Body of Christ and congregations. Denominational teaching and the separation of religion was created by Satan the Devil through man as his spirit representative. Satan is the culprit that has established his works and word in the Church. Some of the largest denominational churches are teaching or believing in his false doctrines.

As a spokesman for God, I believe that's why the Holy Spirit told and directed me to a nondenominational place of worship where God is worship in Spirit and in truth. And the full gospel is taught and preached.

Christians does not serve a denominational God nor Lord. We serve God in Spirit and in truth. I've witnessed the expelling of demon spirits out of people, miraculous healing of the sick, the laying of hands on the ailing. I've witnessed the speaking in tongues and its interpretation. I've had confirmation through prophets and prophetess confirm to me things God had either told me or showed me, which no one else knew of but God and myself.

I've been a member of Lakewood Church for many years where I've never witnessed a false teacher, preacher, prophet, or prophetess in the nondenominational congregation. The works and word of the devil nor his demons will never prevail. I'm a witness of the truth in a nondenominational congregation where a nondenominational God and Lord is worship and served.

Remember, I was told and directed by the Holy Spirit to go to a nondenominational church. Therefore, I'm a witness that Jehovah, the God whom I serve and the Lord Jesus Christ is not a denominational God and Lord.

People, wherever the division of religion and church denominationalism exist, spiritual warfare exist and wherever spiritual exist, doctrine of demons exist. False doctrines and false prophets are works and words of demon spirits. Which mean denominational congregations are in spiritual warfare in the Body of Christ, the Church.

The spirit realm realize the church does not focus on demonize persons in the pulpit conducting a religious service of demon doctrines even though the scriptures clearly says, man cannot drink from the Lord's cup and also from the cup of demons. Man cannot eat at the Lord's table and also at the table of demons.

Minsters are in the pulpit preaching or conducting a religious service as demon spirits speak through them. Some with, while some without knowledge of their presence. Some appear normal in all aspects of life; however, they aren't in their right mind.

The manifestation of demon doctrines and demonic influences in Christianity is more prevalent today in Christian lives than ever before. The purpose of all such demonic activity is to turn people away from God and the pure worship of God.

Their doctrines start in the homes. It is established in the homes to manifest throughout the land. Which mean Christians need to focus on doctrines of demons, the teachings and preaching of demon spirits through the carnality of humankind.

Regardless how smart and intelligent man appear to be, a demon spirit or spirits are greater in spirit and intelligence residing in the body articulating speech and words as its spirits to teach and preach doctrines that are contrary to Bible doctrines.

The utilization of human minds is Satan's weapon in which his spirit and the spirit of demons use as their invisible articulation and supernatural power to manifest through the flesh of that person of whom their spirit dwell's in.

Why religious people often quote scriptures contrary of God's word? All manifestations of demonic doctrines are manifest by way of the carnality of mankind of all ages and denomination. There aren't exceptions in their teaching and preaching. People need not be in the Body of Christ to be led astray by demonic forces in the pulpit or in the world.

Demonic forces are at work in sinners as well as in the Body of Christ. They are out to destroy or tarnish the Word and works of God sound doctrine, which is teaching and preaching the Good News, the full gospel of Jesus Christ.

Sound doctrine is the full gospel of God and Jesus Christ. It tells and explain to mankind what we are up against in the spirit realm. That's why it is imperative for all mankind to study the Word of God to know whether the teaching or preaching is of sound doctrine or is it the doctrine of demon spirits speaking through or manifesting by way of the tongues of false prophets and teachers.

When I was of the world, lost in a world of unbelievers while not knowing the word of God, a doctrine of demons was numerously taught to me by a family members. Whom supposed to have been knowledgeable of the Word of God. I did not know he spoke erroneously of the scriptures until I was saved and begin to study the Word of God for myself.

I've discovered through studying the Word many false teachers quote scriptures erroneously or twisted; or alter to make scriptures sound right and good. The Apostle Paul speak of such false teachers and preachers that will twist God's Word around in order to make themselves look good in the Christian faith.

Church, the teaching and preaching of false doctrines are everlasting. As long there is a devil or demons in the world there will be false doctrines or a doctrine of demon throughout the world.

The world enjoys false doctrine and the teaching of demons which give the world the excuse to live ungodly lives. The world's knowledge is not limit in performing the ungodly works of the world. Also, there is no limit in the world's immorality. Immorality is right in the sight of the world. It is the right life to live. Wrong is right in the world of the ungodly and right is wrong in the minds of the world.

Jesus Christ died on the cross, his death was the basis for removing the law, which had separated the Jews from the non-Jews or Gentiles. Therefore, by accepting the reconciliation made possible by Jesus's death, both Jews and Gentiles (non-Jews) could become "one body to God through the cross," which means Jesus is the Head of "one body the Church" of all mankind.

Church, I believe those who believe in denominational division in Christianity are in spiritual warfare with either themselves or denominationalism because of false doctrines. Any denomination that disassociate their Christianity from other Christians are in for a rude awakening.

Regardless who you are or how strong one's conviction, God is not a denominational God. That's what the doctrine of demons wants to instill or implant into the mind of Christians and Christianity.

People, the preaching and teaching of doctrine of demons are real and alive in the church and it has great influence over denominational congregation. A doctrine of demons represents and believe in separation of prayer in public schools and public places. Wherever a doctrine of demons are taught or preached or exist there is demonic freedom.

Doctrine of demons believe in same-sex marriages that which is contrary to the law, sacramental and principles of God. Some churches throughout the world are permitting and conducting same-sex marriages.

Some states have legalized same-sex adoption of children. Which mean a child of God may be adopted by the same sex or gender as parents. Whether male and male as parents or female and female as parents which is an abomination that God thoroughly detest.

The doctrine of demons is more prevalent today than ever before, age is no exception. Demon possession and the teaching and preaching of demonic doctrines are bringing condemnation into the world by demonization.

Ask yourself why more people want to be the opposite sex today than ever before? People are biologically having their sexual organs alter to assume the role of the opposite. Men who has been men all their lives, some with families now want to be women. Women who has been women all of their lives with families now want to be men. Their sexual preference changed. Why? Because of demon possession. A demon spirit or spirits have entered and possessed their mind and body.

I reiterate, age is no exception. Little boys want to be girls and little girls want to be boys. Why? Demon Possession. A doctrine of demons says, it's right for humankind to choose their sexual preference or alter their sexual gender, whether male or female. Now some religions and denominations are supporting or in support of ordination of gay ministers into the Body of Christ, the Church. Something that will never take place in the Body of Christ. It may happen in the church of ungodly but never in the Body of Christ, the godly. "Never!"

Doctrine of demons isn't something new or happen overnight. Demon Spirits were in the world when Jesus Christ descend into the world. He said, "I did not come to save the world but the world may be saved through me."

People represent the world; however, the spiritual realm or the doctrine of demons represent the world system of things through the people in and of the world. Some people of the world's population does not realize there is a devil and millions of demons in the Earth.

If the devil and demon spirits populate the Earth, false prophets and prophetess populate the Earth as well. Their doctrines are preached and teach to the far most corners of the world among the civilize and the uncivilized. It is accepted in high principalities, statehoods, and governments.

But Jesus warning concerning false prophets paralleled that of Moses. Through using his name and giving signs and wanders to lead astray their fruits would prove them workers of lawlessness.

The true prophet never foretold simply to satisfy human curiosity. Every prediction related to God's will, purpose, standards, or judgment. The three essentials for establishing the credentials of the true prophet as given through Moses were the true prophet would speak in Jehovah name, in which things foretold would come to pass and his prophesying must promote true worship being in harmony with God's revealed word and commandments.

But doctrines of demons which are revealed through the foretelling of false prophets and prophetess and teaching; and preaching through false teachers and preachers are contrary to the Word of God. They are sent as representatives of the spirit realm of Satan and demons to teach and preach false doctrines of the Word of God through mankind.

Demons as such were not created by God. They are invisible wicked spirit creatures sometimes called "fallen angels" having superhuman powers, power to speak through the demonize people who are under the influence of demons' power or demon possession.

The first to make himself one was Satan the Devil who became the ruler of other demons. Their purpose of all such demonic activity is to mislead people and to turn people against the true and pure worship of God.

Therefore, Christians must put up a hard fight against the unseen enemies of the spirit realm. Prophetic warning is given concerning accelerated demon activity on the Earth. When Jesus was on Earth demonic influence was very prevalent, in which some of his greatest miracles consisted of expelling demons from victimized persons.

Since the ascension of Jesus Christ into heaven, think how prevalent demonic influences are in people throughout the Earth. Look around you, the doctrine of demons, demonic activity and influences are in people of the church and outside the Body of Christ.

Today there are many impostors invading the pulpit with deception while conducting religious services with false doctrines stating there are many ways of getting into the Kingdom of Heaven. These impostors who claim to be sent by God never speak of Jesus of being the only way to God. Because Satan and demon spirits has the ability to speak through the mouth of false prophets', preachers', and teachers' words that are contrary of the Word of God.

Church, what this nation need is spiritual revival for setting possessed persons free of demon captivity and the influence demons possess over persons. It is imperative that all non- and denominations join together in spiritual warfare against demonic forces and activity in the Body of Christ, the Church.

Church, many religious leaders are demonized or under the influence of demon spirts but does not recognize their condition as being under the influence of a demon or demons, or even being demon-possessed. Because their minds are focus on money and prestige.

Therefore, it is imperative for Christians and denominational congregations get involve together in the Body of Christ to take upon oneself to expel demons out of anyone suspected of any kind of demonic activity in congregations or the five-fold ministry of the Body of Christ.

Note: Church, if our God whom we worship in Spirit and in truth was a denominational God, I would not have been saved when I was in and of the world. Jesus Christ, the Son of the Living God said, "I did not come to save the world, but the world may be saved through me."

Amen.

Acknowledging the Mind, Not the Perception of Satan

Humankind should thank God for knowing the thoughts of all. Had God not known or perceive man's perception I know I would not be alive today and neither anyone else. It is the mind and God's Spirit He use to guard and guide us away from the perils of life that exist in this evil and wicked world.

Our Heavenly Father realize the minds of mankind in the place Satan's spirit use to enter to set up headquarters. The human mind is the only access or avenue for his spirit of deceptiveness to enter the lives of humankind. There isn't no other avenue in which to enter but by way of the mind.

Man utilize the mind to plan for the future for which Satan use to enter his spirit perception him. Satan's spirit uses the mind to set man up for the use of events that cause them to become disastrous causing great harm or death. Our minds inform the devil of our plans directly or indirectly.

If man allow and he does, the devil or demons spirits will dictate his thoughts or perceptions. When that occur, the results are death. During the adolescent years of my life many of my peers and I not knowingly allowed the devil's spirit dictate their lives as I witnessed their transgressions as demon spirits perform through them including myself.

I believe I was the most demonized or demon-possessed among my peers; however, I nor my peers had never heard the name demon, let along know demon spirits are persons without bodies having the ability to enter human bodies to possess as their own and perform all kinds of inhuman and hideous acts.

The peers I associated with was either alcoholic demonized or demon-possessed, or under the influence of demonic minds. They were disobedient, mean, and destructive. We all were without knowingly were under the power of demonic forces and under the power of influence of the devil and as well in spiritual warfare with ourselves and the world.

We are responsible for some of the evil and wickedness that exist in today's world. Because of it, I've witnessed many of my peers assist the devil and demons that cause them an early death. Several died a senseless death, others died I believe before their time as well. They were either killed or died unnatural deaths, because the devil or demons; or both dictated their lives as well as their livelihoods.

Satan realize it's easy for a person to follow a path of destruction without Jesus Christ as Lord and Savior over one's life. They know a person without Jesus in their life, they possess full control over one's mind, therefore giving them power to dictate and assist their spirit to control their minds perception of how to perceive things.

He realizes God has a plan and purpose for all of whom belongs to him. For all His children is a plan and purpose for well-being in living and to serve and be a servant unto Him. But Satan's plan is to prevent that which God has plan for us.

Therefore, he like to dictate man's life away from God's way of living and bring condemnation upon all mankind by way of the works of his spirit, which is why the works of dictating mankind's thoughts are vital to the devil and demons. That's why it's imperative all mankind guard his mind against the works of the devil and demonic forces.

Man must learn to guard his mind while acknowledging when to guard the mind. We possess the mind of Jesus which explains how we know the thoughts of the devil. How does man know the mind of the devil? Jesus know every thought, perception, and imagination of Satan. Since we, mankind, possess the mind of Jesus that explains how we know the mind and thoughts of the devil and demons.

Thereby, it's imperative that mankind recognize his mind is that of Jesus. But unfortunately, not all mankind are children of God but children of the devil who think like and perform as the devil. Read 1 John 3:9–10.

Since God brought me back to my right mind and senses, I confess I once possessed the mind of Satan's spirits. However, I now profess openly I possess the mind of Jesus Christ. I now recognize every demonic thought or perception the devil's spirit attempt to get me to entertain and dwell on. Church, it is a joy to rebuke the devil and demon spirits literally and spiritually to their faces.

The question is, "How can man be victorious in the battle of the mind?" Be vigilant, stay on the alert and watchful. Whoever is in accord with the flesh, set their minds on things of the flesh but you who is in accord with the mind of Jesus is in accord with the spirit of things. For the mind of the flesh means death, but the mind of Jesus is of the spirit means life and peace.

Also, a mind of the flesh is of the world. One cannot eat of God's table and at the same time feed from the table of demons. That explains a person cannot serve the two, God and the world. Mankind must put up a hard fight against unseen wicked spirits that are trying to capture to control and influence people intellectually of the mind.

There isn't no other method physically or mentally in the spiritual realm a person can be control except by way of the mind. However, God can spiritually, physical, mentally, or intellectually control anyone including Satan and demons.

Church, Satan would like to control your minds. It is the mind whom he uses to control or destroy every facet or life. Without the use of man's mind, they are powerless and ineffective against God creation. Every man, woman and child must know how and when to guard his or her mind.

Therefore, we as adults and children of God must pray not only for our wellbeing but for the wellbeing of our children and loved ones as well. Children are in spiritual warfare as well as are adults and the mind are where it all start.

Spiritual warfare is physical but yet mental and spiritual for which all originate in the human mind and then manifest into physical conflicts with the carnality of the world whom the devil and demon control. Therefore, it's imperative we pray for our children, loved ones and children of neighbors.

The devil has cause and is responsible for multitudes to be deceived of their own mind. A mind of deceptiveness is responsible for many deaths of persons deceived by their thoughts.

Thoughts of deceptiveness is a tool Satan use as a weapon since the beginning of creation and will continue to use as a tool, weapon, or devise against all God's creation.

I've perceived many deceptive demonic thoughts the spirit of Satan attempt to give me to dwell on as my own thought. He told me I was going to die at the young age of thirty-six. Obviously, I did not die.

Since then I've witnessed as well as experienced many false perceptions of myself and of others that came to me with false perceptions of themselves. Whether of an illness or having doubt or being doubtful of oneself.

Mankind must realize the power of false perceptiveness is not to be ignored, all kind of evil exist intellectually, spiritually, and articulately. The spirit of Satan does speak to us through others. It is man's mind and tongue whom his spirit use to articulate effective language that bring individuals under submission of his intellectual perceptions.

Spirit of deceptiveness is responsible of millions of people to become demonize of demons possessed. It is his spirit false perceptiveness the devil use to enter demon spirits of all kinds into the mind and body of humankind to dwell in as their own.

I reiterate it is the devil's spirit false perception that demons enter human minds and bodies. The mind is the only avenue that is accessible to entry. Man's mind including some Christians are the devil's spirit headquarters. If his spirit uses Christian minds as avenues in the spiritual realm, imagine the predicament and condition he has the world in.

I was in the world well over forty years. I was of the world and thought like the world, performed as the world because of my intellectuality opposed my spirituality. It is imperative mankind learn to recognize and distinguish between intellectuality and spirituality to oppose false perceptiveness of the devil or demons.

I'm not ashamed to admit the devil and demon spirits dictated my intellectuality and thoughts of perceptions and literally my life during the years I was under demonic powers. Today, they are destroying the youths of this generation by way of intellectuality.

Today's youth think or believe they know everything to let them tell it. They are the brightest and most intelligent of past and future generations. Some even claim to know far more than parents. In some cases, I've witnessed it to be true. Yet majority of youths are destroying their lives all because of false perceptiveness which they act on and perform. Children of all ages are performing demonic works and acts of demons. What I'm saying demons are performing demonic works and acts through the youths of this generations.

More children ever before are demonized under the power and influence of demonic spirits but yet does not recognize nor acknowledge demonology or demonization that exist in the world today.

Any person who think or possess the act or an instance of intentionally killing oneself has perceived a demonic perception. Suicide is a word that is in the devil vocabulary that is defined as a demonic thought or perception that only the devil or demons possess power to manifest into physical and deadly results through mankind.

The destruction of ruin of one's life or interest in living is cause by an evil spirit, demon. A spirit that is greater than one's natural spirit. It is a spirit of deceptiveness which is a demonic thought of a demon perception perceived in an individual to act on to carry out.

The devil is a murderer that comes to steal, kill, and destroy human lives. However, he or demons cannot perform neither without the use of human minds. It is the mind that they need that activate a person to perform such hideous acts because they are powerless against mankind without man's mind. It is scriptural, "the flesh is weak, but the spirit is willing."

Satan realize the weakness of human minds and because of such weakness demonic thought and false perceptiveness are stronger and more prevalent than ever before.

Mankind need Jesus Christ in their lives and acknowledge Jesus is Lord and Savior in his and her lives. Then man can claim to possess the mind of Jesus Christ. A mind no devil nor demons can come against now nor ever.

Flesh: The Other Spirit Versus the Five Senses

The flesh is weak without the Spirit, the flesh control the mind, the mind controls the five senses, and vice versa the five senses control the mind.

Note: Without the Spirit at hand, humankind does not possess inner strength to control neither. Which Satan know and uses both to control man.

The flesh and mind is used as the devil workshop which he uses to control the entire human race, "world."

Note: Man and Satan acknowledge the mind is essential in our livelihood in making rightful or wrongful decisions or making up one's mind. Therefore, Satan the Devil use the five senses as his own, sight, hearing, feeling, tasting, and smell.

Definition of the five senses.

(1) Sight = The ability to see, to perceive with the eyes, get sight of

(2) Hear = To perceive "sound" by the ear

(3) Feel = To perceive through the sense of touch. To perceive as a physical sensation.

(4) Taste = To distinguish the flavor of by taking into the mouth. To perceive as if by the sense of taste.

(5) Smell = To perceive the Scent of something by means of the olfactory nerves.

Note: How does Satan know these things because Satan is a person walking the Earth. Transition into human form which he appears as a human being, just as you and I are human beings. Walking the

Earth to and fro attempting the steal, kill, or destroy the human race by any means through the mind using the human mind and the five senses to cause man to destroy himself while destroying others as well.

Read 1 Peter 5:8. "Be alert, be on watch! Your enemy, the devil, roams around like a roaring lion, looking for someone to devour."

Note: Satan work and perform off the mind or our thoughts to deceive one another.

Remember Satan walk the Earth appearing as a person just as you or I, a spirit human being, right in our "the world" midst.

Note: Satan knows by the power of the five senses exactly and precisely what each individual male and female like in the flesh but not of the Spirit. "Age nor gender is no exception."

Note: Satan uses each of the five senses of his own mind to deceive the human race by giving off and receiving false deception.

The sense of sight can be deceived of one sees which the result can cause death or other destructions.

That's how he knows the thoughts of individuals of what he sees by acknowledging the thoughts of himself being perform throughout the human race.

There isn't no other human being that know the mind or thoughts of another human being using his or her thoughts to perform his will and purpose on the face of the Earth but Satan the Devil.

Note: Thereby, without the Spirit, the flesh is weak and has no control over itself. Children of Jehovah God that's why we must attend Bible class or Sunday school at an early age to learn how weak our flesh are in the spiritual realm of the devil, Satan.

There is no excuse for allowing someone else besides oneself dictate our (humankind) mind and five senses to perform his will and purpose which is out of the will and purpose of Jehovah God.

Children of God attending Sunday school is vital in all human lives to acknowledge who is in control of one's flesh sometime. We humans take for granted as though the flesh is just to be look upon and recognize of who one is. True but, however, the flesh can be deceiving of one's appearance.

Note: There is an old Proverb, that says, "You can't judge a book by the cover," which is true of the flesh. Remember this is something to think about. Note: "Satan walks the Earth in the flesh but yet a spirit person just as you and I appearing as a human being in the flesh."

Note: This is the "Bible truth," I've had several encounters with Satan who appeared to me as another person. One encounter we even dialogued during that time. I didn't know he was the one whom the Bible says, read Ezekiel 28:13–17.

> You lived in Eden, the garden of God, and wore gems of every kind, rubies and diamonds, tapas, beryl, carnelian and Jasper, sapphires, emeralds, and garnets. You had ornaments of gold. They were made for you on the day you were created.
>
> I put a terrifying angel there to guard you. You lived on my holy mountain and walked among sparkling gems.
>
> Your conduct was perfect from the day you were created until you began to do evil.
>
> You were busy buying and selling, and this led you to violence and sin. So I forced you to leave my holy mountain and the angel who guarded you drove you away from the sparkling gems.
>
> you were proud of being handsome, and your fame made you act like a fool. Because of this I hurled you to the ground and left you as a warning to other kings.

Note: Congregation of God, Satan now walk the Earth as a spirit person deceiving the entire world. Read Isaiah 14:12–17.

> King of Babylon [Lucifer] bright morning star, you have fallen from heaven! In the past

you conquered nations, but now you have been thrown to the ground.

You were determined to climb up to heaven and place your throne above the highest stars.

You said you would climb to the tops of the clouds and be like the Almighty.

But instead, you have been brought down to the deepest part of the world of the dead.

The dead will stare and gape at you. They will ask, "Is this the Man who shook the Earth and made Kingdoms trembles?

"Is this the Man who destroyed cities and turned the world into a desert? Is this the Man who never freed his prisoners or let them go home?"

Note: Children of God, the devil, Satan is on the Earth who walks among us as a human being, a spirit person in search of whom he can devour. Scripture tells us in 1 Peter 5:8, "Be alert, be on watch! Your enemy, the devil, roams around like a roaring lion, looking for someone to devour."

Note: Satan confirmed his presence on the Earth when Jehovah God ask him when the day came for the heavenly beings to appear before the Lord.

Read Job 1:7. "The Lord asked him, 'What have you been doing?' Satan answered, 'I have been walking here and there, roaming around the Earth.'"

Note: Satan answer, "Walking here and there, roaming around the Earth." Which he is doing as a spirit person, a human being, just as you and I are.

However, Satan represent two, a spirit whom human eyes can't see and as a spirit person, a man whom we can see and speak with but cannot distinguish him as a real human being which he possess a similar mind and five senses. We human being are born with.

Therefore, Satan thoughts are similar of the same capacity as we think. It's the thinking capacity which mankind perceive as their own which gives him power spiritually to act in and through human minds and flesh.

Note: Without the Spirit mankind is vulnerable and susceptible for Satan to use the mind and five senses of individuals to perform just as he would or wishes.

The devil, Satan commit and perform acts of all humankind which cause other human beings to perform of their own not acknowledging their performance is that of the devil, Satan. Mankind perform acts of the devil using the mind and the five senses.

Note: Satan acknowledges flesh without the Spirit. Flesh has not control which cause the flesh to become weak but yet the Spirit is always willing. Therefore, mankind must guard the mind by the way of thinking of what is seen because all five senses are tempted by the works of the devil in the physical realm. First is perception and then there is deception. All works of the devil.

Note: Therefore, we must guard the mind and protect our way of perceiving of what we see at all times. No person is immune or exempt of Satan use of the mind or five senses. We are all vulnerable of his machinations and the usage of the mind and senses without one's knowledge.

Acknowledging one's own perception of what is good and what is evil reveal which spirit is performing as its own.

Remember, the flesh is weak and any abnormal or immoral thoughts or perception is of the devil's spirit perception, even thoughts of angel of lights.

Note: Satan also acknowledge the mind and senses are mankind way of distinguishing right and wrong and evil and good. Which is a spiritual fight to do that which is right in God's sight, which is a spiritual war, right in our sight of doing right.

We all struggle against or with the flesh because the flesh is weak. Scripture says, "Keep watch and pray that you will not fall into temptation" (Matt. 26:41).

Note: The Spirit is willing, but the flesh is weak.

Congregation of God, man does not realize how weak the flesh is because God did not give us a spirit of fear.

Read 2 Timothy 1:7. "For the Spirit that God has given us does not make us timid instead, his Spirit fills us with power, love, and self-control."

Congregation and children of Jehovah God, the flesh, human nature cannot please God, people become enemies of God when they are controlled by their human "flesh" nature because they do not obey God's law and in fact, they cannot obey it.

Read Romans 8:8. "Those who obey their human nature cannot please God."

Note: Flesh, the other spirit not of God but of human nature, is at war against the Spirit.

Satan uses every advantage he can against the Spirit of God through the five senses. Therefore, it is imperative of how and what we think because it is the mind that Satan uses to cultivate his insidious plans of attack for and against the human race using the human race as tools and conduits to channel his plans throughout the land against the will and purpose of God for the human race.

Now you know the other spirit.

Jesus Christ, Our Redemption and Redeemer Sermon and Message

Note: Congregation, the word *redemption* referring as to buying back as from slavery or from some obligation. "Redemption," today has more the thought of regaining possession of something.

Note: Jesus Christ came as the "Seed" of Jehovah God, died, and was buried or placed in a tomb. He arose from the dead and bared fruit throughout the Earth.

The Seed that was buried was the Word, "Jesus." Which His followers, the believers is to sow his message or the Word, throughout all nations, therefore, to bearer fruit all over the world.

Note: Congregation, the "Seed" God sent was his Son, Jesus Christ, the Seed of "redemption." And by way of the Seed, God brought the whole world back to himself.

Read Colossians 1:19–20.

> For it was by God's own decision that the Son has in himself the full nature of God.
> Through the Son, then, God decided to bring, the whole universe back to himself. God made peace through his Son's blood on the cross

and so brought back to himself all things both on Earth and in heaven.

Note: Congregation, God brought back that which Satan stolen by deception when he appeared to Eve speaking through a serpent.

However, Satan hadn't any knowledge of Jehovah's plan of getting back that which he lied to take for his own. Satan the Devil through his deception provided a way of "redemption" for all mankind through God's Son, Christ Jesus.

Note: Mankind's need for a ransom came about through the rebellion in Eden. When Adam sold himself to disobedience for the selfish pleasure of listening to his wife's voice to share with her in rebellion standing before God.

"Church, Adam thereby sold himself and his descendants into slavery of sin and to death."

Note: There was a gradual revelation of God's secret concerning the promised "Seed." Would the Seed be heavenly or Earthly? If spiritual or heavenly, it would run an Earthly course to destroy the serpent and free or liberate mankind.

Note: Congregation, the Seed would have to be a mighty spirit person. How would he be provided and who would be his mother? This required God, Son becoming human to correspond with Adam.

God accomplished this by transferring his Son's life from heaven to the womb of the Jewish virgin Mary.

Read John 1:14. "The Word became a human being and full of grace and truth, lived among us. We saw his glory, the glory which he received as the Father's only Son."

Note: Jesus did not owe his life to any human father descended from the sinner Adam. He maintained a sinless state throughout his life.

Note: The Seed Jesus planted was his life for humankind throughout all nations of people for the "Redemption" of life, Muslims, Buddhism, and others. Which properly signifies Jesus paid a price by which captives are redeemed from the enemy, Satan.

Read Romans 5:18–19.

> So then, as the one sin condemned all people, in the same way the one righteous act sets all people free and gives them life.
> And just as all people were made sinners as the result of the disobedience of one man, in the same way they will all be put right with God as the result of the obedience of the one Man.

Note: Jesus was indeed a corresponding ransom not for the redemption of the one sinner, Adam but for the redemption of all mankind descended from Adam. Congregation, He repurchased us so that we became his family.

We by his ransom became His Bride brought from among mankind, the world as a first fruit. Jesus used the authority granted by Jehovah on the basis of his ransom to give life to all those who accepted his provision.

Read 1 Corinthians 15:45. For the Scripture says, "The first man Adam, was created a living being, but the last Adam is the life-giving Spirit."

Note: Though available to all, Christ's ransom sacrifice is not accepted by all and the wrath of God remains upon those not accepting it, as it also comes upon those who first accept and then turn away from the provisions.

> Whoever believes in the Son has eternal life, whoever disobeys the Son will not have life, but will remain under God's punishment. (Jn. 3:36)

> For there is no longer any sacrifice that will take away sins if we purposely go on sinning after the truth has been made known to us.
> Instead, all that is left is to wait in fear for the coming judgement and the fierce fire which will destroy those who oppose God.
> What, then of those who despise the Son of God? Who treat as a cheap thing the blood of

God's covenant which purified them from sin? Who insult the Spirit of grace? Just think how much worse is the punishment they will deserved. (Heb. 10:26–29)

Note: Brothers and sisters, we as Christians and followers of Jesus Christ has the spiritual righteousness to sow seed which is the message throughout all nations. We through Jesus have been given the spiritual right to accomplish his command.

Read Matthew 28:19–20. "Go then, to all people everywhere and make them my disciples, baptize them in the name of the Father, the Son and the Holy Spirit. And teach them to obey everything I have commanded you and I will be with you always to the end of the age."

Note: Wherever the message (seed) is preached or teach, Christ is there in the midst, in Spirit and wherever the Spirit of the Lord, there is freedom.

Read Matthew 18:20. "For where two or three come together in my name, I am there with them."

Note: Paul, the Apostle shows that there is a danger to Christian freedom; therefore, the Christian must set his mind on the things of the spirit in order to win victory over evil.

Read Romans 14:21. "Do not let evil defeat you, Instead conquer evil with good."

Note: Paul also spoke of the need of humankind to be set free from enslavement and corruption; and Jesus Christ told the Jews who had believed in him, "If you remain in my word, you are really my disciples; and you will know the truth and the truth will set you free. Therefore, if the Son sets you free, you will be actually be free."

II

LIFE IN THE SPIRIT

Note: Congregation, Christ Jesus has set us free from the "law" of sin and of death.

Read Romans 8:1–2. "There is no condemnation now for those who live in union with Christ Jesus. For the law of the Spirit, which brings us life in union with Christ Jesus has set me free from the law of sin and death."

Note: Children of God, Jesus Christ provided a redemption price, His life, to set the human race free from enslavement of sin. And the seed, the message which he sowed is still bearing fruit as he is in spirit continue cultivating the land through his followers or servants sowing the fields.

Note: Children of God, there are two kinds of seed which has been sowed into the field or world. The Good Seed that produce people who belong to the Kingdom and the Bad seed which produce weeds. The weeds are people who belong to the enemy, the devil.

Read 1 Peter 5:8. "Be alert, be on watch! Your enemy, the devil, roams around like a roaring lion, looking for someone to devour."

Note: Children of God, there are also children of the Enemy, the devil.

Read 1 John 3:8–10.

> Whoever continues to sin belongs to the devil, because the devil has sinned from the very beginning. The Son of God appeared for this very reason, to destroy what the devil has done.
>
> Those who are children of God do not continue to sin, for God's very nature is in them, and because God is their Father, they cannot continue to sin.
>
> Here is the clean difference between God's children and the devil's children, those who do not do what is right or do not love others are not God's children.

Note: Congregation, Satan has weeds planted or sowed throughout the Body of Christ, right before our eyes, disguised as sheep in wolves' clothing!

Read 2 Corinthians 11:14–15. "Well, no wonder. Even Satan can disguise himself to look like angel of light. So it is no great things if his servants disguise themselves to look like servants of righteousness."

Note: These things reveal the might and power of the spirit creature Satan. He made early efforts to block the promise of the Seed. Satan no doubt identified Jesus as the Son of Jehovah God and the one who was prophesied to bruise him in the head.

Note: Jehovah God pronounces judgment against the "serpent," the devil.

Read Genesis 3:15. "I will make you and the woman hate each other, her offspring, and yours will always be enemies. Her offspring will crush your head, and you will bite her offspring's heel."

Children of God, the efforts to destroy Jesus as an infant were unsuccessful, God continued to protect Jesus during his youth.

Satan done everything he could to destroy Jesus; however, Jesus was ever alert of the danger of Satan's machinations and to the fact that Satan's desire to cause his destruction.

Note: Throughout Jesus ministry, he was in danger, Satan using human agents to oppose and to try either to cause him to stumble or to kill him.

On one occasion, those of his own hometown attempted to kill him. He was constantly harassed by those whom Satan used to try to trap him.

Read Matthew 22:15. "The Pharisees went off and made a plan to trap Jesus with questions."

Note: The Pharisees fail to trap Jesus; however, Satan succeeded in having him put to death by getting control of one of Jesus apostle, then using the Jewish leaders and the Romans to execute Jesus.

Note: The Apostle Satan used was Judas Iscariot who betrayed Jesus. In conjunction with the betrayal, John says, "From the beginning Jesus knew who was the one that would betray him."

Read John 6:64. "Jesus said, 'Yet some of you do not believe,' Jesus knew from the beginning who were the ones that would not believe, and which one would betray him."

Note: Then Satan entered him.

Read Luke 22:3–4. "Then Satan entered into Judas, called Iscariot, who was one of the twelve disciples. So Judas went off and spoke with the chief priest and the officers of the Temple guard about how he could betray Jesus to them."

Note: Congregation of God, it was really Jehovah God, the Father that sentenced or put his Son Jesus Christ to death. The Roman government only carried out Jehovah's plan.

Note: After Jesus death and resurrection, Satan continued to wage a bitter fight against Christ's followers. Paul said that he had been given a thorn in the flesh, an angel of Satan keep slapping him, "But to keep me from being puffed up with pride because of the many wonderful things I saw. I was given a painful physical ailment, which acts as Satan's messenger to beat me, and keep me from being proud" (2 Cor. 12:7).

Note: Satan, also sent false prophets who fought against Paul and those in Ephesus who said they themselves were Jews and yet they were not but a synagogue of Satan.

Note: And in the case with Eve, in the Garden of Eden, Satan disguised his real nature and purposes by transforming himself into an angel of light and had his agents' ministers transformed themselves into minsters of righteousness.

Read 2 Corinthians 11:14–15. "Well, no wonder. Even Satan can disguise himself to look like an angel of light. So it is no great things, if his servants disguise themselves to look like servants of righteousness."

Note: The Apostle Paul says, now I want to remind you my friends of the Good News (the message), which I preached to you. Which you received, and on which your faith stands firm.

Read 1 Corinthians 15:2–4.

> That is the gospel the Message that I preached to you. You are saved by the Gospel if you hold firmly to it, unless it was for nothing that you believed.

I passed on to you what I received, which is of the greatest importance that Christ died for our sins, as written in the Scriptures.

that he was buried, and that he was raised to life three days later, as written in the Scriptures.

Note: Children of God, Jesus Christ is alive in heaven and is at the right hand of our heavenly Father, as Lord and Savior, Redeemer, Mediator, Intercessor, and Healer.

Amen.

Homosexuality

The Holy Bible, God's Word, teaches against homosexuality, lesbianism, and perverted sexual acts. God warns us that it is wrong and sinful for the same biological sex to engage in sexual contact, and it is a sin at its highest level.

Homosexuality and lesbianism came into existence ever since Satan the Devil and demon spirit became inhabitants of the world. And to this day, it is one of the greatest sins if not the greatest to exist throughout the world. It is a sin that bring condemnation through demonic pleasure that destroys humankind.

There are many forms of sexual activity in the world today which many has develop into perverted sexual acts never before heard of nor imagine. Only Satan the Devil could think of because man's natural spirit would never spiritually or intellectually give mankind perceptions of perverted sex or permit perverted sex let alone give man or woman (male or female) the perception he or she is the opposite sex.

First and foremost, why does a person want to believe he or she is the opposite sex or believe some other person is trap in their body that is the opposite sex? Who's responsible of such deception in the mind of people to believe or possess such a thought? The devil's spirit is responsible, that's who.

He's the creator of this false perception in the mind of people throughout the world that they are biologically the opposite sex that is trap in the body of the other sex. The devil's spirit has some people so confuse they do not know whether they are male or female, even though their biological reproduction organs identify their true biological sex. That's how strong his influence is in multitudes of lives.

Satan is the creator of homosexuality of all kinds and levels. He is the spirit being that tell people they are someone other than who they are. He is the deceiver, the devil. The power of influence which Satan and homosexuals' demons holds over mankind is amazing.

There are more homosexuals and lesbians today than ever before, men who prefer men for sex as oppose to women. And women who prefer women for sex as oppose to men. Bisexuals, male and female, who prefer both sexes as oppose of only the opposite.

Those people represent the spirit realm, demons masquerading in disguise in human bodies. Which sexual preference does not exist. Which confirm person that prefer the same sex and those oppose the same sex aren't in their right mind.

No man or woman regardless of age rather be the opposite sex. Only the devil's spirit can influence mankind by his spirit perception to cause a person to believe he or she is the opposite sex, which is a demonic state of mind. Some people are having sex changes to satisfy their sexual preference for which they believe is the right thing to do. Which is an abomination before God.

They believe as though they are correcting a biological mistake. Therefore, man cannot tell him or her anything different about how he or she feel or believe. The devil's spirit has established in their mind they are the opposite sex.

The gay population is a demon-possessed population. Although a person need not be gay to be demonize nor demon-possessed. Many hidden demons' dwell in the bodies of mankind. But they are the culprits that has infiltrated human bodies and minds and established false biological identities and personalities in people.

Even though demons are spirits, they are real and alive, demons are persons without bodies but possess all human characteristics as human beings. And are constantly in search of human bodies to possess as their own. Which over rule man's natural spirit as man's body manifest its spirit as man's body and man's mind manifest its spirit in which the manifestation of its presence is through man's tongue.

In today's society, people prefer perverted sex, as oppose to normal sex. Normal sex isn't the norm any longer. There aren't no ifs and nor buts; a gay generation has emerged by way of the spirit realm right before our eyes through mankind, throughout the world.

Male prefer male; female prefer female for sexual companionships and relationships. And as for some males and females, they prefer both male and female for sexual gratification.

Also, the devil is performing by way of all levels of our government. In some states, wicked spirits of high principalities have made it possible through our government for same-sex marriages and for homosexuals and lesbians to adopt children as their own.

That mean adoption of children of gays as parents will be rear of, brought up in an environment with the belief that such marriages are right. Little boys and girls will grow up doomed for life because of what the devil and wicked spirits has perform through humankind of high levels of government and principalities.

Which mean the gay population by the wickedness and insidious work and operation of wicked spirits, demons in the body of humankind of high levels of government has develop a gay generation. Now the devil has given himself and his agents the right to perform in the physical realm as well as in the spiritual realm.

Remember, the spirit realm is powerless without the aid of mankind. Satan nor wicked spirits cannot perform effectively without the use and aid of mankind.

The gay population is governed by the spirit realm which is the plan I believe he attempted to materialize in heaven, but God expel him out of heaven along with a third of angels or spiritual sons.

Therefore, his attempt in heaven has now created in this world his own spiritual realm and government. A government in both spiritual and physical realms, both govern by himself and wicked spirits by proxy.

Which only Jesus Christ through mankind can defeat the purpose and plan against the human race of the world. And it is by accepting Jesus Christ as Lord and Savior over our lives. There isn't no other way for mankind to defeat the devil's plan in or against humanity.

Look around you, homosexuality and lesbianism and all kind of sexual perverseness is escalating. Child molestation and incest are at its highest level as well as pornography. The devil and demons have people living alternate lives shouting, "We're out, and we're proud."

It's Satan's way in saying, "That which I could not or did not do in heaven, I'm now performing my plan and works through God's Creation in the world whom I'm the god of."

The gay population have forgotten there is a devil on the Earth along with millions of wicked spirits. Demons with many of them dwelling in the body of the human race. There are many types of demons in the world disguise with different identities and personalities masquerading as humankind.

Which confirm gay persons aren't in their right mind but living under the control and power of influence of Satan or demons; or both with some demons masquerading in their body as the opposite sex.

In all reality, Satan has cause people to bring condemnation upon themselves something Jesus has defeated for all mankind. But man's lack of knowledge of himself and the spirit realm is causing man to bring destruction upon himself and others as well.

People of all ages and gender are professing openly their sexual preferences. The question is, why does some men and women prefer to be with the same sex? Some doctors say it's a gene, a chromosome that determines a person's characteristics, as others say homosexuality and lesbianism is genetically hereditary. Which are all lies but an excuse the devil's spirit through mankind is trying to make God's Creation of mankind a biological error.

But God knew the devil's thoughts from the beginning. The devil's plan had already been foretold or prophesied. God knew Satan would try to change all mankind sexual preference and biological perceptions of themselves.

For I've heard homosexuals and lesbians or both genders say "God made me the way I am," or "I was born this way," or "I'm a male trapped in a female's body," or "A female trap in a male's body," or "I'm woman but I've the mind of a man."

However, they are speaking but it isn't their natural spirit speaking. It is the devil's spirit or a demon speaking through such person a perception believes to be of one's own.

Remember, man's natural spirit would never allow a person to lie on God whom man is made in the images of neither would the natural spirit would say, "I'm a male in a female's body" or "I'm a female in a male's body."

It's imperative to remember, you cannot, nor you never will see the appearance of the devil or a demon spirit in a human body. Therefore, you must listen for their approach through man's world or speech and the manifestation of their spirit is through man's (mouth) tongue.

Does the gay population know of demon possession of human bodies? Do they know the power of influence the spirit realm possess in one's life? Don't they know any person that believe he or she is the opposite sex aren't in their natural mind but speak the mind and perception of a spirit other than their natural spirit mind?

These questions must be address to the gay population throughout the four corners of the globe before they condemn and bring destruction upon themselves in hell. They must recognize their condition to realize it isn't their choice or sexual preference but the devil's spirit or a demon in possession of their body and mind that is to condemn it.

It saddens and hurts me to hear a person regardless of gender say, "I'm a man trap in a woman's body," or a woman says, "I'm a woman trap in a man's body" or an adolescent who says, "I'm gay." "I was born this way," or "God made me this way."

No, my brothers and sisters, God did not make you that way and neither did you make yourselves that way. You got that way by demon possession or by way of the demonic and demonize state of mind of your parent.

Therefore, parents can open up avenues for demon spirits of all types to enter their unborn child. Which mean infants can be born into the world possessed by spirits other than their own. But it's the mind that the devil and demons are in control of that which control the body. Demons are the perpetrators unknown to them.

This confirm homosexuals, lesbians, and bisexuals aren't mixed up genetically nor biologically but predestine demonically in the womb of the mother to live an alternate lifestyles and as the opposite sex.

Some parents of both genders are even responsible for their child's false identity. During one's pregnancy they want a son, but God bless them with a daughter or they want a daughter, yet God bless them with a son instead.

Therefore, they bring up their child regardless of gender as the opposite sex or the sex of their preference. Which open avenues to allow demons of all types to enter the body and mind of that child to establish a false identity and personality in that child's mind.

Once the false identity is demonically established, no one but Jesus Christ can clear and restore their true identity. Jesus Christ is the only person that can bring them to their right mind.

However, a relatively small percentage of the gay population of both genders confess God with their mouth but the truth of their sexual preferences is far from their heart. In their heart, they are born biologically of whom God planned them to be but, in their mind, and body they are who the devil's spirit or demon established in their mind and body of whom to be.

Which no Christian nor person in their right mind can infiltrate their right mind nor infiltrate their realm. They need spiritual help in the Name of Jesus Christ to restore their mind of demonic possession to human reality which is the mind of Jesus Christ. Jesus Christ is the way, the truth, and the life. Living any other life without Jesus Christ is demonically.

But regardless of your alternate lifestyle, which isn't by choice but by false perceptions that you perceive of yourself of being the opposite sex. I want you to know God still love you and want to help you by accepting Jesus Christ into your heart as Lord and Savior.

You must understand it isn't you nor your natural spirit in control of your life nor style, nor is it you that speak nor emulate the opposite sex. You and others like you are living under the influence and powers of the spirit realm Satan, demons, evil spirits are all opposing the creation of mankind through you and those like you.

But Jesus Christ want to bring you back to the Father Almighty God. Jesus want to give back your biological identities by curing you and your counterparts of demon possession and take away the devil and demons false perceptions that are established in your mind and body.

The devil is trying to stop all humankind from going to heaven to be with the Lord. Thereby through his work and the works of his agents, demons, and wicked spirits he's doing just that.

However, Jesus tells us, "I'm the way, the truth and the life, no man comes to the Father except through me." It is imperative that you know, you nor mankind cannot serve God without Jesus Christ. People you cannot serve God living an alternate life. Jesus want to bring you back to your right senses, but you must accept him as your Lord and Savior.

Brothers and sisters and you are my brothers and sisters in Christ Jesus. Satan the Devil is a deceiver and the father of lies. Jesus says the truth isn't in him. He brought deception into the world which he is doing through mankind and the gay population.

No one is an exception for him to use as a deceiver nor to deceive and he does it by what man think and sees. And by the power and influence of his spirit as well as wicked spirits, demons.

Therefore, brothers and sisters you must understand, you alone cannot defeat the devil and demons' purpose in you nor your mind. God loves you and Jesus Christ can and will defeat every purpose they have established in your mind and body; and deliver and set free anyone who accept Him as Lord and Savior.

Don't let the devil nor demons condemn you to go to hell. Hell, the Lake of Fire, was made for the devil and demons and not for mankind. However, the spirit realm is trying to bring condemnation upon mankind collectively or individually. It has already been judged and condemned for hell.

Homosexuality and Demons

Then God said, "And now we will make human beings, they will be like us and resemble us. They will have power over the fish, the birds and all animals domestic and wild, large and small." So God created human beings making them to be like himself. He created male and female, blessed them, and said, "Have many children."

During my adolescent years, I grew up with certain individuals, boys and girls my age that acted differently. These boys showed in themselves to have the characteristics of girls and certain girls possessed the characteristics of boys. I knew something was wrong with those people, but I did not understand why they act like the opposite sex.

The boys never participated in any kind of athletics, they always accompanied the girls and participated in female type activities. My peers and I use to joke about them.

It is impossible for them to be born in that condition. God said, "And now we will make human beings, they will be like us and resemble us." God created human beings to be like himself.

I have witnessed young children with the same feminine and masculine characteristics of the opposite sex and I have asked the question over forty years ago, why certain individuals act like the opposite sex?

This day and age, I have discovered the answer for that question, why certain people want to be the opposite sex, because the evil (demons) spirits, Satan demonic forces of evil are preparing their residence in (human beings) bodies and minds in their young age through their parents for a life of sin and immorality in his demonic world of homosexuality and lesbianism activities, which is against God's will (demons will attempt to possess the human body) characterized by sexual desires for the same and one's self.

As the (human beings) bodies are gradually being possessed, demons masquerade in bodies as the opposite sex. The male bodies and minds possesses the characteristics of women, their thoughts, their physical bodies which control's their walk and everything about them is feminine, even the tone of their voice is disguised.

Demons are superhuman intelligent with their plans for individuals. Men have made statements; this is the woman in me. What they do not know to make such a statement, was demonic control by demons that exist in them masquerading as women in their bodies to make them feel what women feel inside. In reality, they are not responsible for the way they act. They are being controlled by (evil spirits) demons.

Demons will masquerade in human bodies until they receive help not from man but from God and you must believe and have faith in Jesus Christ, our Lord and Savior.

Demonic forces have no respectful age limit to possess, they possess children which cause them to act similar as an adult homosexual and the parents are too blind to recognize their funny behavior. Many of us see it and joke about it for a laugh and that I am guilty of. It is no laughing matter; it is a serious situation those children are in.

There are parents who raise their children in that kind of (homosexual) environment because they aren't dissatisfied with their child biological sex, which is God's will and grace. When a human being is born into the world, male or female it is God's preference. He did not give man his consent nor the authority to change his preference, everything God created is perfect. Man's authority came from the evil one, the devil.

Demons with such intelligence knows where and when the parents of the individual will speak. They will control the tongue for their words to come from the mouth and at the same time be in control of the older person to receive and give the right response.

They communicate through mankind with great intelligence so neither person is aware of their existence in them. Demons are shrewd.

Demons are God-fearing evil spirits. Parents if you notice your little ones acting as the opposite sex, you should investigate them. We know small children have the fantasy of acting like the opposite sex and are aware of it, but when they act and are not aware, it is time to thoroughly investigate. If you suspect homosexuality is present, you should know by the warning of the Holy Spirit.

You can cast out any form of demonic presence that might exist in your child with the authority of Jesus Christ's Name. There are demons that might require prayer to be driven out.

Homosexual demonic forces are most comfortable in nonbelievers and possessed families, if a parent or both parents are gay, their children would be raised in their environment and would appear normal to them in that environment.

Homosexuals do not degrade other homosexuals because of the respect of demonic forces have for each other while masquerading their identity, they can hide their presence from humanity but not from God.

Satan have established in the minds of homosexuals and lesbians that they were biological born the wrong sex. Those who changed with knowledge of their biological sex because of something which falsely took place in their life, they are worse off than those who lack knowledge of their gay condition.

Gay people have quoted, "I could not change if I wanted to," or "I am enjoying who I am," or "I wish I could change, but there is something in me that will not let go of me," and "I was born this way," which is an insult before God.

The power of influence which Satan holds over mankind is amazing. His demonic forces are so powerful they are teaching the Word of God and preaching the gospel (the teachings of Jesus and the apostles, also the Christian doctrine of the redemption of man through Jesus Christ, our Lord and Savior and the first four books of the New Testament is the gospel) to their followers in sanctuaries, holy places for worship are homosexuals themselves. Satan is displaying his power through mankind.

What he (the devil) hides from mankind God reveals it to us through the Holy Spirit, but some of us are so involved in committing evil unto others we are too blind to see the evil committed unto us. There is not anything Satan can hide to harm mankind with that God our Father does not reveal to us, Jesus said take heed. Satan cannot hide behind God's Words.

Satan insults to God is through mankind. A homosexual made a statement on live television before a live audience and millions of viewers he said, "God made him the way he is, gay." This was one of Satan many routes and opportunities of insulting God through man (the flesh) in the presence of millions of people.

But for those who believe in God and have faith and trust in our Lord Jesus Christ, it was confirmed through an insult to millions of people, believers and nonbelievers that Satan cannot hide nothing from God which God does not reveal to man. What takes place in the dark must come to the light and be revealed to humanity.

Human beings are the source and target he can attempt to use against God's will. He can only go as far as God allows him. He is not allowed to do anything without God's permission. People should realize the supernatural power this evil spirit possesses that can control mankind.

The only way a demon-possessed person can become clean is by turning to God and asking in Jesus's Name for deliverance, believe and have faith in Jesus Christ, our Lord and Savior.

Their residence is not permanent in our bodies for those who believe in Jesus Christ. Remember God did not put them there, they enter through the power of Satan, the chief of the fallen (demons) angels.

Demons possess bodies for the purpose to defile and process for condemnation and to use against God's will.

"This evil nation is like a man or woman possessed by a demon." For if the demon leaves it goes into the deserts for a while, seeking rest but finding none. Then it says, I will return to the man or woman I came from. So it returns and finds the man's or woman heart clean but empty. Then the demon finds seven other spirits more evil than itself, and all enter the man or woman and live in him or her. And so, he or she is worse off than before.

Lesbianism and homosexual relationships regardless how you characterize a woman to woman; or man to man sexual relationship it is a sin insulting to God.

There is no excuse for women to lust for woman or man lust for man for sexual companionship and gratification.

I do not believe there is a woman alive today who lacks knowledge of their sexual or biological birth and knowledge of woman creation. God created woman from man's rib for man companionship and blessed them and said, "Have many children." God did not create women for women sexual partner.

Women who desires women oppose to men for sexual purposes and men who lust for men for sexual gratification, those people are demonically influence. It is not by choice of their sexual partner nor sexual preference, but by the choice of that which exist (demons) in them.

Demons are controlling their lives which they think is normal. A majority of them will say to anyone, what I do is my business. The statement clearly means, "I know what I am doing." Satan have established in their minds they have the right to choose their own sexual preference and God does not. The demon spirits do the action while the bodies does the performance. The demonic action is invisible, but the results can be seen.

The gay population is not a sick society mentally nor physically, but they are mentally and physically possessed by masquerading evil (demons) spirits.

The Life and Preparation of homosexuality and lesbianism begin at an early age, some parents notice and detect it in their child and prevent it from happening through prayers. While others go unnoticed of their child developing a sexual preference and there are gay parents who raise their children in a gay environment.

It is not a sudden change in their life but a gradual change which develops slowly unnoticeable over a period of years, so it can be well established in the minds of one's sexual preference.

As he or she grows older, demons have well established themselves in their mind and bodies. They have created a false identity for them which they act out themselves which ever identity of the opposite sex in their minds that's who they believe they are. Gays have made the statements, "I am who I am supposed to be." Such words they speak are demonic that is beyond their control. There are many who are unknowingly possessed by demonic forces that are influenced into gay activities by their own counterpart.

Remember Satan and his demonic forces of evil are superhuman intelligent and they use their intelligence and power of influence on mankind. As individuals grow, they grow stronger into their false identity and there is no human being who can change their minds.

It is humanly impossible to change or help a person who is under the power and control of (demons) evil spirits, unless you ask God for help to deliver an individual from demonic control and from under condemnation held over them.

They must believe in God, have faith and belief in Jesus Christ, our Lord and Savior. It is the only way to be delivered, there is no other way to be cured from that deceitful, wickedness, immoral and sinful life.

Believing in God, he will communicate with the Holy Spirit which dwells in human beings, based on your faith and belief in Jesus Christ, our Lord and Savior.

Satan have humanity fooled; you must see with your mind to see what the eyes cannot see. With your eyes you are blind, but with the mind, you can see in the dark.

You must learn to use your mind to see the unseen and to understand how this evil spirit operates in man and mankind. You can learn to see his performance around you and with your mind you can also see how he and his demon forces prepare to perform in yourself and others. This is why Satan attempts to keep mankind blind, not by eyesight but by mind power.

He has fooled mankind for many years. Man tried to see his work with his eyes, the only time you will recognize his work with the eyes is after it has been performed and the results are visible. The mind and ears tells man what can be seen that cannot be seen with the eyes. Satan does not want it revealed to mankind.

I am going to attempt to open up the mind and ears for those of you who are blind in the world of the unseen, the demonic world of evil (demons) spirits that exist in and around us and throughout the four corners of the world.

They are making their presence known to those who are aware of their existence, they know with or without knowledge mankind cannot harm them without God in his plan. This is not a fairy tale, they are superhuman intelligent, they will attempt to go beyond what the human body are capable of enduring.

Gay population, there is nothing Satan can bestow upon you that God will not change or remove. The identities and titles which he has created and bestowed upon you and a multitude of people as gays are devastating.

Gay population, you are not by choice, but individuals possessed by one or more demons masquerading in your bodies as the opposite sex and their control over you are overwhelming.

Demonic forces masquerade in male's bodies as females with personalities and characteristics as women, which the male has no control over. They create physical attraction between themselves and the same sex who are also possessed. What you recognize (results) is obvious, a homosexual relationship, which is against God's will. Demons masquerading in female as males produce the same characteristics as males and affection for women companionship.

Lesbianism relationship are not as obvious as a homosexual relationship, why? Because women are accustomed to hugging and kissing on special occasions, but demonic forces are there in them masquerading as males in female bodies and exhibit their feelings in public as a man would for a woman, without arousing the public suspicion of their lesbian relationship.

There are bisexuals among the gay population. There are singles, married couples and parents. Demons that exist in their life have schizophrenia personalities and characteristics of both sex, male and female. Demonic forces which can possess human bodies and change their personality to accompany any occasions in any situations.

One of the personalities remains as the original male or female and the other becomes the split personality to accompany the opposite sex. The original personality in the male and female desires the companionship with the same sex.

The schizophrenia personalities that exist in bisexuals are (demons) evil spirits masquerading as the same of the opposite sex in one person and the same as the original in the other person, remember they are masquerading in both individuals.

Demons do everything normal through human beings as human beings and they will attempt to go beyond human being endurance applying their superhuman power to accomplish their plans against an individual.

Homosexuals, bisexuals and lesbians or any other gay group of people are not by choice but by the power of the (devil) evil one, you are targets whom Satan is firing his invisible fiery darts at and sooner or later, you will be pierced by his fiery darts to become another victim of his deadly plan.

Satan opposes all human beings even his followers that are dedicated to him, because he knows God can and will change mankind at his will and he cannot prevent it.

He used his power of influence that changed directions in my life and a multitude of others to create false identities in them to use in his plan.

Any gay person that says he or she feels great about their sexual preference and their relationship with the same sex, their belief and statement come from the evil one.

A married or single person that says they feel wonderful about their bisexual life and their other personality to assume the personality of the opposite sex to be with the same sex, he becomes a female in the mind to have sexual relationships with females. Those sinful acts are performed through demonic power. Remember demons are performing in both partners.

A married or single person that says they feel wonderful about their bisexual life and their other personality to assume the personality of the opposite sex to be with the same sex, he becomes a female in the mind to have sexual relationships with females. Those sinful acts are performed through demonic power. Remember demons are performing in both partners.

The multitude of gay human beings are gay not by choice but by the possession of their bodies by demonic forces and the power of influence of Satan over family members, relatives, and strangers.

The gay population speak as normal human beings, their outside appearance is normal as male and female. The damage is being done on the inside by demons that is invisible to the human eye. They cannot hide from God and those who God have given his consent to see, their outside appearance of how they are performing on the inside of individuals.

You are either controlled by God's will and the Holy Spirit or become rebellious, disobedient and be controlled by the (devil) evil one and his evil forces, demons. There is no other god, person, or spirit to attempt to control you. This evil spirit as an angel of light can transition into any category of personalities and nationality he so desires for his plan and yours.

He is the creator of all sinful categories and his demonic forces acts out his plans of possessing human beings of all ages to attempt to accomplish his many missions. Some he will accomplish and some he won't.

A multitude of human beings who are victims, potential victims and those who have been victimized because of Satan and demonic forces performance through the parents to do their evil work, do not hold ill feelings of malice in your heart against the parents or whoever you think is responsible for your condition.

Neither should take full responsibility for your condition, because Satan and his demons are the perpetrators who controlled the parents, yourself, and others to commit his sinful and evil deeds.

There is a multitude of married couples who have families and are scared of being expose of their secret preference. You are hiding your fear from mankind but who you should fear is God.

What I am telling you is what is in the dark must come out into broad daylight. Do not be afraid of those who can kill the body but cannot kill the soul, rather be afraid of God who can destroy both body and soul in hell.

Children of gay parents or who suspect their parents are gay, pray for your parents. Ask God in Jesus's Name to deliver your parents from something beyond their control. Jesus said, "ask the Father in his name and you shall receive."

The gay population is controlled by (demonic forces) evil spirits. They are very shrewd and intelligent with concealing their presence. They communicate through the possessed bodies to offer encouragement to other demons possessed bodies. They realize they can travel throughout the country seeking someone to dwell in or join others who has already established a dwelling (body) place. They also realize they can always attempt to return with others stronger than before to their old (bodies) dwelling places.

A majority of their old dwelling (bodies) places they return, and re-enter and others cannot be re-entered because the homes (bodies) are clean.

I attended several elementary schools with two demon-possessed boys and I also attended high school with one of them. As young as I was, I knew something was not right with their personalities and characters until recently I realized they were demon-possessed.

Just recently thirty-five years later, both men met a horrible death, they were killed several months apart. Neither one knew the other.

During their short lives, demons possessed their bodies masquerading as a feminine person. Were they aware of their hidden sexual preference? I believe they were, it was obvious, but they were not aware of the homosexual demons and neither was I, that possessed their bodies and minds to masquerade and control them to act like the opposite sex.

Did they doubt their sexuality? We will never know whether they did or not. Today I know they were not responsible for something they had no control over.

The only explanation I heard for their opposite sex characteristics even as child was, "they are born with that condition" and it is still in circulation today. Such statements will remain in this world as long as Satan remains. Satan wants mankind to accuse God for something he is not responsible for.

Man is not to doubt himself; he is created in God's image. Man's doubts come from the (devil s) evil one, which cause man to delay someday an important segment of his life.

If doubt exist in you, ask God in Jesus's Name to remove it. You will feel as great as you ever felt in your life. You thought it felt great with unknown demons masquerading in you as the opposite sex, you should feel the effect of God's Holy Spirit in your body.

Amen.

Does the World Acknowledge Satan Is the World's Biggest Enemy? Sermon

Note: Not only in the Earth, but in and throughout the human race. Satan's spirit is right before one's eyes, when a person lie or lies for you.

Jews says Satan the Devil is a liar and manslayer in the spiritual realm as well as in the physical realm of the human race.

Note: A lie is the opposite of truth. Lying involves saying something false to a person who is entitled to know the truth and doing so with the intent to deceive or to injure him or another person.

"Satan done just that with a lie of deception, the first recorded lie of enmity in the universe was the action of the serpent, later identified in the Bible as Satan the Devil."

Read Revelation 12:9. "The huge dragon was thrown out the ancient serpent named the devil or Satan, that deceived the whole world. He was thrown down to Earth, and all his angels with him."

Satan approached Eve with a challenge as to God's truthfulness. Read Genesis 3:1–4.

> Now the snake was the most cunning animal that the Lord God had made. The snake

asked the woman. "Did God really tell you not to eat fruit from any tree in the garden?"

"We may eat the fruit from any tree in the garden" the woman answered.

Except the tree in the middle of it. God told us not to eat the fruit of that tree or even touch it, if we do, we will die.

The snake replied, "That's not true, you will not die."

God said that because he knows that when you eat it, you will be like God and know what is good and what is bad.

Note: Jesus Christ described this spirit creature as a manslayer and also as a "liar" and Father of the lie.

Read John 8:44. "From the very beginning he was a murderer and has never been on the side of truth, because there is no truth in him. When he tells a lie, he is only doing what is natural to him, because he is a liar and the father of all lies."

Since that time Satan has been the chief enemy of God. He has exercised influence over mankind and they have yield, so have I to that influence so the whole world is lying in the power of "deception" of the wicked one.

Read 1 John 5:19. "We know that we belong to God even though the whole world is under the rule of the Evil One."

Note: The world, "people" doesn't realize to be friends with the world is to be enemies with God. No human being should want to be God's enemy!

Read James 4:4. "Unfaithful people! Don't you know that to be the world's friend means to be God's enemy. If you want to be the world's friend, you make yourself God's enemy."

On the other hand, brothers and sisters, there are many who become God's hard-set enemies including Satan and the wicked demons who set themselves in opposition to God.

"The enemies of God are also the enemies of Jesus Christ!"

Read John 8:42–47.

> Jesus said to them, If God really were your Father you would love Me because I came from God and now I am here. I did not come on my own authority, but He sent me.
>
> You are the children of you father, the devil, and you want to follow your Father's desires. From the very beginning he was a murderer and has never been on the side of truth, because there is no truth in him. When he tells a lie, he is only doing what is natural to him, because he is a liar and the father of all lies.
>
> He who comes from God listens to God's word. You however are not from God, and that is why you will not listen.

Note: When on Earth, Jesus Christ suffered much at the hands of the enemies of God. Nevertheless, He treated them being kind, Jesus even healed one in the crowd that came out with clubs and swords to seize him.

Read Luke 22:49–51.

> When the disciples who were with Jesus saw what was going to happen they asked. Shall we use our swords, Lord?
>
> And one of them struck the High Priest's slave and cut off his right ear.
>
> But Jesus said, Enough of this! He touched the man's ear and healed him.

Enemies of Mankind

Note: These enemies of Jehovah God and his Son, the Anointed One Jesus Christ are shown to be composed of nations and national groups of people of the Earth, including high officials.

These enemies of God are at the same time enemies of mankind because they fight against mankind reconciliation with God and God's purposes toward human livelihoods and families and also oppose the truth and are, therefore, against the interest of all mankind claiming the truth.

Man cannot be living a lie, claiming to Love God while hating his brother.

Read 1 John 4:20–21. "If we say we love God, but hate others, we are liars. For we cannot love God, whom we have not seen, if we do not love others whom we have seen. The command that Christ has given us is this, "Whoever loves God must love others also."

Note: The extension to others, love is restricted toward those whom Jehovah shows are unworthy or toward those set in a course of wrong doing such as Ananias and his wife playing false to the Holy Spirit by lying.

Malicious lying is definitely condemned in the Bible; however, it does not mean that a person is under obligation to divulge truthful information to people who are not entitled to it.

We know as Christians; Jehovah God Word is based on truth from beginning to end. The spirit that proceeds from Jehovah God is pure and holy. It is the spirit of the truth.

Jehovah is the God of truth. He is faithful in all his dealings. His promises are sure for he cannot lie.

Read Number 23:19. "God is not like people who lie. He is not a human who changes his mind. Whatever he promises, he does. He speaks and it is done."

Note: Children of Jehovah God, mankind cannot serve two masters. Man cannot serve the devil, Satan, and God, you either serve one and hate the other.

Those who serve God must walk in the truth to gain God's approval and serve Him in truth.

Read Joshua 24:14. "Now then, Joshua continued, honor the Lord and serve him sincerely and faithfully."

Also, read 1 Samuel 12:24. "Obey the Lord and serve him faithful with all your heart. Remember the great things he has done for you."

Note: Do not allow the devil, Satan make you believe there is no other God, which would include not serving nor worshipping the Living God. This would include abiding by God's requirements and serving Him in faithfulness and sincerity.

"God is a Spirit and those worshiping him must worship with spirit and truth."

Read John. 4:23–29.

> But the time is coming and is already here, when by the power of God's Spirit people will Worship the Father as he really is offering him the true worship that he wants.
>
> God is Spirit and only by the power of his Spirit can people worship him as he really is. "Which is in Spirit and in Truth."

Note: The Christian congregation is a pillar and support of the truth, therefore, don't believe all that you think because Satan has deceived the whole world with "deception," which mankind has perceived as his own. His spirit is at work this very moment in mankind throughout the Earth with thoughts of deception of deceiving the world.

However, Jesus Christ is the truth like his Father Jehovah. Jesus Christ is full of underserved kindness and truth. While on the Earth, he always spoke the truth as he had received it from his Father. He committed no sin nor was deception found in his mouth.

Read 1 Peter 2:22. "He committed no sin, and no one ever heard a lie come from his lips."

Jesus, being the Spirit of truth, God's Holy Spirit could never be the source of error but would protect Christ's followers from doctrinal falsehood's while protecting them from worldly deception of the devil, Satan.

The Book of Revelation reports, Satan is hurled down out of heaven to the Earth, no longer having access to the heavens as he did in the days of Job and far centuries thereafter.

But through God's Word Christians are enlightened to realize Satan's existence, his power, is designs of deception and above all his purposes and manner of operation, so that they (we) can fight this spiritual foe with the spiritual weapons God provide.

Read Ephesians 6:13–19.

> So put on God's armor now! Then when the evil day comes, you will be able to resist the enemy's attacks and after fighting to the end, you will still hold your ground.
>
> So stand ready with truth as a belt tight around your waist, with righteousness as your breastplate.
>
> and as your shoes the readiness to announce the Good News of peace.
>
> At all times carry faith as a shield, for with it you will be able to put out all the burning arrows shot by the Evil One.
>
> and accept salvation as a helmet, and the word of God as the sword which the Spirit give you.

Amen.

Spiritual Warfare Fought through Faith

Congregation, we are in spiritual warfare even through Christ in us. Even now as you sit in the sanctuary, praising and worshiping God and the Lord, we are in spiritual warfare.

Note: I've discovered in spiritual warfare, it is a person's faith that the devil attacks. He knows if he can defeat a person faith, he'll win the war every time. Just a little faith can stop or defeat the attacks of the devil.

Christians, yes Christians believe they are free of spiritual warfare with Satan. I like you to know, Christians are more vulnerable of Satan's attacks today more than ever before.

Note: Jesus tell us if you have faith as big as a mustard seed, you could say to this mulberry tree, "Pull yourself up by the roots and plant yourself in the sea and it would obey you."

Jesus want the people to acknowledge the devil is a defeated foe and all a person need is faith the size of a mustard seed to overcome the works of the devil.

Congregation, a majority of Christians does not acknowledge nor realize he or she are in spiritual warfare and certainly not the Church because the men of God aren't teaching nor preaching spiritual warfare as it should be taught.

The message many are preaching has nothing to do with spiritual warfare, sin, or the fear of Almighty God. Many preach a gospel that speaks of self-reliance, how to beautify self, how to build self, how to enrich self and succeed in business.

Note: If you notice and paid attention, their teaching and preaching has gotten shorter, while their advertisement of their products has lengthened.

They aren't aware or in denial of Satan machination, his crafty scheme and cunning design for the accomplishing his sinister works that he is using against them and the congregation.

Satan has turned some away from the pulpit to be salesmen of the Gospel of Jesus Christ, instead of preaching the Gospel.

Note: The congregation and even themselves are being fool and misled right before the Lord with the message in their mouth. Sweet and better words cannot come from the mouth of a person in spiritual warfare, only deception. That's how Satan fool men of God, who is responsible of shepherding the flock of the Church.

Note: Every one of us are vulnerable of the tricks and schemes of the devil. The entire world is being led by the works of Satan and he knows as long as he can capitalize on people ignorance and faith in the Body or outside the church, the more successful he is.

Note: It's a person' faith that help, claim individual victory over the devil and demonic influence over one's life. Persons that are in spiritual warfare, does not realize it to be extreme and faith in the Lord Jesus Christ to have victory over Satan and his force.

Church, spiritual warfare isn't seen visible, you can hear it with spiritual ears and see it with your spiritual mind. Satan know that individually spiritual warfare can't be seen without Christ, however, the effects can and when the effectiveness is seen in most cases it's too late, the damage has been done.

Note: We often look at the other person's mistake but never one's own mistakes and if we happen to grasp our mistake, we accept it but not others. That's the craftiness of Satan turning you away of someone you could have help.

Congregation, I said in the beginning we all are in a spiritual war believe it or not we are at war. A war like no other and never will be like any other. Because this war isn't visibly seen only the effect of it cannot be seen physically because it takes place in a spiritual realm.

Regardless how unique it maybe, you can hear the war being verbally fought among people. However, you must be spiritual discern. To be spiritual discern, a person must possess the "spirit of discernment," which is a gift of God's spirit. "Discernment of inspired utterance."

Congregation, spiritual warfare is an embattlement (war) being fought internally and externally but not visibly; however, it can become physical. That's the reason spiritual warfare is a battle like no other, age nor gender is no exception in this war.

Internally, a person is battling within him or herself, influence with demonic emotions of all degree of who they are. People are battling against their biological gender, males and females, which start in their adolescents' years and develop into a life-or-death situation.

Externally, look around at people, people are so loose living, their lifestyle. They only think of themselves, even though that's how they think but heinous perception of demonic influences at work.

Immoral lifestyle is the norm of today which it's not about to go away if anything it going to get worse, the world hasn't seen nothing yet.

Satan has the world system of things in his grasp and if you think or believe otherwise, ask a person portraying as the opposite sex for an answer regarding their alternate lifestyles.

Many will answer, "I'm who I am supposed to be." Men posing as women. Women posing as men even young adolescents are at war with this biological agenda. All of which is spiritual warfare.

Note: Spiritual warfare isn't just fighting an enemy or an opponent, the enemies we are engaged with internally and externally are invisible enemies who has declared an all-out spirit war against the human race of the world.

It's not a discriminatory war, every race, gender of people on the face of the Earth is in spiritual warfare. Christian and non-Christian, Jews and Gentiles and all denominations across the country.

Now you know, mankind cannot please God without faith, it takes faith to please God and the faith we have to please God is the kind of faith to defeat the devil and his works through Jesus Christ.

Note: "Man's faith in Jesus Christ determine is strength."

Note: The beginning of spiritual warfare

Spiritual warfare began with Job. Job didn't have the fainted clue or belief that he was under the attack of Satan the Devil.

The issue was raised when Satan appeared before Jehovah in the courts of heaven. Congregation spiritual warfare happen with a challenge.

Note: Now it come to be the day when the sons of the true God entered to take their station before Jehovah and even Satan proceeded to enter right among them, Jehovah God said to Satan. "Where do you come from Satan answered Jehovah and said, "From roving about in the Earth and from walking about in it." God asked, "Have you set your heart upon my servant Job, that there is no one like him in the Earth."

Jehovah went on the say to Satan, there is no one like him in the Earth, a man blameless and upright fearing God and turning aside from bad.

Read Job 1:6–8.

> At that, Satan answer Jehovah and said, have not you yourself put up a hedge about him and about his house and about everything that he has all around? The work of his hands you have blessed, and his livestock itself has spread abroad in the Earth. But, for a change, touch everything he has and see whether he will not curse you to your very face. Satan was making an excuse for Job's faithfulness to God. Job's serves you because of the things you give him, not because he loves you.
>
> Jehovah answered, "Everything that he has is in your hand, but you must not hurt Job himself."

Note: Job's children and wealth are destroyed

Right away, Satan began causing trouble. The beginning of spiritual warfare of Job for Job. He had all Job's livestock either killed or stolen. Then he saw to it that Job's ten children were killed. Job lost almost everything yet he remains faithful to Jehovah.

Read Job 1:22. "In spite of everything that has happened Job did not sin by blaming God."

Satan again appeared with the other angels before Jehovah. Once again, Jehovah asked Satan if he had seen the faithfulness of Job.

At that Satan answered, skin in behalf of skin and everything that a man has he will give in behalf of his soul. For a change thrust out your hand and touch as far as his love and his flesh and see whether he will not curse you to your very face.

> Jehovah gave Satan permission to do whatever he could to Job, God said, "You are not to kill him." (Job 2:1–5)

> So Satan struck Job with a terrible disease, Job's suffering was so great that he prayed to die. His own wife turned against him saying, "Curse God and die!" (Job 2:7)

> But Job refused to do that, "Until I expire, I shall not take away my integrity from myself," he said. (Job 2:9)

> Job remained, faithful to God. So it was proved that Satan was wrong in his challenge that Job only serve God for material gain and not out of love. It was also showed that Satan could not turn everybody away from serving God. (Job 27:5)

Job gave God, an answer to Satan challenge that human beings would—serve Him under test. Read Isaiah 54:17. "However, the challenge Satan challenged God that he can turn persons away from God, that challenger still stand to this very day, that challenge was the beginning of spiritual warfare in the Earth."

Read 2 Corinthians 10:4. "The Apostle Paul describes the war waged within the Christian between "sin's" law and God's law or the law of the mind."

Spiritual warfare is the purpose of one's faith. Man cannot please God without faith it takes one's faith to please God and that faith which we Christians possess is the kind of faith to defeat the devil and his works through Jesus Christ.

The greatest example was the perfect man Jesus Christ. He held fast his loyalty to God despite all the tests and trials that Satan brought upon him. Jesus Christ was in spiritual warfare his entire course of life upon the Earth.

Whether you know or not, Satan's chief aim is to get persons to weaken their faith to break God's govern laws that require us mankind to live by.

Christian Warfare

Note: While the Christian does not engage in a physical war against blood and flesh, he is engaged in warfare. None the less, a spiritual fight.

Read 2 Corinthians 10:4. "The Apostle Paul describes the war waged within the Christian between 'sin's' law and God's law or the law of the mind."

Note: The warfare of the Christian is, therefore, an agonizing one requiring every effort of faith to come off winners. But we can be confident of victory through the underserved kindness of God through Christ and the help of God's spirit.

Read Romans 8:35–39.

> No, in all these things we have complete victory through him who loved us.

> For I am certain that nothing can separate us from his love. Neither death, nor life, neither angels nor other heavenly rulers or powers. Neither the present nor the future.
>
> Neither the world above nor the world below, there is nothing in all creation that will ever be able to separate us from the love of God, which is our through Christ Jesus our Lord.

Spiritual warfare is more prevalent than ever before and the reason for it is because mankind does not recognize it existence in and around them because they aren't aware, we live in a spiritual world that is more real than just as real as the physical world we live in.

Congregation, 75 percent of the world population does not realize we live among spirit enemies, that is here to steal, kill, and destroy human lives any way possible. We cohabitate with evil spirits in the flesh and in the atmosphere of homes and in the spiritual realm or world.

Read Ephesians 6:12. "And in addition to it, the warfare against sins law, the Christian has to fight against the demons who take the advantage of the tendencies of the flesh by tempting the Christian to sin by lust of the flesh; lust of the eye; and lust of the heart."

Note: In this warfare, demonic spirits induce or encourage those under their influence to tempt or to oppose and persecute Christian in an effort to break or weaken their faith and integrity to God.

The Bible reveal that the resurrected Lord Jesus Christ with all authority in heaven and on Earth granted to him by his Father will engage in a warfare to destroy all God's enemies and will establish ever lasting peace.

In spiritual warfare of the Christian, God views the Christian as his soldier and, therefore, provides him with the necessary spiritual weapons.

Remember, Christians you aren't fighting against flesh and blood; therefore, our weapons are not carnal but mighty in using every Word of God that proceed from the mouth.

Note: A person does all he can to keep free but he may still come under attack by wicked spirits. Recall that the voice of the devil himself was heard by Jesus Christ tempting him to break God's law.

The Apostle Paul said we have a wrestling against the wicked spirit forces in the heavenly place which means that every servant (Christians) of God must take up the complete suit of armor of God that he may be able to resist the devil attacks. Read Ephesians 6:10–18, "The whole armor of God."

Amen.

The Holy Spirit: Satan Waging War against the Holy Spirit Sermon and Message

Note: "Our Father which art in heaven, Hallowed be thy name. Thy Kingdom come, Thy will be done on Earth, as it is in heaven."

Children of God, God's will shall be done in us, through us, as it is done in heaven. God's will for all mankind bring to pass that which has been done in the spiritual heaven.

God's will for mankind is made known by the Spirit, but not the flesh, which I know without a doubt, "When I was part of the world, disobedience was constantly at work through the "flesh of my heart."

Note: "Being born again of the Spirit and not of the flesh. I truly say without any doubt, "Greater Is He in Me, than He that is within the world."

Read 1 John 4:4. "Ye are of God, little children and have overcome them, because greater is he that is in you, than he that is in the world."

Note: How do I know, "Greater is He in me, For the Bible, God's Word told me so, plus Jehovah God have shown me. I'm Greater than he, the devil, Satan, he that is in the world and greater of those of the world, by the Power of God's Spirit, the Holy Spirit which dwell in my body which is the temple of the Holy Spirit."

Read 1 Corinthians 6:19–20. "Don't you know that your body is the temple of the Holy Spirit who lives in you and who was given to you by God? You do not belong to yourselves but to God. He bought you for a price. So use your bodies for God's glory."

Note: Congregation of God, Satan at this very moment attacking the Holy Spirit. Satan only avenue of attacking God's Spirit is not in a physical manner but in a spiritual manner internally and externally against God's will for humankind of "born-again believers."

Note: The devil is waging war against the Holy Spirit through the flesh of man, who hasn't any clue the devil's spirit is at work in himself, not only in the flesh, he has control over but against He that is in him, the Greater One, God's Spirit.

Note: The Holy Spirit in born-again believers is under attack internally without the assist of man's knowledge.

The Holy Spirit is also God's free gift, which he grants to those who sincerely seek and request it. A right Heart is the key factor of God's requirement of His free gift.

But Water and Spirit is the requirement of born-again believers, which all mankind must be "born again of water and of the Spirit."

Flesh

Note: Children of Jehovah God, you should know flesh can't war against flesh which God created perfect from dust of the ground; however, Satan chose to war against the flesh while using simultaneously the flesh to war through against the Spirit of God in man.

Read Galatians 5:16–17. "For what our human nature wants is opposed to what the Spirit wants and what the Spirit wants is opposed to what our human nature wants. 'These two are enemies and this means that you cannot do what you want to do.'"

Note: It's an internal spiritual war being individually fought, Spirit against the flesh, which the Holy Spirit serve as Helper which helps mankind to understand God will and purpose in their lives, that which the devil is against.

Satan told Jehovah God that he could cause mankind to curse him to His face which he fails to do.

Satan appeared to me as a transparent spirit whom I saw at the age of six; I didn't know it was the devil, who telepathically communicated with me; to tell me to curse God; however, I knew not to.

Note: "I revealed my age because age is no exception in the devil's attacks against the "will and purpose" of God in human lives.

Read Job 2:4–5. "Satan replied, 'A person will give up everything in order to stay alive.' But now suppose you hurt his body, he will curse you to your face."

Note: The devil has a will and purpose of his own, to steal, kill, or destroy human lives by any means. He Counteracts and oppose all God's wills and purposes against the human race by deception of deceiving the whole world.

Read Revelation 12:9. "The huge dragon was thrown out-that ancient serpent named the devil or Satan that deceived the whole world. He was thrown down to Earth and all his angels with him."

Note: He's a counterfeiter, a duplicator, and a deceiver, he appears at times as an angel of light, even after he told God he could cause man to curse Him to his face.

Satan has openly changed his once conceal strategy attacks against the flesh, he's now attacking the "works of the Holy Spirit internally of man, using man and himself as spirit against God's will and purpose in human beings' lives.

This message of truth isn't preached in pulpits nor taught in seminaries by theologians because Satan possess power and ability which he uses to blind the physical eyes and mind of man to hinder or prevent mankind from performing the will and purpose of God in our lives.

Note: "I was in the process of praying, when I received this Revelation internally his "works and strategy," which he has changed to prevent Jehovah God's will and purpose to not take place or come to pass, not only in our lives but throughout the entire Earth.

Note: Children of God, Jesus Christ tells us how to pray, the Lord's Prayer, of God's will be done on Earth as is in heaven. Confirmation of God's will for all human beings has already been done or taken place in heaven, which shall now come to pass individually through us human beings of the Earth.

Note: Congregation, laymen, clergies, servants, pastors, ministers, theologians of all denominational seminaries, I, a servant of God, write, "God's will and purpose" of this message of truth, did not come from any Earthly source but from above; if it had come from an Earthly source, Satan or demons would've prevent, stop, or hinder me of receiving and revealing this message of truth.

Note: The spirit realm of Satan and demon spirits are attacking and waging war internally against the Word of God throughout nations all around the world, which is global.

However, humankind can rely on the Holy Spirit as helper to bring to pass God's will, plan, and purpose prevent disobedience or rebellious living.

However, sad to say, the message of truth isn't being taught in seminaries nor told or preached in pulpits across the Earth.

Note: Believers and nonbelievers, there are Bible Scriptures throughout God's Word where Satan spirit is counteracting against the Word of God internally through the five-fold ministry of some apostles, prophets, evangelists, pastors, and teachers, which are for edification of the Body of Christ, the Church.

Satan is counteracting through the flesh without one's knowledge! As proof, read Matthew 16:21–23 where Jesus spoke of his suffering and death.

> From that time on Jesus began to say plainly to his disciples, "I must go to Jerusalem and suffer much from the elders, the chief priests, and the teachers of the Law. I will be put to death but three days later I will be raised to life."
>
> Peter took him aside and began to rebuke him, "God forbid it, Lord! He said, "That must never happen to you!"
>
> Jesus turned around and said to Peter, "Get away from me, Satan! You are an obstacle in my

way because these thoughts of yours don't come from God, but from human nature."

Question, "Was Satan present? Jesus spoke of him being present there among them. Where? In the spirit of a thought or perception of Peter which he spoke out of the flesh which is evidence of Satan's control of the flesh or Nature of human beings without their knowledge. Waging war internally against the Spirit of God through believers and against the Name, Jesus Christ of nonbelievers.

Note: Children of Jehovah God, believers and nonbelievers, we (you) can't see the devil's approach. You must listen for his approach through a person's spoken Words which his spirit manifest himself in and through the person's tongue!

Therefore, pay attention to the Spirit but also discern who is speaking to you and through whom.

Discernment is one of the nine gifts of the Spirits. He that is in you, a believer is greater than he that is within the world, and those of the world.

Note: Satan and demons sometimes addressed or called evil or wicked spirits of the Earth. They are real and alive without a body. We, humans, are real and alive on the Earth with bodies.

However, some have set up residency in human bodies, performing internally. While expressing their action externally through whom they reside in or possess.

Note: We believers and churchgoers, often quote the Scripture.

Read 1 John 4:4. "But you belong to God, my children, and have defeated the false prophets because the Spirit who is in you is more powerful than the Spirit in those who belong to the world."

Note: Which is true; however, Satan has now placed this scripture on display of the hearts of believers while he challenges believers, quoting this Scripture verse, actually believe, greater is He in them, than he that is within the world. "The devil speaking of himself."

"Congregation of God, the devil will test every person on the face of the Earth, beyond one's imagination and self-endurance quoting that Scripture." You shall be tested, whether a believer or nonbeliever, just quoting scripture.

Note: One must remember, he that is within the world, the physical and spiritual world can very well enter the mind in spirit to work or challenge or attack believers or nonbelievers in and through themselves.

Quoting the Bible verse 1 John 4:4, "Ye are of God, little children and have overcome them, because greater is he that is in you, than he that is in the world."

Note: "He that is in the world," is responsible for many who has "backslid" back into the world, even some "servants, males and females who was called into ministry."

Quoting this scripture verse is evidence, the entire world is being attack or being challenged in the spiritual realm, internally and externally of mankind.

I reiterate, all mankind shall be tested, whether a believer or nonbeliever, just quoting scripture.

Note: All children of God are under attack, age is not an exception. Man need not be provoked in a war he can't see because we aren't fighting against "flesh nor blood," which takes place internally of man as well as externally, which is a battle aren't physically seen, however, can be seen and heard spiritually with the ears, "Yes, the ears."

Note: Yes, children of God, we all possess the ability to see and hear the devil's spiritual works and actions right before you through your hearing.

"Satan, demons acknowledge their waging war against us can be seen and heard only through human ears and vision of the Holy Spirit."

All spiritual and physical action of the devil or demons can be seen and audibly heard in spirit, by way of human ears.

Humans can't literally see with the ears, but can see spiritually with the ears. Spiritual things, you cannot imagine of ever seeing visually with the eyes.

Note: Children and congregation of Jehovah God, He that is in us believers, the Holy Spirit, hasn't lost a battle nor spiritual war nor never will internally nor externally.

Every spiritual war that has been waged against the human race, internally and externally in the past, present, or in the future has already been defeated but because of man lack of knowledge some failed the test and challenge.

"The devil and his household, demons of the Earth acknowledge they are defeated foes." I am a living "witness and testimony" of their defeat!

Amen.

SCHIZOPHRENIA

It disturbs me to hear of people with several personalities which the medical field describe and clarify such people as schizophrenic. It bothers me to read about something as far fetch from the truth than a man in the moon. It disturbs me even more to see a human being with more than one personality which he or she can't acknowledge nor distinguish their own natural personality.

A human being has three spirits that dwells in the body. The three spirits are the Spirit of God whom give and take life. Man's natural spirit and the devil's spirit. There are others that can also dwell in the body of mankind, demons which by avenues the devil open's up to enter many kinds, types of demons. Jesus reveal demon existence in mankind during his stay on the Earth.

The devil's most common route among others to open up an avenue to enter demons into the mind and body is through alcohol and drugs. The devil use alcohol to enter alcohol and many other habit control demons into my body. Which dwelled in my body for over thirty years where I heard voices and conversations for as many years in my head.

Note: Many spirits can exist in the human body, only two are required. God and human beings' natural spirit. Any others are demonic. However, there is an opposite spirit that can exist in the human (flesh) body which is Satan the Devil's spirit by with a thought or perception.

Even though mankind has three spirits dwelling in the body, he has only one personality and any other than his or her own is demonic. What I'm revealing to you is that a person, human being who has more than one personality is demonized or demon-possessed.

He or she might have many personalities and as many demons, evil and ruling spirits as personalities to dwell in their body.

God didn't give us, mankind multiple personalities, neither did God give man the intellect for multiple personalities. Man can't develop or multiple real personalities, which I read that professional opinions in the medical field have diagnosed such cases and classified them as mental and medical cases.

I reiterate, it disturbs me to hear of people with multiple personalities which the medical profession classifies as schizophrenic which the population in the world suffers from schizophrenia which give a small indication of the percentage of evil spirits, demons that exist (dwell) in mankind and the world.

People confuse themselves of mental illness, retardation, and demon possession of the body. Retardation (schizophrenia) is a defect in the brain that may result from various causes. That is, they occur before birth. For example, a child may be born with an incomplete develop brain.

Mental illness means "sickness of the mind"; it involves a mental break down so serious that a person must have special care or enter a mental hospital.

Much of the world mental illness is demonically motivated. A person or persons who are under demon power, man automatically set judgment upon them as insane. Man has no time, nor does he or she put any effort to investigate or examine such person. Which is like judging the book by its cover before reading it.

A person under personalities traits anything can occur as having or knowing imaginary friends along with various personalities. Or it may mean personality traits that lead to abnormal behavior which lead into committing unnatural and inhuman acts. Any personality other than their own or any unnatural or inhuman acts committed are demonically motivated.

The spirit world is real; why can't man understand that? Schizophrenia and the spirit realm operate together, one in the physical and the other in the spirit realm, which they are both demonic. In the schizophrenic, man witness the work of the demon's spirit in a human body and the results of his and their work manifest in the physical realm as a man give title created by the devil's perception in those who has jurisdiction over the demon possess. Schizophrenic is the terminology the devil use in man to disguise demon possession.

I never experience a personality conflict but heard voices of all kind. I've heard so many voices I actually felt as though I was surround by people. Had I sought medically help at the beginning of hearing voices for over thirty years, I believe I would've been committed to an asylum and possible still remain committed because people would've formed their own wrong medical opinion of me.

My problem was demonically motivated and spiritually cured. It was not until God cured me of alcohol demons of over thirty years that the voices which I heard for as many years left. There was nothing medically wrong with me which I know. And yes, those voices are real, there is nothing imaginable about them. I'm a witness not by sight but by hearing. Hearing spirit voices in my head. Which they will tell you, "We are real," which they are real. And they can make you speak back to them in public or any place.

The demon's spirit or spirits in the schizophrenic (demon-possessed) communicate with the spirit realm through such persons. Schizophrenia is not a disease or what some claim it to be. There is no medical cure for it (demon possession) the only cure is spiritual which is in the Name and through Jesus. Schizophrenia is demonically motivated, and it is in the Name of Jesus and through prayer for the schizophrenic to be cured but man must believe in God.

Yes, the spirit world is real, a person who has multiple personalities is living proof it's real and also demons, evil and ruling spirits exist in every home, house or shelter that exist and is standing throughout the world which should indicate the number of evil spirits that inhabit the Earth. And it is just as many that possess and exist (dwell) in human bodies.

Believe me they are in your home observing you, they ride along with you in your automobile. Demons will physically harass mankind in their own disguise way, they will appear to children as imaginary friends. All of this is a part of the spirit realm which part of it exist in you, mankind.

There is a spirit realm in mankind body which I called a third dimension in mankind's life, which there is communication between man and the spirits in the physical realm through the schizophrenic.

But because lack of knowledge mankind is allowing the spirit realm to destroy him and for some reason man does not want to increase his knowledge about demons, the evil spirits. Yet people ask is there a spirit world? Which the answer is, "Yes, there is a spirit world and we live in it, have lived in it since man inhabit the Earth." That question is asked but many still doesn't believe in the spirit world and they are in big trouble.

My experience tells me the spirit realm is not outside of the normal human norm in some instances. But Jesus reveal to mankind that there is a spirit realm when he cast out demons throughout his stay on Earth and above all when Jesus was resurrected from the dead, prove beyond a doubt that a spirit world exists and by his death man also receive power and authority over it, which the spirit world is aware of.

The spirit realm can't be viewed as a subject matter to be study and examine to determine whether it exist because the spirit realm won't allow man to study nor expose it and anyone who has ever attempt to or has, have had some kind of confrontation with the supernatural. I know, I'm currently in the midst of one, been in it all my life but I didn't discover it until I begin to write to expose it.

I'm not here to prove evil spirits exist or is there a spirit world, Jesus has already revealed their existence, I'm here to reveal the reality the spirit realm imposes on our mankind everyday life in the flesh as well as in the physical realm.

People with multiple personalities is not aware of their condition and neither should man's flesh be a mystery for obvious reasons. Jesus revealed and showed mankind what power evil spirit possess that inhabit the Earth and the power they have over the flesh and mind of mankind. Jesus also reveal they can enter to live in human or animal bodies. They can speak through man as their spirit possess the body and mind as it performs and manifest in it. Yet the results are in the flesh we witness in our everyday life but tend to ignore it.

Mankind's question should be, "Does demons exist in my body, or am I possessed with evil spirits?" You can answer the question yourself. Anyone who perform unnatural or inhuman act is demonize or possessed with some kind of demon spirit in their body. Any person or persons who perform uncontrollable habits or urged to perform unnatural acts are demon-possessed or demon motivated by the power of the devil.

Your thoughts of perception do not indicate demon possession every time an unnatural thought or desire appear in the mind, but it does warn you that the devil is present. But to dwell on such perception can be a potential access that the devil is planning to open the body and mind to enter demons which only the knowledge of God and God's word can prevent them from entering. And the knowledge of God can cast them out, but mankind must believe in God and our Lord Jesus Christ.

Without Jesus Christ a schizophrenic (a demonized person) with multiple personalities (any human being who has two or more personalities are demon-possessed) will forever exist in mankind. There is not a person in the medical field can medically treat demon possession unless they give spiritual advice which is in Jesus Christ to be cured.

Schizophrenia (demon possession) is not medically treatable which is should not be taught as such because schizophrenia is a spiritual problem which it should be treated as such.

If the devil had his way with me, he would kill me; believe me, he has tried over the years. Man might ask, "Why I make such a statement?" Because he knows what I'm doing is for the Lord.

I've been into the spirit realm. I've witnessed a demon spirit exit from Abyss, "the place in the depths of the Earth where the demons were imprisoned until their final punishment." I know who they are, where and who demons, evil and ruling spirits exist and who they exist in.

I know how the spirit world operate and communicate through mankind and how it communicates between man and spirit. I know when demon spirit speaks directly or indirectly through human bodies to or against me or mankind. All those things, evil spirits perform through people I'm acquainted with.

I was possessed with alcohol and many other habit control demons for over thirty years, near the last stage of that period. A church goer said to be a Christian said to me, "Bring your crazy a———on." Because I refuse to eat at their home. Should I ask that person today does he recall that statement, he would deny or refuse to admit to it. This is an indication a spirit spoke through him directly to me, that's the reason he will deny or refuse of making such a statement. I reiterate because people with multiple personalities are not aware of their demonic condition.

I don't believe the word *schizophrenic* is mentioned in the Holy Bible, if it is I must have missed it. Schizophrenics should be mankind's terminology for demon possession of the human body because mankind in the medical field doesn't know spiritually how to analyze it but medically, he attempts to but to no avail in its duration because schizophrenic is not link with the medical field.

I believe Jesus knew Luke, the evangelist and physician would be baffle by demonically cause illness by demon's spirits which he couldn't recognize but through himself no illness could be conceal from him. Therefore, Luke would consult Jesus to diagnose cases to determine whether it was demonically motivated or natural. I believe there were occasions Luke consulted Jesus for cures and reasoning. So shall man today consult God's word, believe me there's an answer.

Why did the Lord choose a physician as a disciple? I believe in order for physicians of today to consult his word because of the devil's plan against mankind's health. The devil knows man's health is the most important thing to him with the exception of God but in some he has made health their most important thing and you know who you are.

Mankind must face reality. He is dealing with a spirit world which is to be complicated for the medical field because there is nothing medically wrong with a person who has multiple personalities also schizophrenia is not a mental disorder as some claim it to be.

A person is mentally unstable only if such person is born with abnormal brain or the brain develop a disease during their life. If there are no abnormalities in the brain but abnormal behavior due to multiple personalities, which means demon possession exist in the body.

Genetically, genes are not a factor in a person's personality nor his or her sexual preference as some have speculated or might believe.

Ask yourself how can a person who are schizophrenic claim to or want to be someone rather than themselves? Which should explain to man, a person that claim to be someone else know who he or she want to be. Occasionally such person wants to be anyone else other than their self, then there is other occasion such person rather be their self than someone else.

They know when and where to be their self or someone else whom to identify with. Homosexuals, lesbians, trans, and bisexuals are demonized people (schizophrenics).

Schizophrenia is demonically motivated, demons possessing the human body, but people use an excuse for those like themselves as having a behavior or personality problems.

The only cure for schizophrenia (demon possession of the human body) is through Jesus Christ. Demons, evil, and ruling spirits can't be talked, bribed nor compromise out of the human body. They must be cast out in the Name of Jesus or driven out by prayer, but mankind must believe in God and our Lord Jesus Christ. Believe me the spirit realm know whether you believe.

Many of the possessed (schizophrenic) has no faith nor do they believe in God. Believe me, the spirit realm knows who you are and so do you. It's imperative you understand, I'm only confessing the truth what mankind, the devil and the spirit realm is in the midst of.

Should the medical branch consult the Holy Bible for things which are medically relevant in their research, I believe the medical team would be far better off spiritually in the medical field.

Doctors whom this book will fall into the hands of, it will not be coincidental.

Uncontrollable Spirits

This nation and the world must realize, we live in an evil spiritual realm with uncontrollable demon spirits at work and on rampage that only the Name of Jesus and the Word of God control them. Therefore, it is so vital in mankind lives to know God our Father in heaven and the Word of God and the Lord Jesus Christ.

The power to control the spirit realm is in the Name of Jesus Christ. The spirit realm knows Jesus and tremble just to hear his name because it knows there is supernatural power in the Name of Jesus. Power that does not exist no place in the world.

People, it's time to focus on the spirit realm, the uncontrollable demons, evil spirits that are on rampage throughout the four corners of the world and wherever mankind exist demon spirits exist in the body (flesh) of mankind and in the Earth atmosphere.

These uncontrollable evil spirits are here to steal, kill, and destroy you and mankind. And we are all vulnerable of their insidious attack mentally of demon possession and physically through the flesh of humankind, which age isn't no exception.

There are more children and adolescents today control by controllable demon spirits than ever before and don't realize it. Some know something is obviously wrong with them but don't know what and others just don't care because they like being wicked and evil. They perceive it to be cool and the right way to be.

They don't realize nor comprehend uncontrollable demon spirits are here to kill or get people killed. That is their purpose in all human being lives, kill or be killed and friend, they aren't fooling around.

Confirmation of the truth, look around you, observe the multitudes of people young and old alike committing wicked and evil acts against their will. Even though some are minor, and others are major still they possess no control over what they do and feel.

However, some feel remorseful, where else others don't. Those feel remorseful hear the voice of the Holy Spirit, but don't heed to "He that is in them is greater than he and demon forces in the world and in the body of mankind." Because demons' spirits or forces are possessive once their spirit enter the mind and body.

I'm speaking of evil spirits that is alive in the body as one's natural spirit. Demon spirits are more powerful and aggressive and overrule the natural spirit of man and that spirit cause others to perceive it's cool to kill or be kill.

Friend, no human being in his or her right mind think it's cool to kill or destroy themselves. No human being unless there is a spirit or spirits in their body greater than their own natural spirit. I've been victimized when demon spirits possessed my body and mind, also by demon spirits in the flesh of others as well.

But now I'm a witness of the truth, uncontrollable spirits will cause mankind to destroy oneself. God didn't bring mankind into the world to die before he starts living. And it saddens me to see my brothers and sisters out of control because of some kind of demon spirit or demon force controlling their destiny to die at an early age or before their time.

People, it's imperative to know it is the works of the devil and demon spirits that here to steal, kill, and destroy mankind and it's happening at an alarming rate. Young and innocent people go out into the world to die senseless deaths, it's occurring all around us.

Loved ones leaves home never to return alive or never seen again. Why? Because of uncontrollable evil and wicked spirits are on rampage to destroy all mankind, young as well as the elders, and age isn't an exception.

Brethren, the world has accepted wickedness and evilness as the norm. That's the demon spirit or forces of evil mentality perceived in their mind. And you can't tell them or the world anything different or make them obey, except in the Name of Jesus.

The spirit realm in the flesh of human bodies or in the Earth's atmosphere cannot hide nor conceal itself from the Name of Jesus.

The Name of Jesus control the unseen enemies that are all around us twenty-four hours a day in our homes, on our jobs, in the atmosphere and everywhere we travel, we are in the presence of uncontrollable demon spirits and forces.

Believe me, the Holy Spirit is my witness: Demon spirits are assigned to us and control us, mankind. And people, they are super bad. There is no respectful of persons for demons to come against nor possess the body of to use as manifestation of its spirit.

Children of all ages are vulnerable to demon possession. Time and time again people are saying, "I don't have control of my children; I've raised them right and they used to be obedient and mind me. I don't know what gotten into them to cause them to be evil and wicked."

They don't mind nor obey me; they are disrespectful, curse, and fright; and now they've stopped attending church service and have taken residency with neighborhood gangs.

Parents and friends, the devil open up avenues in your sons and daughters mind to enter uncontrollable demon spirits to control them to perform his will. However, demons can't enter the mind nor body of human beings under their own demonic power. It takes the power of influence and any created habit of the devil's spirit to allow demon spirits to enter the mind, body, and manifest by way of its spirit.

Therefore, those who reluctant to act the demon or demons will use their body and mind as the manifestation of its spirit to perform. The flesh becomes it body as the mind manifest as its spirit.

Which simply mean a person's flesh serve as the body and mind as the manifest demon spirit; therefore, possessing the mind and body to act and serve as its spirit without the person's knowledge. Therefore, the person is performing the devil's will by way of demon forces against their own natural spirit's will.

Which cause the person to not have or loss control of their body and mental perception to perform. Demon force are now in control of him or her. Now they are demon-possessed and out of control and you certainly can't control him.

Uncontrollable spirits cannot be control by mankind alone. Man must be a believer to make the spirit realm obey in the Name of Jesus. There isn't no other Name, the devil or demons will obey and friend the spirit realm knows whether or not man is a believer. Demons won't obey nonbelievers. Therefore, don't attempt to dispel or make demons obey you in the Name of Jesus.

Because you'll make a big mistake, remember the spirit realm knows nonbelievers. It knows who's hot and who's not. I'm a witness of the truth. The devil and demons know who believes and doesn't believe in Jesus and friend, the power is in the Name of Jesus of the believer.

Therefore, I reiterate, nonbelievers don't make the mistake nor attempt to make the spirit realm obey you or cast demon spirits out of the flesh of mankind or the Earth's atmosphere. Because the demon spirit or spirits will attack anyone whose isn't a believer by way of whom the spirit or spirits dwells in. And cause such person to harm or even kill you. Therefore, don't try to make the spirit realm, demon spirits or uncontrollable spirits in the flesh of your loved ones obey you because that loved one will hurt or even kill you.

In reality, it isn't the person; it's the evil spirit dwelling and in possession of their mind and body that cause him or her to become uncontrollable and attack (parents) you or mankind. Uncontrollable demon spirits cause people to be uncontrollable.

Now there are people (parents) in general that's demonize, under the influence of the devil's power or demon-possessed by uncontrollable spirits. However, one admits something isn't right in you, you still can't control your emotions physically nor mentally.

Which that should tell you there is a spirit or spirits in your body that is in control of your mind and body that is greater than your own natural spirit. Therefore, confirming the human mind and body isn't in control but the manifestation of the demon or spirits are by way of the flesh physically and the mind mentally creating its own intellectual perception to perceive in the mind that make the body obey.

Friend, all human beings are vulnerable sometime in their lives to this condition under demon possession. I was demon-possessed for over forty years and didn't realize it, but I knew something wasn't mentally right in me because sometimes I did things, I didn't want to do which I thought was normal.

There I used the excuse that it is normal to do things I possess no control over things that was detrimental to me as well as others. Friend that's how strong, real, and alive demon forces are in (our) mankind body and life.

Which mean man personally can't do anything about his condition because it is not, he that is in control and never will be without Jesus Christ in his life as Lord and Savior. It takes the supernatural power of Jesus to control the inner self of man, that no devil nor demon spirit can come against.

Therefore, unless Jesus Christ is in your life, you do not possess, nor your natural spirit possess power over a demon or demons in possession of the mind and body. I didn't discover I was demon-possessed until after God cured me of alcohol demons of over thirty years and for over thirty years, I heard demon voices in my head. I didn't know it was demon voices I heard until God cured me, and the voices left.

During those thirty years, I was without Christ in my life as my Lord and Savior. And mankind without Christ as his Lord and Savior is subject to demon possession regardless of age. However, man that is demon-possessed without acknowledgment of his condition and with Christ in his life is better off with Christ in him because when he's weak that's when Christ Jesus is strongest in him. Always remember, "He that is in you is greater than he that is in the world and the Earth's atmosphere."

Multitudes of Christians and believers has some kind of uncontrollable spirit dwelling in their body but not knowing. Even though some admit something is wrong or isn't right with their mind's perception and body.

Demon forces attacks humankind in many areas of one's life. Uncontrollable habits are caused or created by demon spirits manifesting their presences by way of habits that you think is cool such as cigarette smoking, tobacco chewing, all kinds of drug abuse habits, alcohol and overeating that cause obesity. All these habits and disorders are demonically control habits manifest in human form and action.

Friend, a demon spirit or an uncontrollable spirit (demon) can and will cause you to do and perform all kinds of abnormal acts that seem normal to you. A demon spirit can cause pain in the body and create abnormal thoughts and perceptions by the manifestation of its spirit. It will cause man to think, act, and perform physically and intellectually it's perceptions or its spirit will perform them through man.

Therefore, mankind throughout the world need Christ as Lord and Savior. Friend, mankind cannot live alone nor believe he can without Jesus Christ as Lord and Savior. It is impossible that the spirit realm is aware of. Demons know Jesus and have seen Jesus.

Demon spirits acknowledge power over the spirit realm is in the Name of Jesus but even Christians and believers must exercise this power in faith and belief against the spirit realm. Because demon spirits in the atmosphere as well as the flesh (mind and body) of mankind, believers, and nonbelievers see, hear, and know everything man does and say in the flesh.

Demons know whether man is a believer or nonbeliever. There isn't anything in the flesh or carnal demon spirits does not know of mankind. Because we are forever in their presence. Demons know whom it can enter and control and whom it cannot control to perform its will or the will of the devil. Because we who has Christ as Lord and Savior perform and abide by the spirit and not by way of the flesh.

Remember uncontrollable spirits (demons) control's the carnal, flesh, body, and mind of mankind and not the spiritual aspect of man. Therefore, at all times we are to abide in the Spirit. "He that is greater in man." Recognize and acknowledge the power of Christ in you is more powerful than the devil and all demon spirits combine. And always remember the Name of Jesus Christ supernaturally reach across the four corners of the globe. There isn't no person, place, or thing the Name of Jesus cannot penetrate.

Amen.

The Lamb of God

Look, this is the Lamb of God. Look, this is He who takes away the sins of the world (John 1:29). Jesus Christ, the Son of the Living God came into the world, the Son of man. Symbolically, Jesus became the Lamb of God, a young sheep to die for the sins of mankind, the world.

"The Lamb was often used as a victim of sacrifice because of its innocence and mildness. Therefore, it was an emblem most suited to the character of the Messiah."

The fact that John, the Baptist called Him, The Lamb of God is most significant. He was neither the people's lamb nor the lamb of the Jews nor the lamb of any human owner but the Lamb of God.

When the Lamb was finally sacrificed, it was not because He was a victim of those who were stronger than Himself but rather because He was fulfilling His willing duty of Love for sinners. It was not man who offered this sacrifice although it was man who slew the victim. It was God who gave His Son for ransom for those who believe in the Son of God would have eternal life.

Jesus, the Son of God also appear as the Good Shepherd, not because He provided economic plenty but because He would lay down His life for His sheep. "In the Scriptures, sheep denotes the defenseless, innocent and at times abused people of God."

The Shepherd is one who herds, guards, and tends sheep, one who cares for and guides a group of people as a minister. In relation to sheep herders. Jesus appeared as the Son of man, born of a virgin, "Emmanuel, God with us."

We were like sheep without a shepherd, "the Cross appears under the symbol of the Shepherd." We were like sheep and without a shepherd. We were helpless and fearful; therefore, we mankind were lost, scattered and were at the complete mercy of our enemies; Satan the Devil and demons.

The Son of God took another title, "The Son of Man." Not to deny His Divinity but to affirm the new condition he had taken. Since he was humbling himself and making himself obedient, even to the death on the Cross. Once again, the Cross appears; however, this time under the symbol of the Son of Man which stood for the shame, abasement and grief which is the human lot. It is descriptive of what Jesus became, rather than where Jesus is from. Because the name implied not only humiliation but identification with sinful mankind. Remember John, the Baptist acknowledge, "Look, this is the Lamb of God. Look, this is He who takes away the sins of the world" (John 1:29).

"Sheep have from earliest time been offered in sacrifice under the law. All first-born male lambs were to be sacrificed. But not until at least eight days old. The same number of days Jesus was circumcised."

Jesus entered the world the Son of Man to suffer our transgressions and iniquities. Jesus Christ, the Son of Man experienced and minister the title of high priest. A title that gave him authorization to enter the Holy of Holies. The Tent of the Lord's Presence's or Tabernacle which only the High Priest could enter for the atonement of sin.

Human sin caused division between God and man for God does not approve of sin. Only by fulfillment of the requisite of a true covering or atonement for sin could the breach between man and his Creator be healed.

It was on the Cross, Jesus shared his Blood wearing the titles of "Son of Man" of whom sin entered, "The Good Shepherd." One who herds, guard and tends sheep. "One who cares for and guides a group of people as a minister." Jesus, The Lamb of God. "Who takes away the sin of the world suffering death. Jesus tasted death for every human and provided a corresponding ransom for all mankind. Jesus "the High Priest" died on the cross once and for all for the atonement of sin. "For God so loved the world that He gave his only Son so that everyone who believe in Him may not die but have eternal life" (John 3:16).

God sent His Spirit in the Son of Man, Jesus Christ to conciliate through faith in the blood those who in faith accept God's provision for atonement through Jesus Christ can gain salvation. Which points out that God is the Source of salvation through Jesus.

The ransom sacrificed is the basis for salvation and as King and everlasting High Priest, Christ Jesus has the authority and power to save completely those who are approaching God through him. He is Savior of the Body, the congregation of his anointed followers and also of all who exercise faith in him.

Jesus Christ became the Anointed because of being appointed by God. The coming of Christ or Messiah, the one whom God would anoint with his Spirit to be the universal King had been foretold centuries before Jesus's birth (Dan. 9:25–26). However, at his birth Jesus was not yet the Anointed One or Christ.

The personal Name of Jesus followed by the title "Christ" calls attention to the person himself who became the Anointed One of Jehovah. This occurred when he reached thirty years of age, was baptized in water and was anointed with God's Spirit visibly observed in the form of a dove descending upon him (Matt. 3:13–17).

The story of every human life begins with birth and ends with death. In the Person of Christ; however, it was His death that was first and His life that was last for eternity. Every other person who ever came into this world came into to live. He came into it to die. The only Person ever pre-announced to never die a second death.

It was not so much that is birth cast a shadow on His life and thus led to His death, it was rather that the Cross was first and cast its shadow back to His birth. Jesus's life has been the only life in the world that was ever lived backward. "Remember, Jesus came into the world to die."

Born of a woman, He was a man born with all humanity. Born of a virgin who was overshadowed by the Spirit and full of grace. He would also be outside currently of sin which infected mankind.

The first sin offering acknowledging himself as a sinner was Able, who led by faith to present an offering requiring shedding of animal blood thereby accurately foreshadowing the real sacrifice for sin. But Jesus was the first human sacrifice for sin. But Jesus was the first human offering his Blood as a sacrifice for sinners forever lasting and a symbol of deliverance from spiritual slavery of sin.

Jesus's Blood was evidence of his death on the Cross. It was the ransom that freed mankind. You know well enough that it was not paid in Earthly currency, silver or gold. It was paid in the precious Blood of Christ. No Lamb was ever so pure, so spotless a victim.

The sacrifice commanded under the law covenant all pointed forward to Jesus Christ and His sacrifice as Jesus Christ was a perfect man, so all animal sacrifices were to be sound, unblemished specimens.

Christ, the redeemer came by way of human sacrifice. Ransom, the redemption referring to a buying back. Jesus perfect human life offered in sacrifice is the antitypical sacrifice. One that is foreshadowed by or identified with an earlier symbol or type, "Lamb."

Ransom came by way of human sacrifice of Jesus Christ becoming a human being, the Son of Man, becoming the "Lamb of God," and "High Priest" in heaven's atonement. The Day of Atonement may just as properly be called Day of the Ransom through faith in the Blood. Those who in faith accept God's provision for atonement through Jesus Christ can gain salvation.

Apostle Paul show that Jesus Christ is the antitypical High Priest. Paul also indicates that the high priests' entry into the Most Holy once a year with the blood of sacrifice animals foreshadowing the entrance of Jesus Christ into heaven itself with His own Blood, thus to man atonement for those exercising faith in his sacrifice.

Christ comparably presented the value of his human Blood to God in heaven where it could be applied to benefit those who would come to rule with him as priests and kings. "The appointment of a priest must come from God. A man does not take the office of his own accord."

What I'm saying is Jesus whose priesthood I've just described is our High Priest. And is in heaven at the place of greatest honor next to God himself. He ministers in the temple in heaven the true place of worship built by the Lord and not by human hands.

The Temple or the Tabernacle, the Tent of the Lord's Presence was constructed in the wilderness with human hands. God had spoken to Moses in the wilderness during the departure of the Israelites from Egypt, giving him the complete pattern for the Tabernacle. "See that you make all things after the pattern that was shown to you in the wilderness." It served in providing a shadow of heavenly things and, therefore, had to be accurate to the least detail (Heb. 8:5).

Their work is connected with a mere Earthly model of the real Tabernacle in heaven. Tabernacle literally mean tent habitation or Tent of the Lord's Presence erected for the worshipping of God in the wilderness. It was divided into two rooms or partition.

The first was called "The Holy Place," here were placed the table of showbread, the golden candlesticks and the golden alter of incense. When all was ready, the priests went in and out of the first room whenever they wanted to do their work.

The second was called "The Most Holy Place, here the "ark of the covenant" was kept which was a symbol of God's gracious presences. Only the High Priest enter the Most Holy Place and then only once a year all alone and always with the blood which he sprinkled on the Mercy Seat as an offering to God to cover his own mistakes and sins of all the people.

The Most Holy was divided from the Holy Place by a curtain or veil that was torn from top to bottom when Jesus died on the Cross which became immediately accessible for all believers and priests to enter the Most Holy of Holies in heaven into the very presences of God's heavenly Tabernacle.

The High Priest enter the Most Holy only on the annual Day of Atonement (a covering of sin) at no other time could any other person go between the curtain that hung between the Holy Place and Most Holy Place.

Scripture outline three entries of the High Priest into the most Holy Place on Atonement Day, first with the golden censer of perfumed incense fired by coal from off the alter, a second time with the blood of the bull, the sin offering for the priestly tribe and finally with the blood of the goat, the sin offering for the people.

Under the old covenant, the priest stood before the alter day after day offering sacrifice that could never take away our sins. But Christ gave himself to God for our sins as one sacrifice for all time when he died on the Cross. Thereby, removing the curtain that separated the Holy Place from the Most Holy Place thus allowing believers as priest to enter the Most Holy Place in heaven to see God on His Throne as God really is.

Christ became High Priest. He went into that greater perfect Tabernacle in heaven not made by man nor part of the world. And once for all took Blood into that inner room, the Most Holy of Holies and sprinkled it on the Mercy Seat. Not the blood of goats and calves. He took his own Blood, "The Lamb of God" and with it he by himself made sure of our eternal salvation.

He then sat down as High Priest in the highest honor at God's right hand. For by that one offering he made forever perfect in the sight of God all those whom he is making Holy.

Jesus sacrificed himself on the Cross, "The Lamb of God." He appeared as High Priest to enter the "Tent of the Lord's Presences" in order that we as priests could enter not the Tabernacle on Earth that was made by human hands but the Tabernacle in heaven made of God.

Jesus Christ the Son of Man took on many titles that brought him great suffering for our transgressions and iniquities. Christ experienced every hardship and pain mankind would ever experience.

God, the Father, the Holy Spirit performed by way of His Son to reconcile mankind and for believers in the Son to have eternal salvation through Jesus Christ, The Lamb of God. Jesus's death on the Cross brought redemption from sins and reconciliation with God are made possible.

Amen.

Abortion: A Great Sin

Multitudes of protestors, young and old of all nationalities. Men, women, and children protesting against the gift of life, rejecting the Holy Spirit, God's free gift is now an obstacle to others from receiving it.

In committing this horrible sin of abortion mankind have brought to completion all sins that has been committed including swearing against the Holy Spirit.

These things we're witnessing throughout the world is the work of the devil through humanity opposing God's will to live life and live abundantly and God's commandment, "Thy shall not kill."

Jesus, Our Father's only son died for our sins, he did not die for something which was already dead. Jesus died because God knew sin is alive and lives in mankind. Jesus did not die just for sin; he died for mankind because sin comes alive through mankind.

Had sin died when Jesus died on the cross, mankind of this generation and future generations would live a sinless life but since sin is alive Jesus defeated sin through his death in order for mankind to be forgiven for his sins which is alive.

Jesus was raised from the dead and is alive, his Spirit lives in mankind that can defeat the sin which also lives in mankind.

Since Jesus's death, therefore, Satan has no more control over sin but mankind does. That is why Satan tempts mankind through the flesh because he cannot control sin through the Spirit, he is aware of that but not all of mankind. Therefore, mankind becomes vulnerable to sin because lack of knowledge. As long as mankind lives sin also lives but only through the flesh.

Jesus said, "the mind's willing but the flesh is weak." I also believe a body without knowledge of the Spirit is dead. But yet Satan have no power over sin but through temptation is Satan plan to cause mankind to sin. When we say the Lord's Prayer, we ask our Lord to lead us not into temptation by his spirit that lives in us.

There is a great likeness between the Sadducees and today's abortion protesters. Whenever Jesus's name is mention or called out in their presences, they become angry.

Why do those people become angry whenever his name is called out or visible? Is it because the presence of Satan or his demons are present? Yes.

Because any human being with or without knowledge of God but with the presence of the Holy Spirit in them should rejoice just hearing the Name Jesus because the Father's spirit is in them which allows Jesus to confirm that the presence of God is communicating with the Holy Spirit base on their faith and belief in him.

Also, there are demonic possession among the multitude of abortion protestors performing Satan's will through all ages, which confirm Satan have no respectful person nor race to act against the will of God nor does his demons possess no respectful person to act through opposing God's will. One should remember God's will do what is right. He will bring suffering on those who make the innocent suffer.

God said, "Thy shall not kill." We're God's temple and that God's Spirit lives in us. So if anyone destroys God's temple which is Holy and you yourself are his temple.

Abortion law, there is no law in the world that give mankind the right to oppose God's law and commandment, "Thy shall not kill."

Mankind must always remember where the Spirit of the Lord is present, there is freedom and the Spirit of the Lord is present in the fetus of the unborn, therefore, through abortion mankind serve and act as Satan executers.

People, wake up. Use your mind to see Satan and his demons performing in yourself and those around you. Their presence can be seen but you must use your mind to see their work with the eyes before the wrath of God come down upon you.

Abortion right by manmade law, Satan is attempting through man to rewrite and defile God commandment. "Thy shall not kill" is a spiritual law because it is God's temple which he speaks of a temple for his Spirit to be received in.

Satan can't take it upon himself or his demons to write an abortion law, the right to live he must use mankind as his tools to oppose God's will and also cause mankind to defile and persecute himself.

God said, "I set life and death before you," so if a fetus is destroyed before God set life before it, then mankind has denied God's will and commandment.

Who give mankind the right and authority to destroy human lives? Who gave women the right which God is responsible for to live in her until its natural time arrives for it to be born into the world to receive his spirit to live?

Satan and demons work secretly together while plotting against those who are acting out their plans in abortion.

Satan possess the power to defiant God's will which he uses boldly in mankind to cause mankind to be disobedient and display disrespect toward God.

Every human being that protest the right for abortion, whether they realize it or not are reflecting their disrespect toward God.

I believe the Holy Spirit has spoken to every human being who are involved protesting the right for another human issue and it shouldn't be an issue today but it is because Satan is the creator of it.

Satan says since God is the creator of man and life. He will be the creator of death between the two and the earliest stage of death between mankind and life is the death of fetuses that is as close of preventing human lives by human lives.

Satan is the curator of abortion and mankind is in the dark but the issue has become a spiritual issue involving human lives because man is made in our Father's (God) image. You must understand anything that is spiritual is Holy and God possess the power over it, and therefore, it must come into the light.

Because of this spiritual issue (abortion) between life and death, God's Holy Spirit is to be receive by those unborn human beings.

I believe God's anger will be distributed throughout the world among those who are protesting the right to live.

Mankind should not protest against the will of life because it is a spiritual gift and grace to live. He that is greater than you which lives in you are just as great in the other life you are protesting against.

But Satan, the creator, has established in the minds of those that he is greater than He (God) that live in them and this angers God and our Lord and Savior.

People, throughout the world, you do not rebuke God, nor do you display action against his will and purpose. God sees everything we do, He knows everyone's thoughts; therefore, you can't fool God. You can't say I didn't know right from wrong or distinguish good from evil because even the unknowledgeable is warned by the Holy Spirit of right and wrong; and good and from evil. God knows everything. God is omniscient, having total knowledge, knowing everything!

Amen.

Healing for This Generation, Mankind Can Be Made Whole Sermon and Message

Note: Healing come to those who "believe and trust" the Word of Jehovah God, which is the restoring of health to the sick. Making sound or whole that which is broken or injured, the "curing" of various disease and defects and returning of a person to the general state of wellbeing.

Note: Children of God, the Bible describe such healings. Sometimes the healing was gradual at other times, it was instantaneous.

Among the blessings, Jehovah God bestowed on (us) all mankind the regenerative power and the ability of the body to heal itself when wounded or diseased.

In restoring the health of a person by a Doctor maybe recommend but in reality, it is God given power within the body that accomplish the healing. Jehovah God restored the bodily health of afflicted Job.

> Then, after Job had prayed for his three friends, the Lord made him prosperous again and gave him twice as much as he had before. (Job 42:10)

Praise the Lord, my soul, and do not forget how kind he is.

He forgives all my sins and heals all my diseases. (Ps. 103:2–3)

Note: Children of God, it is written that He both wounds and heals; and He does this literally and figuratively.

With Him there is a time to wound and a time to heal.

Read Deuteronomy 32:39. "I, and I alone, am God, no other god is real. I kill and I give life. I wound and I heal; and no one can oppose what I do."

Note: Jesus Christ recognize that teaching and preaching the Good News of the Kingdom was of first important in his ministry but he showed compassion on the multitudes that followed in the hope that he would heal their physical ailments.

Read Matthew 12:15. "When Jesus heard about the plot against him, he went away from that place, and large crowds followed him, He heal all the sick."

Also read Matthew 14:14. "Jesus got out of the boat, and when he saw the large crowd, his heart was filled with pity for them, and he 'healed' their sick."

Note: Jesus's miraculous healing work served as a visible sign to his and this present generation which give evident of his Messiahship.

Jesus miraculous healings also foreshadows the healings, blessings that is extended to mankind (us) under God's Kingdom. Jesus's healing, then, is still of today in Jesus's name!

Read John 14:12–14.

I am telling you the truth, those who "Believe" in Me will do what I do, yes they will do even greater things, because I am going to the Father.

And I will do whatever you ask for in my name, so that the Father's glory will be shown through the Son.

If you ask me, for anything in my name, I will do it!

Note: Jesus healed and restored the health of many persons, the lame, maimed, blind, and dumb. Jesus healed the epileptics and paralytics. He healed them all.

On many occasions, those who were demon-possessed were released from their satanic enslavement and bondage.

Read Matthew 12:22. "Then some people brought to Jesus a man who was blind and could not talk, because he had a demon. Jesus healed the man, so that he was able to talk and see."

Note: In another instance, Jesus just spoke the word and the ailing or sick one, though a distance away was healed.

At other times He personally laid his hand on the sick one or touched a wound and healed it.

Read Luke 22:50–51. "And one of them struck the High Priests slave and cut off his right ear. But Jesus said, Enough of this! He touched the man's ear and healed him."

True Testimony

I, a Servant of Jehovah God, Called by God

Note: Some persons opposed Jesus not appreciating the healing work he was performing, some religious leaders being greatly angered when Jesus healed persons on the sabbath.

Note: "True testimony. Maybe openly read to a congregation in the midst of Jesus Christ." For where two or three come together in my name, Jesus says, "I am there with them."

Note: Still today not all denominations in the Body of Christ, the Church recognize Jesus's presences in their sanctuary nor the everlasting benefit of healing made available through the ransom sacrifice of Christ for those who are in need of being made whole or heal of any infirmities or any bodily ailments.

Read Isaiah 53:5. "But because of our sins he was wounded, beaten because of the evil we did. We are healed by the punishment he suffered, made whole by the blows he received."

Note: Child of God, Christ himself carried our sins in his body to the Cross, so that we might die to sin and live for righteousness. It is by his wounds that you have been healed! "Therefore, Claim and receive your healing!"

"True testimony: Jehovah God is my witness." Maybe read openly to the congregation.

Note: Congregation of God, this divine power of healing. Jehovah God delegated to me, was not my own power nor knowledge nor wisdom that healed the sick whom I was sent to neither was any method used rather it was the Spirit and supernatural power of Jehovah God that effected such healings.

I have full faith and confidence in Jehovah God and knowledge that Jesus had that the curing and restoring of health was accomplished by God's Spirit and supernatural power.

True testimony

Note: In a vision of Jesus Christ and Myself, Jehovah God said to me, "Those who come to me, through My Son, I will work for them through you. Speaking of me, His servant!

However, I've been opposed, persecuted, and insulted among and by members of the Body of Christ which is the Church of Christ by an associate pastor, a retired pastor who told me to, "go home and pray" and even a family member for praying for a member of their congregation who had cancer in her body which I hadn't any knowledge of her bodily condition.

I asked her to stand for me to pray; she refused, so I asked her several times to stand, yet she refused, shaking her head left to right, as in a no manner.

She had been a member of the congregation her entire Christian life under her brother's ministry, who pastored over the congregation for over fifty plus years.

True testimony

Note: "I knew of him when he was a young minister and I was a demon-possessed alcoholic hearing demonic voices in my head.

Jehovah God cured me and set me free of demon possession of over thirty-six years and the voices left as well.

Years later, God called me into the five-fold ministry that are apostles, prophets, evangelists, pastors and teachers and that which I am not in fear to say, "Yes I am Jehovah God's prophet and in an audible voice said, "You are a prophet." While at another place and time, said quote, "If you love Me, tell the truth," which God confirmed, I heard correctly, quote, "If you love Me, tell the truth," in an audible voice.

Note: Congregation of God, a true Christian who were taught the Word of God without compromise would've stood and acknowledge Jesus Christ was in our midst.

Read Matthew 18:20. "For where two or three come together in my name I am there with them."

"Which mean, she refused to stand in the Midst of Jesus Christ whom I believe would have healed her of cancer, had she stood."

Note: I reiterate: Jehovah God spoke to me, "Those who came to me through My Son, I would work for them through you!" referring to His servant, me.

I'm a Visitor

Note: The following Sunday in the sanctuary before morning service, I was told by one of the associate pastors, quoting, "You know you're embarrassed, sis." (She died several weeks later.) "If I was on the podium or in the pulpit, I would not allow that to happen." Then later the retired pastor, who is now blind after fifty years plus of ministering, to quote, "Go home and pray, if that weren't enough persecution, the devil, Satan pushed it even farther, my brother (family) spoke out." What do you call yourself doing? "We don't do that here. You do that (prayer) at your church."

I'm not a member of their congregation. I visit there even though I'm in God's congregation, the Body of Christ, the Church.

At the time of this true testimony, I was a member of another congregation (church) where I was told by Holy Spirit to attend, which I've been a member for over twenty-two years, and I am a "prayer partner." Where miracles happens, the lame walk, the sick is healed and made whole, the laying on the hands which I've done and they recovered, the paralytic returned to normal, cancer and heart patients were healed and where tongues are spoken which are gifts of the Spirits at work in and through believers.

"I was persecuted for which I was called to do. I was persecuted just as Jesus Christ were persecuted for healing the sick."

True testimony, Jehovah God is my Witness.

Thank You, Father God!

Note: Sons and daughters of God, in a vision, "Jehovah God showed and spoke to me, those (mankind) who come to Him (God) through His Son Jesus He (God) would work through me" his servant for them. "Yes, through me."

Children of God, it's important that the person performing the cure have full faith and confidence in faith and confidence in Jehovah and acknowledge as Jesus that the curing was accomplished by God's supernatural power and not of his own.

Read John. 5:19. "So Jesus answered them, I tell you the truth, the Son can do nothing on his own, he does only what he sees his Father doing. What the Father does, the Son also does."

Note: It isn't necessary for the afflicted ones to have faith before being cured. Miraculous healing is a sign of divine backing. Those who refuse to recognize and acknowledge this sign were blind and deaf.

For this reason, divine healing were to serve as a sign to unbelievers also on the other hand true spiritual healing comes from Jehovah God to repentant ones.

Note: Such healing has the effect of strengthening the weak hands and wobbly knees, opening blind eyes and restoring hearing to the deaf, healing to the lame and giving speech to the dumb in a spiritual way.

Note: Congregation of God, spiritual healing comes from Jehovah God to repentant ones.

Healing

(1) To heal is restoring of health to the sick.
(2) The making sound or whole that which is broken or injured.
(3) The curing of various diseases and defects.
(4) The returning of a person to the general state of wellbeing with a sound mind.

Note: Preventiveness of One's Healing

(1) "Faith" = failing to act upon or have faith in God. "Faith without action is dead." One must act upon faith in Jehovah God.
(2) "Unbelief" = lack of belief or faith, especially in religious matter.
   The world sin is unbelief in Jesus Christ.
   Read John 3:18. "Those who believe in the Son are not judged, but those who do not believe have already been judged, because they have not believed in God's only Son."
(3) "Trust" = failing to trust or place reliance in God.
   Note: The person seeking true understanding prays to God, "Make me understand that I may observe your 'law' and that I may keep it with the whole heart."
(4) "Sin" = A transgression of a religious or moral law. Deliberate disobedience to the will of God.
   The introduction of sin on Earth came through a spirit creature referred to as the resister, adversary, the principal false accuser or slanderer.
   Note: He who carries on "sin" originate with the devil because the devil has been sinning from the beginning.
   Note: Also sin put mankind out of harmony with Jehovah God.

(5) Unforgiveness = reluctant or refusing to forgive.

Read Matthew 6:14–15. "If you forgive others the wrongs they have done to you, your Father in heaven will also forgive you. But if you do not forgive others, then your Father will not forgive the wrongs you have done."

Note: Child of God, those five reasons prevent persons of beings heal, which applies to all human beings." Healing is one of the gifts of the Spirit.

The nine gifts of the Spirit are (1) speech of wisdom, (2) speech of knowledge, (3) faith, (4) gift of healing, (5) powerful works, (6) prophesying, (7) discernment of inspired utterance, (8) different tongues, (9) interpretation of tongues.

Note: Neither of the gifts come from human beings or any human source, the Gifts of the Spirit is from God. It is Jehovah God who is responsible for performing of the Gifts of the Spirit in and through believers.

Note: One and the same Spirit gives "faith" to one person, while to another person he gives the power to "heal."

Church, these gifts of Jehovah God spirit not only benefit the giver, but also benefits the others, "believers and nonbelievers."

True spiritual healing comes from Jehovah God to repentant ones.

Amen.

About the Author

Growing up in my adolescent years, I didn't know we live among demons, spirit persons. No one ever mentioned the name *demon* to me, and when I heard that name, I thought it was just a figure of speech because no one ever seemed concerned when the name *demon* was spoken of, not even family members.

My family members never spoke of demons. Neither my relatives. Their terms of speaking of demons, those spirit persons without bodies, not made flesh and blood, I believe, were their terminology for ghosts and spirits of loved ones, which I, a young adolescent, heard from members of both sides when they spoke of seeing deceased "loved ones" standing near the bed or in some other room of the house. Wicked spirits are powerful. Demons are the wicked spirit persons, not of flesh and blood. They are the ghosts that the false perception of seeing something when they're not visibly seen, which is the terminology used to describe demons, those spirit persons pretending to be spirits of deceased loved ones to advance spirits of the dead are still on Earth.

Whether it's true or not, I don't know; my father told me a ghost chased my mother out of the house. I never asked my mother whether it was true or not! Today, I believe it could possibly have happened because of past experiences I've encountered in the spirit world to the point that the Holy Spirit told me, "Do not be afraid!" And I was given a warning about future spiritual encounters in the spirit world.

As I grew in biblical knowledge, I discovered that the culprits were pretending to be spirits of deceased loved ones. Not only loved ones, but many have also entered the bodies of loved ones and may have entered you without your knowledge. They may be across the land performing whatever their wish and purpose in and through families and relatives.

Note: I've witnessed apparitions of spirit person. Demons not of flesh and blood but never a ghost, pretending to be a spirit of a deceased loved one. I didn't know what a ghost was then and now. I still don't know after seventy-plus years later.

The Word says, "To be absent from the body is to be present with the Lord!"

I've witnessed a demon spirit person not of flesh and blood, Satan the Devil. However, I've seen Satan transition in human form as a spirit person, a living human being, just as you and I are spirit beings with a body transition back to an invisible spirit being without flesh and blood. This I witnessed. God is a witness of this truth!

Note: Satan the Devil is the only demon that has transitional power to materialize, appearing as a real person, a human being, yet spirit.

Children of God, we live and cohabitate with real live spirit persons, demons, right under our roofs and throughout the land.

Today, after seventy-plus years, I still do not know who or what a ghost is. It's still a ghost story to me, something you hear of, yet can't see.

Why isn't it being preached or taught in the body of Christ, the church, that demons can pretend to be spirits of deceased loved ones in our homes and throughout the land? Demons, those spirit persons without bodies, are observing us in our homes and everything we do or perform. They hear every word spoken to retaliate or counter against you and through others! Children of God, I've defeated the spirit world and, with it, the spirit persons, demons!

Thank you, Lord.

Milton Keynes UK
Ingram Content Group UK Ltd.
UKHW010728231023
431165UK00001B/100